# History 5–11

## A guide for teachers

Second edition

Hilary Cooper

Routledge
Taylor & Francis Group

LONDON AND NEW YORK

First published 2006
by David Fulton Publishers

This second edition published 2012
by Routledge
2 Park Square, Milton Park, Abingdon, Oxon OX14 4RN

Simultaneously published in the USA and Canada
by Routledge
711 Third Avenue, New York, NY 10017

*Routledge is an imprint of the Taylor & Francis Group, an informa business*

© 2012 Hilary Cooper

*British Library Cataloguing in Publication Data*
A catalogue record for this book is available from the British Library

*Library of Congress Cataloging in Publication Data*
Cooper, Hilary, 1943–
   History 5–11: a guide for teachers/Hilary Cooper. – 2nd ed.
   p. cm.
   Rev. ed. of: History 3–11. Abingdon [UK]: David Fulton, 2006.
   Includes bibliographical references and index.
   1. History – Study and teaching (Elementary) – Great Britain. I. Cooper,
   Hilary, 1943– History 3–11. II. Title.
   LB1582.G7C66 2012
   372.890941 – dc23
   2011043090

ISBN: 978-0-415-69359-2 (hbk)
ISBN: 978-0-415-69360-8 (pbk)
ISBN: 978-0-203-15356-7 (ebk)

Typeset in Bembo and Helvetica Neue
by Florence Production Ltd, Stoodleigh, Devon

Printed and bound in Great Britain by
TJ International Ltd, Padstow, Cornwall

# History 5–11

*History 5–11* addresses the key issues surrounding the teaching of history in the primary curriculum. With an emphasis on the importance of learning about the past through the processes of historical enquiry, this textbook will be an invaluable resource to all trainee and practising primary teachers interested in teaching history in an accessible, dynamic and above all enjoyable way.

This fully updated second edition highlights:

- examples of good practice
- meaningful assessment and record keeping
- planning for progression and differentiation
- the primary to secondary transition
- cross-curricular approaches to history.

This book also analyses the most recent and salient reports concerning primary education, including the 2011 Ofsted report *History for All*, the *Historical Association Primary History Survey 2011* and the findings of the *Cambridge Review*. It contains case studies, lesson planning guidance and methods to develop pupils' historical understanding as well as offering creative and innovative ways to teach the subject of history in the primary classroom.

**Hilary Cooper** is Professor of History and Pedagogy at the University of Cumbria, UK. She has published numerous books on history teaching and is an internationally renowned keynote speaker.

The 5–11 series combines academic rigor with practical classroom experience in a tried and tested approach which has proved indispensible to both trainee PGCE students and to practicing teachers. Bringing the best and latest research knowledge to core subject areas, this series addresses the key issues surrounding the teaching of these subjects in the primary curriculum. The series aims to stay up to date by reflecting changes in government policy and is closely related to the changing curriculum for the primary core subjects.

Each book contains lesson planning guidance and methods to develop pupils' understanding as well as offering creative and innovative ways to teach subjects in the primary classroom.

Titles in this series include:

**Physical Education 5–11,** Jonathan Doherty

**History 5–11,** Hilary Cooper

**Modern Foreign Languages 5–11,** Jane Jones and Simon Coffey

**English 5–11,** David Waugh and Wendy Jolliffe

# Contents

# Acknowledgements

*History 5–11* draws on examples of practical, school-based research into the teaching and learning of history, case studies applying research to practice, and case studies illustrating innovative and creative approaches. I should like therefore to express my appreciation to recent research undertaken by history teacher educators from the United Kingdom and around the world who have explored primary school children's thinking. Their studies are discussed in Part 1. They include: Keith Barton, University of Indiana; Alan Cully, University of Ulster; the late Hilary Claire, London Metropolitan University; Dursun Dilek and Gulcin Yapici, University of Sinop; Penelope Harnett, University of the West of England; Pat Hoodless, Leeds Metropolitan University; Alan Hodkinson, Liverpool John Moores University; Peter Lee and Rosalyn Ashby, London University Institute of Education; Peter Vass, Oxford Brooks University; Gail Weldon, Western Cape Education Department, Capetown; Yosanne Vella, University of Malta; and Jayne Woodhouse, history education consultant.

I am grateful to the teachers whose case studies, described in educational papers and journals, demonstrate that energetic and lively new approaches to primary history can still be found, despite the constraints. These include teachers in Keyworth School in Kennington; Stephenson Way Primary School After School Club, County Durham; Southbank International School, Hampstead; St Illytd's School in Swansea; Pat Lewis in Blaenavon; the Lancaster City Museums Project; Wendy Scott from Fortune Park Day Centre, Islington; and Alison Hocking, Goetre Infants' School. I am grateful to those who have published examples of their work in ICT and history and given recommendations of useful sites: Elaine Dawe, David Mason, Hugh Moore, Steve Mynard, Jo Peat, Stuart Roper and Ben Walsh.

I thank the students at St Martin's College who worked with me on some of the illustrative examples: Elizabeth Hart and Sarah Spink, for their Foundation Stage plans in Chapter 5 and colleagues at St Martin's, Sam Twiselton and Kath Langley Hamel on history and literacy, the late Robin Foster on history and mathematics, and Pete Saunders who commented on the section on history and ICT.

Thanks are due to the children and teachers who have worked with me on case study examples, including: Greenvale Primary School, Croydon; Stramongate School, Kendal; and Eaglesfield Paddle School, Cumbria.

Finally I remember those who have encouraged and supported my interest in the teaching of history in primary schools over the years: the late Joan Blyth, author of *History in Primary Schools* (1982); Roy Hughes, University of Leeds; and Jon Nichol, editor of *Primary History* (Jon and I created and manage the History Educators' International Research Network and edit *The International Journal of History Teaching, Learning and Research*). I should also like to applaud the Historical Association for its website, where many of the themes of this book can be explored further (www.history. org.uk).

# Introduction

## Aims of this book

The aims of the second edition of this book remain the same as for the first edition. It is written as a core text for both experienced primary teachers and initial teacher training students. It shows readers, through a series of case studies, working with children and teachers across the primary age phase, how to plan interesting history lessons that develop pupils' historical understanding in increasingly complex ways and how this can be assessed. The processes of historical enquiry are embedded in the case studies: making deductions and inferences from sources, selecting and combining sources to create accounts that explain changes over time and communicating these in interesting ways. The case studies are illustrated by pupils' work and talk. Links are made between theory, practice and research, encouraging readers to reflect upon and develop their own practice.

## What is new about this edition?

The second edition is different from the previous one in three ways. It spans the ages five to eight, rather than three to eight. It omits precise references to the *National Literacy Strategy* (DfEE/QCA 1998), the *National Numeracy Framework* (DfEE 1999) and the *National Curriculum for England and Wales* (DfEE/QCA 1999) but recognises that the objectives the strategies and curriculum espoused remain relevant. Whatever a new national curriculum for history may involve, the processes of historical enquiry will not change. Indeed there are important reasons why children should continue to learn history through engaging with historical enquiry. These are addressed in Chapters 1–4.

The most important difference in the second edition is that it reflects the findings of three significant, recent surveys that report on the way history is currently taught in primary schools. Their findings are all similar. They address: why history is important, the strengths of history teaching and learning, and areas for development. The surveys are: *Children, their World, their Education: Final report and recommendations of the Cambridge*

*Primary Review* (Alexander 2010), *History for All* (Ofsted 2011) and the *Historical Association Primary History Survey* (Historical Association 2011).

The *Cambridge Primary Review* (Alexander 2010; referred to hereafter as the *Cambridge Review*) is a report on an enormous research study, drawing on commissioned surveys by experts, reports from organisations and from over 1,000 individuals, and regional meetings with teachers, parents and children. The aim was to collect research evidence about primary education and evidence from practice, to discover what parents, teachers and children want from primary education and to make recommendations, based on this evidence, about future policy and practice.

*History for All* (Ofsted 2011) contains evidence from history inspections of 83 primary schools between 2007 and 2010. It shows ways in which standards have risen since 2007, identifies key issues to be addressed and describes the essential components of effective learning in history. The *Historical Association Primary History Survey* (Historical Association 2001; referred to hereafter as the *Primary History Survey*) is based on questionnaires submitted by 344 foundation stage and primary school teachers. It investigates leadership, curriculum organisation, and planning and assessment in primary history education.

Therefore it seems useful to outline the findings of the surveys on which this edition is based in the introduction. A detailed needs analysis to enable readers to reflect upon and evaluate their own strengths and areas for development, based on the findings of the surveys as they read through this book, is given in the Appendix, pages 238–42. It includes references to pages in each of the reports and to pages in this book where each of the aspects of teaching and learning identified in the reports can be found.

## Why is history important?

Roy Hughes is quoted as saying that, 'History can help children to make meaning. Conceptual development is a vital part of children's developing work in history. Children's classroom activities should be framed by cause, consequence, interpretation and evidence' (Alexander 2010: 229). The *Cambridge Review* found broad consensus on what children should learn, which included history, because of its impact on 'culture, consciousness and identity and the lessons it offers for present and future' (p. 259). On page 272 it continues that, 'place and time need proper public and political recognition of their importance to children's understanding of who they are, of change and continuity, cause and consequence, why society is arranged as it is'. 'History', it says, is 'central to respect and reciprocity, interdependence and sustainability (local, national, global), citizenship, culture and community'. *History for All* (Ofsted 2011) considers that history is well placed to enhance pupils' sense of social responsibility, enabling them to see the diversity of experience and understand more about themselves, although in 4 out of 28 primary schools visited the contribution history made to the this understanding was insufficient. There was however some excellent practice.

The *Primary History Survey* indicated that history for 5–11 year olds has a central role in school curricula, grounded in the needs of children, parents and society. History education, it says, is 'a major element in children's political, social and emotional education, in terms of identity, a sense of belonging and the informed, evidence-based sceptical thinking of citizens in a plural, liberal democracy' (pp. 5–6). The survey concludes that history in the primary phase of education is a major element in pupils' political education, particularly in relation to national master narrative, identity and a sense of belonging, and the perfect subject to educate young citizens. It is also an excellent medium for the highest quality literacy education (p. 27).

## Strengths of history education 5–11

### Children enjoy their history lessons

The *Cambridge Review* found that children singled out history among subjects they enjoyed because it gave them opportunities to be active through 'hands-on' experiences and to be involved in their learning (p. 213). *History for All* (Ofsted 2011) found that pupils' attitudes to history were good or better in all the schools visited. They were well-motivated and thought history was fun (p. 9). The *Primary History Survey* also found that both children and teachers enjoy history.

### Teachers enjoy teaching history

In the *Primary History Survey* between 90% and 75% of teachers who responded felt that the following aspects of history were well taught in their schools: development of knowledge and understanding; making links between the past and today; learning through museum and site visits; using a variety of teaching methods; social history and the lives of ordinary people; and local and community history. *History for All* (Ofsted 2011) found that the most effective teachers brought history to life through a range of experiences, including use of local expertise and local provision, made effective cross-curricular links, and added additional topics in response to children's needs and interests and with regard to developing chronology and an over-arching narrative.

### History is a rich dimension of pupils' learning

Authors of the *Primary History Survey* comment that

> the breadth of key historical episodes and the contrasting and complementary narratives teachers said they taught reflect the sea change in academic history from being rooted in the British master narrative of civilisation's progress . . . to one that is diverse and reflects the importance of the histories of all members of our society.
>
> (p. 16)

This reflects changes in the last twenty years in the role of women and the wider range of ethnic backgrounds within our community.

## High standards in 'the basics' and in history are positively related

*The Diversity and Citizenship Curriculum Review* (DfES 2007) stated that the evidence of inspections over decades consistently shows that a belief in the pursuit of standards in the 'basics' is unfounded; they are positively related, and high-performing schools achieve high standards both in the basics and in history (p. 439).

The *Primary History Survey* states that the map of the teachers' knowledge that the National Curriculum for history develops produces a rich comprehensive and multi-faceted dimension of pupil learning. The survey found that the history taught in primary schools featured British, European and global history and that children had good knowledge of topics and episodes but not of changes within and beyond periods. It was not a narrow curriculum.

# Achievement in history is good

*History for All* (Ofsted 2011) found that achievement in history was 'good or outstanding' in 63 of the 83 primary schools visited between 2007 and 2010, and outstanding in 9 of these schools. It was not inadequate in any of them (p. 9). The report continues that 'where history was thriving pupils were developing a good knowledge of historical topics, acquiring a detailed understanding of the past and learning to ask questions, research evidence, draw conclusions, communicate their findings and make valid judgements'.

# Areas for development

### Teachers' pedagogical knowledge: understanding of the processes of historical enquiry

In the *Primary History Survey* only 54% of the respondents said that they felt confident in understanding progression in historical thinking and that the concepts and processes of historical enquiry were not well-developed in their curricula, although 90% felt that knowledge and historical understanding was good (p. 16). It seems that teachers are more concerned with historical knowledge than with historical thinking; 62% said that they would like to develop children's historical thinking more.

The *Cambridge Review* (Alexander 2010: 257) emphasises the importance of understanding the processes of enquiry which lie at the heart of a discipline. But it also recognises that this was an arid process that gave subject teaching a bad name if learning the processes of enquiry does not involve active, enthusiastic engagement, imagination and joint activity, because this is what motivates children. *History for All* (Ofsted 2011) found discrepancies both within and between schools in planning to develop subject specific knowledge.

## Chronology

*History for All* (Ofsted 2011) found that children had good knowledge of topics and episodes but their chronological understanding and ability to make links across the knowledge they had gained was weaker. Teachers found it difficult to establish mental maps of the past for their pupils, partly because they lacked the expertise and also because of the fragmented nature of the National Curriculum. Pupils in schools where history teaching was relatively weak experienced history 'simply as a series of episodes' (p. 31).

## Planning for assessment and progression

This section received a lower response rate than any other aspect of the *Primary History Survey*. It may reflect teachers' lack of confidence in understanding historical thinking and progression. Of the 182 who answered the question, 'do you assess in history?', 69% said they did and 31% said that they did not. Of those who did assess, 50% assessed termly, 35% yearly and only 6% (9 teachers) assessed weekly or monthly. The level descriptors were not seen as useful by 30% of respondents. This suggests that teachers see success in history in terms of engagement and enjoyment rather than in terms of progression in historical thinking. This survey found some contradiction between the infrequent assessments teachers said they made and the claim that 86% planned for progression; this suggests that teachers see progression as content covered rather than progression in historical skills and conceptual understanding. Teachers did however offer understanding assessment and progression as an area for professional development.

## The curriculum

The *Primary History Survey* found that teachers said that the curriculum needs modifying to reflect political, cultural and social changes since 1999. Teachers said that they would like to include more about multi-cultural Britain, gender history, diversity and world history in the curriculum. The *Cambridge Review* considered that the most conspicuous curriculum casualties have been those kinds of generic learning across the curriculum that require time for thinking, talking, problem-solving and that depth of exploration which engages children and makes their learning meaningful and rewarding. The case, it says, for art, music, history, drama and geography needs to be rigorously reasserted. So does the case for reflective and interactive pedagogy on which the advancement of children's understanding largely depends (p. 238). On page 256 the review stresses the need for local flexibility and recommends that each aspect of the curriculum should have a local dimension.

*History for All* (Ofsted 2011) found that where teaching was cross-curricular, planning for progression in developing historical knowledge was limited and that pupils' perceptions of history were sometimes unclear. It considered that a thematic approach did not undermine the integrity of the subject providing the knowledge and thinking of each subject was emphasised. When this was done well and the curriculum focused on developing historical thinking pupils made good progress.

### Primary–secondary school liaison

The *Primary History Survey* found that there was virtually no liaison or planning for progression between primary and secondary schools. *History for All* (Ofsted 2011) also found links between secondary and primary schools were weak, so that secondary schools were not exploited to support non-specialists in primary schools (p. 6). It recommended that formal and informal networks, clusters and federations should be developed to provide greater opportunities for teachers to work together on subject-specific training.

## How does the second edition of *History 5–11* reflect the three surveys?

### Part 1: Teachers' pedagogical knowledge: understanding the processes of historical enquiry

Part 1 considers further the reasons why history in the primary school is important, which was discussed in the *Cambridge Review* and in the *Primary History Survey*. Then it responds to the findings in each of the surveys that teachers need, and want, to develop their pedagogical knowledge in history; their understanding of the processes of historical enquiry. Each strand of enquiry is analysed in turn: selecting sources to investigate for a chosen enquiry, making inferences about historical sources, understanding the reasons for, and evaluating different accounts or interpretations of the past and developing historical concepts. There is an extended section on what is meant by chronological understanding, since *History for All* (Ofsted 2011) found that there was a particular need for development in this important strand of children's understanding in history. Each aspect of historical enquiry is explored through action research, showing ways in which children of different ages can engage with each strand of thinking.

### Part 2: Planning and assessment

The *Primary History Survey* found that most teachers did not assess pupils' work in ongoing, formative ways and made summative assessments only termly, yearly or not at all. Those who did assess appeared to do so on the basis of topics covered or children's enjoyment. Many teachers claimed that they planned for progression, but this was not progression in children's thinking. This is understandable since teachers did not understand the nature of historical thinking, because it had not been part of their training or professional development and many did not find the level statements helpful.

Part 2 takes as its starting point the finding in the surveys that teachers and children enjoy history and suggests a variety of dimensions to consider in planning for enjoyable teaching and learning in history. This section celebrates the things that teachers and children said that they enjoyed, in the *Primary History Survey* and the *Cambridge Review*: hands-on activities, visits, a variety of teaching methods, working with the community, and effective cross-curricular links. There are suggestions about ways in which teachers might include greater diversity in their planning, as they requested in the *Primary History Survey*.

Then it responds to the finding that planning and assessment in history is an area in which teachers requested further understanding. Chapter 6 shows how, based on enjoyable activities, the processes of historical enquiry described in Part 1 can be integrated into each level planning and assessment: whole school, medium-term and long-term planning. It explains how to construct effective medium term plans for history, how these inform lesson planning and how assessment is an integral part of planning at each stage, demonstrated in a planning cycle. Types, purposes and methods of monitoring and promoting individual progress through formative assessment are discussed and manageable and imaginative forms of summative assessment, recording and reporting to parents are explained.

## Part 3: Examples of planning and assessment in practice

Now that the processes of historical enquiry, and how these may become an integral part of planning and assessment have been explained, case studies at Key Stages 1 and 2, supported by examples of children's work, illustrate the process and ways in which it can be modified. This is followed, in Chapter 9, by a discussion, based on case studies, of ways in which mutually beneficial liaison between teachers and children in Years 6 and 7 might facilitate smooth transition between primary and secondary school, another area that the surveys found problematic. Part 3 ends with a consideration of the kinds of generic learning across the curriculum that involve time, reflection, interaction and problem solving and that the *Cambridge Review* found to have been marginalised, by an overcrowded curriculum, in recent years.

## Part 4: Principles, theory and practice

The final part of the book returns to the theory/practice links referred to in Chapter 1. A case study on the Saxons explores ways in which children can be encouraged to make inferences and deductions about a range of sources, then makes suggestions about how busy teachers can reflect on, analyse and develop their practice.

## Needs analysis

The professional needs analysis at the end of this book (Appendix, p. 238) will enable you to consider your personal areas of strength and areas for development, based on the three reports that this book addresses (Alexander 2010; Historical Association 2011; Ofsted 2011), as you read through the book and reflect on your developing professional experience.

## References

Alexander, R. (ed.) (2010) *Children, their World, their Education: final report and recommendations of the Cambridge Primary Review*. London: Routledge.

DfEE (Department for Education and Employment) (1999) *The National Numeracy Framework: framework for teaching mathematics from Reception to Year 6*. Sudbury: DfEE Publications.

DfEE/QCA (Department for Education and Employment/Qualifications and Curriculum Authority) (1998) *The National Literacy Strategy*. London: DfEE/QCA.

DfEE/QCA (1999) *National Curriculum for England and Wales: handbook for primary teachers in England*. London: DfEE/QCA.

DfES (Department for Education and Skills) (2007) *Diversity and Citizenship Curriculum Review*. London: DfES.

Historical Association (2011) *Primary History Survey (England): history 3–11*. London: The Historical Association.

Ofsted (Office for Standards in Education) (2011) *History for All: history in English schools 2007–2011* (www.ofsted.gov.uk/publications/090223).

# Teachers' pedagogical knowledge

## Understanding the processes of historical enquiry

# 1

# Changes in the teaching and learning of history

---

**DRAKE'S DRUM**

Drake he was a Devon man an' ruled the Devon seas,
(Capten, art tha sleepin there below?)
Rovin' tho his death fell, he went wi' heart at ease,
An' dreamin arl the time o' Plymouth Hoe.
'Take my drum to England, hang et by the shore,
Strike it when your powder's runnin' low;
If the Dons sight Devon, I'll quit the port o' Heaven,
An drum them up the Channel as we drumm'd them long ago.'

(Sir Henry Newbolt 1897)

---

You really need to listen to the music to thoroughly appreciate this! It represents the view of the past as generally taught in elementary schools from about 1865 until about 1965: nationalistic, moralising, rousing. An example of this approach is H.E. Marshall's *Our Island Story* (1905), widely used in schools in the first half of the last century, recently republished by readers of the *Daily Telegraph* and enthusiastically reviewed by Debo, Duchess of Devonshire, in the *Spectator* (Devonshire 2005: 45). The text accompanying the illustration of our hero on page 321 must be the original 'cool Britannia': '"There is time to finish the game and beat the Spaniards too," said Drake.' The text continues: 'Day by day the wind grew fiercer . . . [the Spaniards] were shattered on unfriendly rocks . . . At last, ruined by shot and shell . . . about fifty maimed and broken wrecks reached Spain . . . Elizabeth ordered a medal to be made saying, "God blew with his breath, and they were scattered".' I have no problem with national pride but *Our Island Story* simply does not square with what is known. In the section on 'Good Queen Bess' it goes on to quote William Collins (1788–1789).

> There were so few rogues that would plunder and rob sir,
> That the hangman was starved for want of a job sir.
> Good neighbourhood too. There was plenty of beef,
> And the poor from the rich never wanted relief
> For the sovereign and subject one interest supported,
> And our powerful alliance was by all nations courted,
> Oh, the golden days of good Queen Bess.

So what about the land taken over by wealthy sheep farmers, deplored in a contemporary work, *Utopia*, by Sir Thomas More, the resulting, homeless, 'sturdy beggars' passed on from village to village, what about the anti-Catholic laws, the Catholic plots, the fear of Spain?

This experience of history lessons was brilliantly satirised in 1930 by Sellar and Yeatman. The section on 'The Great Armadillo' recounts that,

> The Spaniards complained that Captain F. Drake had singed the King of Spain's beard, or Spanish mane as it was called . . . Drake replied that he was in his hammock at the time and a thousand miles away. The King of Spain however insisted that the beard had been spoilt and sent the Great Armadillo to ravish the shores of England.
>
> (Sellar and Yeatman 1930: 66)

If you do not think that is very funny – good. You did not experience this kind of history teaching! We have come a long way, as illustrated by the multi-perspectival Armada press releases written by Year 6 children on pages 130–2. But perhaps you experienced no history at all. History was optional in primary schools until 1989. After the Plowden Report (1967), the emphasis was on direct experience through the senses; history was generally considered unsuitable for young children, being seen as concerned with the affairs of adults and abstract ideas that could not be meaningful to young children.

> History, it is said, again and again, is an adult subject. How can it be studied by children without being so simplified it is falsified? There is first the problem that it is not until the later years of primary school that some children develop a sense of time . . . Yet we visited an Infant school where one exceptional child had memorized the dates of the Kings and Queens of England, 'except for all the muddling Anglo Saxons.'
>
> (Plowden 1967, paragraph 620)

Only since the 1980s have we identified what exactly is involved in finding out about the past at any level and explored ways in which young children can actively engage with this process, in ways which develop critical and discursive thinking, rather than brainwashing, and justifying the reasons why they should do so. I read history at university, but found teaching young children, in the Plowden tradition, much more interesting than teaching history in the sort of high school for girls that I had attended. After some time I was seconded to take an advanced diploma in child development, at the Institute of Education in London. There I realised that no one had ever systematically tried to apply theories of constructivist learning to the processes of historical enquiry, so I made this the subject of my dissertation. When I returned to school I used my work as a Year 4 class teacher to collect empirical data that informed my Ph.D. on 'Young Children's Thinking in History' (Cooper 1991). Colleagues abroad, ranging from previously communist countries of Eastern Europe to previously fascist countries of Western Europe and South America, have also begun their own researches into the teaching of history to young children in their own contexts, which engage children in active enquiry rather than giving them a simple 'story of the past', which can be politically manipulated.

For, of course, young children are aware of times before their own, although their understanding may be incomplete and even stereotypical, if not mediated through education. From their earliest years, children have some awareness of 'the past' through illustrations of traditional stories and rhymes, family photographs, old buildings, then later through film, television and heritage sites. But to begin to understand the past children must learn, from the beginning, the questions to ask and how to answer them. Historical enquiry involves making deductions and inferences from sources, traces of the past that remain, then selecting and combining sources in order to construct accounts of the past, tracing changes over time. This chapter has explored the ways in which interaction between the processes of historical enquiry and the content of history have evolved. Chapter 2 goes on to consider the first strand of historical enquiry, making inferences from sources. Chapter 3 considers how accounts or interpretations of the past are created by making inferences and deductions about sources. Chapter 4 discusses the special language of history: key historical concepts. Each chapter, therefore, considers a strand of historical enquiry, how this relates to theories of how children learn, and recent research exploring children's ability to engage with historical enquiry in increasingly complex ways.

## The content of history

Originally the story of a society's past was handed down orally, and in some societies it still is. In others it was written down: by the Greeks as epic poetry, in *The Odyssey*; by medieval monks as chronicles, lists of events, of battles lost and won; in Shakespeare's histories as the story of a nation's kings. The story was always told for a particular audience and a particular reason.

Over the past 150 years, history has become recognised as an academic discipline and its scope has broadened. Frederick Maitland (1850–1906) justified history as the study of the law, in any society. Marc Bloch (1886–1944) drew on new disciplines to study human settlement: place name study, technology and social sciences. Lewis Namier (1888–1960) analysed political life, and Mortimer Wheeler archaeology. Fernand Braudel (1902–1985) linked geography and history, making connections over time and space and exploring the role of large-scale, socio-economic factors in finding out about the past.

A history, then, may be broad or in-depth. It may be about an individual, about social groups, economic or political movements, local, national or global. Historians have their own interests: women's history, black history, the history of childhood, the history of a particular class, left-wing or right-wing perspectives. And since history is an umbrella subject that includes all aspects of life there are histories of music, art, science, religion, geographical histories, sports history.

But history is not just a story or a list of events. Whatever content an account of the past may focus on, it must be investigated through the process of historical enquiry.

## The process of historical enquiry

The process of enquiry, too, has evolved gradually. Leopold von Ranke (1795–1886) studied records. How did this document come into existence? How has it come down to us? How do the answers to these questions influence its trustworthiness? How do they explain the differences between two accounts? For Marc Bloch, clarity of analysis and asking the right question were consistent criteria. What do we know? What can we know? How do we know? How can we communicate that knowledge? Herbert Butterfield (1900–1979) employed imaginative sympathy in describing characters and events.

R.G. Collingwood clarified the process of historical enquiry in his autobiography (1939). He saw historical enquiry as beginning with a complex of ordered, specific questions in the tradition of the great philosophers, Plato, Bacon, Descartes, Kant. He said that, just as philosophy had found it necessary to accommodate a revolution in thinking about the natural world, based on empirical observation and deduction in the seventeenth century, it must encompass a similar revolution in the way it studied man in constantly changing societies.

Collingwood worked out this philosophy of history through constant practical application in archaeology. He proceeded from specific questions about sources, the significance and purpose of objects, whether they were buttons, dwellings or settlements, to the people who made and used them. The sequence proceeded from what can be known about an object, then what can be 'guessed', then, finally, what he would like to know, in order to support, extend or contradict his guesses. For instance, he knew from concrete evidence that a Roman wall from the Tyne to the Solway existed. He guessed that its purpose was to form a sentry walk with parapets as protection against snipers. He wanted to know if there were towers as a defence against vessels trying to land between Bowness and St Bees, in order to support his guess. A resulting search revealed that towers had been found but their existence forgotten, because their purpose was not questioned. History, then, involves interaction between the known content and the process of enquiry, in order to try to make sense of it. First, then, we need to find out how historians use sources and how we can use them with children.

When I was invited to write a second edition of *History 5–11*, it was recognised that many primary school teachers feel that their own knowledge of the content of history is weak. This is understandable since, as the three reports that frame the changes in this edition pointed out, many primary school teachers are required to teach history in schools, yet history was not necessarily included in their initial training and there has been virtually no continuing professional development training in recent years.

It was suggested that the book should therefore be accompanied by a CD containing an outline of key knowledge. But how could this be selected? Inevitably there would be bias in the selection. When the National Curriculum was mooted there were fierce political discussions about what was essential information. The Historical Association caused an outcry with its paper 'History in the Core Curriculum' (Historical Association 1987), recommending sixty chronological topics for pupils from five to sixteen.

In any case, no teachers can have a comprehensive knowledge of every period of history in every civilization, so it is important to do your own research in planning a topic and also to engage with the children in their enquiries. Children need to understand that teachers do not know all the answers and it is good to see teachers modelling the enquiry process and getting as involved in and as excited by it as their pupils. For if they do not find it interesting why should anyone else?

Books and websites for adults, for example websites for art galleries and museums, frequently have good illustrations and photographs that can be projected as a PowerPoint® presentation and that children of any age can use as sources, although seeing sources first hand, whenever possible, conveys a far more exciting connection with the past. Your local history librarian and archivist will offer invaluable support for local history. References to some websites to support teachers are given below.

BUT BEWARE!

It is important to remember that children need to understand the process of historical enquiry, to integrate content with process, if they are to learn history, to understand why there are different perspectives and interpretations and not simply to learn what Charlotte Mason, an innovative educationist writing in the nineteenth century, called 'miserable little chronicles of feuds, battles and death which are presented as "a reign"' (Mason 1993, vol. 1: 281).

So, although websites may give useful information and suggestions for pupil enquiries, it is essential that these are mediated by the teacher, not downloaded in their 'raw state'.

Ofsted (2011), Alexander (2010) and teachers themselves (Historical Association 2011) all emphasise that teachers do not feel confident in their understanding of what is involved in historical enquiry. This affects the learning objectives they plan, the activities they devise in order to achieve these learning objectives and their ability to assess, both formatively and summatively, in order to plan for progression. Progression depends, not on the content covered but on progression in historical thinking.

So the next three chapters, exploring the different strands of historical enquiry, are essential reading.

## Indicative websites

www.learningcurve.gov.uk (useful sources and suggestions for enquiries)

www.bbc.uk/history (includes history of Scotland, Ireland and Wales)

www.historymole.com (timelines)

www.history.org.uk (The Historical Association website. This has a wealth of material accessible to members)

www.Ask.co.uk (search for 'primary history content' – lots of primary sources and oral history)

www.blackandasianstudies.org (role of black and Asian people in Britain for centuries)

www.co.uk/history/forkids (good for content information)

www.phm.org.uk. (working people in Britain)

www.nationalarchives.gov.uk

www.bl.uk (British Library)

If planned carefully by the teacher some of these websites could support individual and group pupil enquiries within a topic studied.

## References

Alexander, R. (ed.) (2010) *Children, their World, their Education: final report and recommendations of the Cambridge Primary Review.* London: Routledge.

Collingwood, G. (1939) *An Autobiography.* Oxford: Oxford University Press.

Cooper, H. (1991) 'Young Children's Thinking in History', unpub. Ph.D. London University Institute of Education.

Devonshire, D. (2005) Review of *Our Island Story, Spectator,* 19 November.

Historical Association (1987) *History in the Core Curriculum.* London: The Historical Association.

Historical Association (2011) *Primary History Survey (England): history 3–11.* London: The Historical Association.

Marshall, H.E. (1905) [2005] *Our Island Story.* Cranbrook: Galore Park.

Mason, C. (1993) *Charlotte Mason's Original Home Schooling Series, Vols 1–6* (www.ambleside online.org).

More, T. (1997) *Utopia.* New York: Dover Thrift.

Newbolt, H. (1897) 'Drake's Drum', in *Admirals All and Other Verses,* set to music by Charles Villiers Stanford: The Very Best of English Song, CD2 EMI Classics.

Ofsted (Office for Standards in Education) (2011) *History for All: history in English schools 2007/10.* London: Ofsted (www.ofsted.gov.uk/resources/history-for-all).

Plowden (1967) *Children and their Primary Schools* (The Plowden Report). London: HMSO.

Sellar, W.C. and Yeatman, R.J. (1930) *1066 and All That.* Harmondsworth: Penguin.

# 2

# Historical sources

Historical sources are any traces of the past that remain. They may be written sources: documents, newspapers, laws, literature, advertisements, diaries, place names. They may be visual sources – paintings, cartoons, film, video, maps, field patterns, plans – oral sources or music. They may be artefacts, sites, buildings.

## Questions to ask about sources

The questions we ask about sources are valid if they lead somewhere. Collingwood (1939) identifies key questions: How was it made? Why? How was it used? By whom? Were there others? What did it mean to the person who made and used it? For example, a superior example of a Roman shoe found at Vindolanda – the equivalent of one made by Gucci or Lobbe – may tell us something about the social or economic structure of the fort. A letter from a first generation 'Dutch' Roman at the fort, asking for underpants and socks from Rome, may tell us about the economic and transport systems of the empire and the attitudes of the Dutch tribes to cold, clothes, and culture. It is the graffiti on the door of Newgate Prison or the Robert Burns song scratched into the glass of a casement window that quickens the pulse – tangible links with other people who lived in other worlds.

## Problems with sources

What makes sources intriguing is that they do not yield their secrets easily. We usually have to 'guess' what they may be telling us, based on what else we may know. There may be more than one possible inference to make about a source. Children particularly enjoy 'guessing' about a source, justifying it, arguing with other interpretations, when no single 'correct' answer may be known. Even if their hypotheses seem unlikely they are learning to engage with the process of historical enquiry; with maturity and greater knowledge children's 'guesses' become more valid, in that they conform to what is known about the period, what is likely and whether there is contradictory evidence. With experience and maturity they become more aware of the factors to take into account in asking questions about sources.

## Asking questions about sources

- Sources may be of varying status, because they were created for different purposes: a diary, a newspaper account, an advertisement; portraits of, for example, Elizabeth I, are masterpieces of propaganda, often conveyed through the symbolism of power and ambition (see p. 134).

- Sometimes new evidence comes to light. Harlow (1996) describes the discovery of the site near St Paul's Cathedral of a 'forgotten' battle between Normans and Saxons, which took place three months after the Battle of Hastings and was actually the point when the Normans conquered England. Norman propagandists wanted to portray William as a military genius capable of overwhelming the Anglo Saxons with one overwhelming blow at Hastings so they forgot about this final bloody confrontation. But other contemporary sources, such as William Jumieges, a French monk, dedicate as much space to this battle as to the Battle of Hastings and Guy de Amiens describes how Duke William of Normandy took the battle so seriously that he constructed siege engines and battering rams.

- Sources may be reinterpreted as society changes. In Monte Alban, the great abandoned city of pre-conquest Mexico, in tomb seven, the focus of the 500 precious grave goods was said to be a priest associated with the god Xollotl. However, this was because, in archaeology, figures associated with wealth and power are generally assumed to be male. Dr Sharisse McCafferty has not come up with any new evidence but applied a modern feminist perspective to the grave goods. The weaving battens are a badge of femininity, which boys were prevented from touching. There is also spinning equipment. What were originally thought to be false fingernails are, in the new interpretation, thought to be thimbles (Burne 1995). The skeleton, McCafferty argues, is therefore female.

- Sources may be cult or ceremonial objects that we do not understand. The Iron Age 'Waterloo Helmet' in the British Museum or the Uffington chalk horse in Berkshire may represent ideas or social practices about which we can only surmise. The recorded discussion of my Year 4 class about the meaning of the Uffington horse involved geology and the social organisation needed to make it and its practical and symbolic significance. They follow through and weigh each other's points of view, form imaginative ideas into logical arguments and use abstract concepts: co-operate, community, ceremonies, beliefs, customs. Here is a short extract.

It looks like a bird.

It's a horse.

They could draw horses.

So they had horses.

They were hard workers . . . skilful . . . artistic . . .

There must be a lot of chalk under the surface.

So there won't be trees like oak trees – not many trees.

They could live on the chalk; it's well-drained – the water would run away.

The soil would be thin – it's easy to plough.

Whatever tools they used it must have taken a long time. They must have co-operated. They lived in a community.

It's not an ordinary horse. It's much more different from the ones we see.

It must be a special one or they wouldn't go to all that trouble.

It's probably a symbol for something – a clue.

To bring a good harvest?

A symbol of strength?

To an enemy? Perhaps the horse brought bad luck so they stayed away.

Perhaps if someone was ill they prayed to it. It gave them power when they were ill.

Or perhaps they just had fun.

Maybe they danced around it – or put fires on it and burnt something, maybe for the chief's birthday.

I don't think they had birthdays.

But they had beliefs and ceremonies . . .

■ We have to accept that sometimes we cannot know. A recently unearthed pot of Roman face cream has been described as showing the 'finger marks of the woman who used it' – but is this merely a stereotypical assumption? What had happened to the fifty-six, taller-than-average Romans, all prime-of-life males, whose cleanly beheaded skeletons were found in York in 2004? Were they legionaries killed in battle, the result of a pagan ritual, victims of each other as gladiators, punished as a unit found guilty of cowardice, loyalists of the Emperor Caracalla's brother? The opinions of experts vary. What is certain is that they died horrible deaths, were a mix of nationalities, that they were of high social status. What is probable is that they were the elite victims of military persecution. What is possible is that they were killed for disloyalty or cowardice. The rest we can probably never know (Girling 2006).

■ Traces of the past may tell us something of people's actions, but we can never know the thoughts and feelings that underpin those actions. We cannot even know what a contemporary may be thinking and feeling. Sarah Wheeler, writing about historical biography, asks,

> What is motivation? It is a deep sea fish swimming around in the fecund depths of the subconscious. Which of us can say that we understand the tangled skeins of fears and desires that control our own behaviour, let alone those of our husband or wife, letting even more alone that of a long dead stranger.
>
> (Wheeler 2006)

Collingwood (1939) attempted to clarify the relationship between interpreting evidence and the thoughts and feelings of people. Historical evidence, whether it is an artefact, a building, a picture or writing, is the result of an action. An action is the result of rational thinking. Rational thought has its roots in feeling and imagination. Feelings and thinking only continue to exist to the extent that they are represented in the action, in the evidence. Collingwood says, for example, that we know that Julius Caesar invaded Britain in successive years, we can suppose that his thoughts may have been on trade or grain supply or a range of other possibilities and his underlying feelings may have included ambition or career advancement. Collingwood points out that a historian can share the thoughts of someone in the past because he has experienced similar feelings and thoughts within his own contexts through shared humanity but that, nevertheless, they are different thoughts because the person was thinking them in response to a particular, ongoing situation at the time.

■ It is necessary to understand societies in the past from the standpoint of a person living at the time, in a society that may have had different attitudes, values and beliefs from our own. Collingwood (1946) says that man does not live in a world of hard facts, to which thoughts make no difference, but in a society with moral, economic and political structures and rules; as the structure changes, man's thoughts and behaviour change too. People may have had different values and beliefs from our own, because they had different knowledge bases. We need to try to see the world from the standpoint of other times to try to understand why the Saxons relied on ducking or burning to determine guilt or innocence; why sixteenth-century people thought the plague was a punishment from God; why Victorian children worked in factories or were sent to the workhouse.

■ New evidence may be discovered. For example, the Mildenhall Treasure in the British Museum, a hoard of Roman silver plate dug up in 1943 in East Anglia, was thought by the farmer who discovered it to be pewter and he put it on his mantelpiece. When it was identified later by a visitor as Roman silver and examined by experts in the British Museum, historians were forced to reassess their ideas about the quality of silverware used in Eastern Britain in the fourth century AD. (www.britishmuseum.org→Explore→Highlights)

■ Evidence is often incomplete. Historians need to use imagination in order to do what Elton (1970) calls 'filling in the gaps' in a narrative, when evidence is incomplete. Ryle (1979) sees this as cashing in on the facts and using them: ammunition shortage and heavy rain before a battle cause the historian to wonder about the hungry rifleman and delayed mule trains. But historical imagination is not free floating. It needs to be based on the most likely explanations of what is known.

For all these reasons several hypotheses about a source may be different but equally valid. Making inferences from sources involves giving reasons for your argument, listening to the views of others and being prepared to change your mind, or to accept that often there is no single, correct answer. We have to make reasonable hypotheses about what we can infer. Such 'guesses' are valid if there is no contradictory evidence, if they are reasonable and if they fit in with whatever else is known about the period.

## Impact of learning theories on children's use of sources

### Inferences, probability, argument, progression

The key constructivist theorists are Piaget, Bruner and Vygotsky. Their work has been both modified and developed over the years by many others but essentially their contributions to our understanding of learning remain central.

#### Inferences about sources

Piaget offers some insights into the progression in children's ability to make inferences from sources. His work suggests a sequence in development in which, at first, children's thinking is dominated by intuitive trial and error, by the child's own experiences and feelings. Wood and Holden (1997) found, in discussing old domestic objects with

Key Stage 1 children, that the younger children drew *randomly* on their experience, including factual and fictional knowledge, although they were able to use this knowledge to make informed suggestions about how the artefacts were used; one child drew on his knowledge of Mrs Tiggy-Winkle. The older children's knowledge was more organised, and they were increasingly able to draw on relevant information from their home and school experience.

At the next stage of concrete operations Piaget found that a child can take in information from the tangible and visible world, fit it into existing mental patterns, adjusting these when necessary to accommodate new information, and so store it, in order to use it selectively to solve problems. A child at this stage is therefore able to form a reasoned premise and support it with a logical argument. In Chapter 12, children retain vocabulary they have learned in one context and transfer it to new contexts. They interpret evidence in a previously unseen map by drawing on a field visit to a similar area, on previous class discussion and also on their own ideas. They transfer the thinking skills they have learned in whole-class lessons to group discussion when no adult is present.

At a third stage of formal operations, it is possible to think in terms of abstract and negative propositions (if . . . then; either . . . or; when . . . is not; both . . . and) and to weigh all the possible variants in an argument. The Year 6 newspaper accounts of the Armada (pp. 130–2) show children just embarking on this stage.

## Argument

Piaget's work on language (1926; 1928) suggests that a young child is able to communicate a valid statement of fact or description. This is followed by a stage of 'primitive argument', in which the statement is followed by a deduction going beyond the information given but the explanation is implicit. At the next stage a child attempts to justify and demonstrate an assertion using a conjunction (since, because, therefore), but does not succeed in expressing a truly logical relationship. The child eventually arrives at 'genuine argument' through frequent attempts to justify an opinion, and is able to use 'because' correctly. An example of this is found in the archaeologist's report sheet on page 221. However, in history this sequence depends on the complexity of the evidence and the questions asked. Donaldson (1978) recognised that children's ability to reason depends on what the question is, how it is relevant to a child's concerns, the child's expectations of the questioner, the extent to which they concentrate on language and that language is related to non-verbal cues. She concludes that young children must develop their ability to reason and make inferences as early as possible by receiving the right kind of support.

## Rules

Piaget (1932) suggested that children at first see no reason for rules. At the next stage they think that rules must be rigidly obeyed, then later they recognise that there are circumstances in which they should be challenged or changed. In a historical context, initially people's behaviour is idiosyncratic. Then people are seen as good or bad, heroes or villains, friends or enemies. At a later stage children can begin to understand and discuss the reasons for people's behaviour, the values of a society different from their own, why perspectives differ. This is illustrated by the three perspectives of the Armada (pp. 130–2) and especially in the cartoon 'I thought God was on our side'.

## Probability

Piaget's work on probability (Piaget and Inhelder 1951) also shows that at first children cannot differentiate between chance and non-chance but at a concrete level they have an increasing understanding of what we can know and what we can guess. Eventually they can differentiate between what is certain and what is probable. (See examples in Chapter 11.)

## Teaching approaches and progression

Bruner (1963) introduced the notion of a 'spiral curriculum'. He set out the processes whereby a discipline may be structured so that the thinking processes which lie at the heart of a discipline can be tackled from the very beginning in their simplest form, then in increasingly complex ways. He said that this involved translating a subject into appropriate forms of representation that place emphasis on 'doing', on appropriate imagery, and a set of rules for making deductions and inferences. Problems, he said, must involve the right degree of uncertainty in order to be interesting, and learning should be organised in units, each building on the foundations of the previous one. He also said that we should define the skills children need in order to extrapolate from particular examples, from a memorable specific instance, to the general, in order to transfer the thinking processes learned to other similar problems; this gives confidence and avoids 'mental overload' of facts. Children learn, in whole-class lessons, how to ask and answer questions about sources, then are able to transfer this process to new sources (Chapter 12). They need opportunities to answer questions about tactile, visual and symbolic sources. This approach is also employed in the case study in Chapter 12. Each period is explored through site and museum visits, artefacts, pictures, diagrams, plans and written sources. Observations were recorded in a variety of ways using kinetic, iconic and symbolic approaches: through art techniques (painting, embroidery, lino cuts and silk screen prints, pottery), through science experiments (dyeing, firing clay, cooking food), through technology (building a model Roman kiln, an Iron Age hut), through writing in different genres (notes, poems, fiction, reports) and tape-recorded discussions. Bruner described the role of the teacher as 'scaffolding' children's learning, for example by questioning, cueing, providing resources. This was part of the whole-class lessons and is also exemplified in the structure of the archaeologist's report (p. 221), which aimed to structure thinking by developing causal thinking, differentiating between what is known and what can be 'guessed' and what cannot be known, and by encouraging the use of abstract concepts to reach conclusions – 'hard words'.

## Discussion

Vygotsky made two contributions to our understanding of children's ability to make deductions and inferences about sources. First, he demonstrated the importance of social interaction and trial and error through discussion, forming a point of view, listening to others, modifying the original viewpoint (1962). Second, his work on the 'zone of proximal development' (1978) showed how, by working with an adult or more competent peer, children's thinking can be taken forward. Both aspects of Vygotsky's work, discussion and concept development, are illustrated in Chapter 12.

## Recent research into children's use of sources

### Understanding different attitudes and values

Bage (2000: 26) says that leading learners willingly into worlds different from the societies in which they exist is a moral and creative act of the highest order. Barton (1996) found that children often seem to feel impelled to respond to the challenge of explaining attitudes and values in the past. For example, younger children (Ashby and Lee 2001) suggested that the Romans executed slaves 'because they did not know about God and Jesus'; Saxons resorted to deciding guilt by oath-taking because 'They did not know about police courts – or medicines – or about floating and sinking', or 'because it was their religion'. Older pupils tried to unpack the values and beliefs behind the institutions, referring to culture and norms. However, it is important to notice that some Year 2 children responded in ways characteristic of fourteen-year-olds. They behaved as if they believed that even puzzling institutions could be made intelligible by understanding how people saw their world, not by reference to our world.

### Distinguishing between validity and truth

Ashby (2004) investigated the development of the ability of pupils in Year 3, Year 6, Year 7 and Year 9 to grasp the difference between a true and a valid statement. She asked them how they could decide if the claim by the Welsh monk Nennius, that 'Arthur killed 960 Saxons at Mount Badon', was true. Their answers illustrated progression. The younger children wanted to find out from an authority, an adult or a book. They did consider the credibility of the author; 'monks would write the truth' (hem!). By Year 7 pupils recognised that books may differ, in which case they would see what most books say. Most Year 9 pupils questioned the author's claim on the basis of his ability to know. They recognised that inferences could be made from sources and considered whether these were likely. This study does explore progression in historical thinking but the methodology was based on a secondary school approach rather than starting from holistic primary practice so do not be pessimistic about the levels achieved here by some younger pupils.

## Developing historical imagination

Vass (2004) described a way of developing historical imagination through story. He based his approach on the view that the outcome of the historian's labours is 'any patterned account, intended to be true, of any past happenings involving human intention or doing or suffering' (Hexter 1971: 3). He gave pupils artefacts from the Second World War (e.g. blackout curtain, ration book, gas mask) and invited them to 'fill in the gaps' to make their own stories, set in London in the Blitz. They used event framing. This enabled the stories to take place within a given chronological framework. One child, evaluating the stories, concluded that, 'I think Jodie's story is more like it was than mine. There is more evidence.' She was, Vass reflects, 'discovering that historical evidence is not as tangible or obvious as imagined'. Children decided on a 'key factor' that determined the origin of the stories (e.g. the ration book was lost in the dark). This gave rise to interesting discussions about 'unique events' – 'No two stories are ever the same, even in history books . . . It depends on who is writing the story' – and to discussion about chance: 'Most things happen by chance . . . this, therefore that . . . There was a good chance of an air raid during the war but you never know do you, if that was how the ration book was lost?' Second, Vass drew on the work of Ferguson (1997), who argues for a 'chaotic' model of historical forces, where the actuality of the past is seen as only one of many possible outcomes; he claims that this helps historians to understand better what actually happened and why. The children constructed 'counterfactual histories', beginning with a Bethnal Green air raid in 1943 and ending, via six event frames, with the commemoration of the victims thirty years later. One child's perceptive conclusion was that, 'It was the rockets that did it [caused panic in which people were crushed to death]. The sirens worried people but it was the rockets going off that caused the panic. They were new. People had never heard that sound before. It was the rockets that did it.'

## Moving from abstract to concrete

Dilek and Yapici (2004) at the University of Marmara, in Istanbul, have challenged the notion that learning develops from concrete to abstract and, drawing on the research of Egan (1988) and others, suggested how a concept they call 'abstract thinking specific to childhood' might be developed through stories about the past. Gulcin Yapici read a story about 'Grandfather Seljuk' to a class, giving them opportunities for questioning and explanation during the story. The story was written to include descriptions of artefacts based on photographs in museum catalogues (Altun 2001). When the story ended children were asked to draw certain artefacts described in the story. Similarities with and differences from the original artefacts were analysed.

Three levels of abstract thinking in the children's responses to the story were identified. The story described servants pouring rose sherbets into glasses from a ceramic flask 'round like a globe with peacock decoration and two handles next to the rim'. Pupils' drawings correctly reflected this description. Dilek and Yapici called this 'static imagination' because it simply recorded what had been described (Figure 2.1).

SULUK

**FIGURE 2.1** Example of 'static imagination'. Drawing of water flask described in the story as 'shaped like a globe, with two handles near the rim and decorated with a peacock'. (Information is recorded but no detail added.)

They identified the next level of response as 'transition' from 'static' to 'dynamic imagination'. Pupils were asked to draw a coin depicting Suleiman Shah on his horse, carrying weapons with three prongs. There were six pointed stars on each of his shoulders and down his legs. Around the edge of the coin was written 'Destroyer Prince'. In general, pupils' coins looked very like the original but some had added details: headgear, saddle, boots not described in the story. They were 'filling in the gaps' in the information given, in valid ways. Similarly, one pupil added musical notes to a tray depicting wedding food (Figure 2.2).

At a third level Dilek and Yapici identified what they called 'dynamic imagina-tion'. Some pupils devised historically acceptable symbols representing abstract concepts. For example, a coin, described in the story simply as a 'symbol of sovereignty' (Aydin 1994) was depicted by a pupil as having a two-headed eagle, a symbol of the Anatolia Seljuks, on one side and Kabadabad Palace, symbol of the state, on the reverse (Figure 2.3). So the identified sequence was: description without addition; inclusion of valid details not given in the story; translation of undisclosed symbols into images representing abstract concepts.

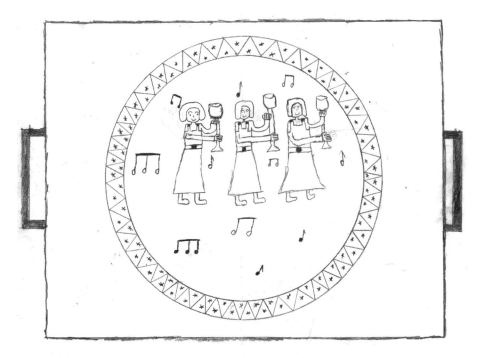

**FIGURE 2.2** Example of 'transition from static imagination to dynamic imagination'. Drawing of a bronze tray described in the story as decorated with women in long dresses, some holding glasses. The pupil has added musical notes to reflect the musical instruments mentioned in the story.

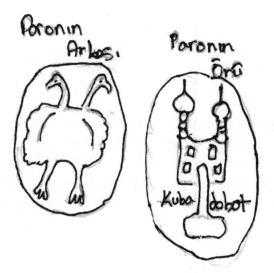

**FIGURE 2.3** Example of 'dynamic imagination'. The two-headed eagle on the front of the coin is the symbol of the Seljuk Turks and Kabadabad Palace on the back represents the economic and political power of the state. Information in the story is shown symbolically.

## Distinguishing between what is known and what can be guessed

A group of eight-year-olds (Cooper 1991) who had been learning about the Saxons through class lessons that involved making deductions and inferences (good guesses) about a variety of sources were given previously unseen sources to discuss. One of these was a slide of a replica of the Sutton Hoo Sceptre. They interpreted this within the framework of the knowledge acquired through their sequence of lessons.

1   Where did the Saxons come from, where did they settle, when and why? This lesson was based on Saxon artefacts (wrist clasps, brooches, etc.) linked to maps showing where the artefacts had been found, written evidence of the Roman withdrawal and Saxon records of where they settled (www.vortigernstudies.org.uk; Bede 2008; *Anglo Saxon Chronicle* 2007).

2   Inferences about Saxon life based on extracts from *Beowulf* (Heaney 1999).

3   Map of the seven kingdoms in AD 700, information about kingship from Bede (1990) and the *Anglo Saxon Chronicle* (Swanton 2000), and some seventh-century Anglo Saxon laws in Kent and Wessex.

4   Evidence of the spread of the Roman church and the Celtic church from Bede, linked to a map.

5   A local visit to Coulsdon to trace evidence of Saxon settlements from spring line, place names and hedge dating.

Here are some of the children's (written) responses to the questions: what do you know, what can you guess and what can't you know about the Sutton Hoo sceptre?

- I know: they had kings. Therefore they must have had to be obedient, they must have had to be loyal. They had a sceptre with an animal on it (deer). Therefore it must have been a symbol. It was precious. It took a long time to make. Therefore it must be unique.

- I can guess: the gold sculpture deer may be saying 'save our lives or where we live'. Therefore the sceptre may mean 'Kill us and be warned; you'll die'. That might be why the ruler carries it; to show he is the ruler for God on earth.

- I'd like to know: why it's made out of stone because it must be heavy and why there is no picture of himself on it, because it could tell us what sort of a king he was.

These eight-year-olds are discussing an artefact and applying information and thinking processes previously learned to a new source (Bruner 1963). They are distinguishing between what they know, what they can guess and what they would like to know

(Piaget and Inhelder 1951). They are using 'because' and 'therefore' to justify their statements about how it may have been made and used (Piaget 1926) and what it may have meant to the people who made and used it (Collingwood 1939). There are also attempts to consider the possible thoughts and feelings of these people (Collingwood 1946) and understanding that they probably had different values and beliefs as represented by the 'symbol'. Children were using their imagination, based on what they knew, and learning to make suppositions. The more they make, with maturity, the more valid these will become.

In an interesting study with seven-year-olds in Malta, Yvonne Vella (2004) describes a series of activities that were designed to help pupils to make inferences from pictures. At first the children were shown a painting and asked to 'say anything you wish about this painting'. The discussion was video-recorded. Activities followed that were intended to accelerate the children's ability to interpret visual sources.

- An early-twentieth-century photograph of a milk seller with goats was shown. Children were asked what they thought was going on. Then the photograph was divided into four using two strips of paper and the children were asked to look at specific areas of the picture and were asked much more specific questions.

- The children were given a magnifying glass to look at a small eighteenth-century picture of a toddler in a baby walker made of cane. This picture was part of a larger painting, which was later uncovered. The children could see whether they had been correct in their first analysis.

- A nineteenth-century painting of sailors looking out from a boat. The children were asked to play a game in which the paper was lifted for a brief moment. Each time they were asked to say what they had spotted.

- Children were shown a nineteenth-century picture of a Maltese lady and were asked, 'Do you think this lady really looked like this?'

Then the children returned to the original picture. Again their discussion was recorded. They focused much more on the detail in the picture and the points they made were more complex.

## Student teachers investigate children's inferences about sources

Paula Andrews wondered what sorts of questions her Key Stage 1 class should be encouraged to ask and what was the teacher's role. Is there progression from Year 1 to Year 2? What artefacts stimulate the most questions and why? She found that the youngest children made observations but needed help in turning these into questions. As they got older they were able to formulate their own questions and increasingly asked open questions that led to discussions: how things were made, how they were used and why. The artefacts that stimulated the most interest and discussion were things that worked and could be explored through manipulation.

Beverley Wright used a literacy session on adjectives to ask her Year 3/4 class to make inferences about the people depicted in Tudor portraits. She, like Claire (1996), found that children attributed strengths and weaknesses to male and female portraits respectively. Beverley used the plenary session to discuss this with them and challenge their assumptions.

## Some ideas for practical activities using sources to engage you in reflection on your own practice

### Writing, maps, pictures, artefacts

■ Portraits. Put a portrait in the middle of a sheet of paper and invite children to make a spider graph of what they can infer from the portrait. Can they divide their ideas into categories; what categories? Do children get better at this activity with experience? In what ways? What was your role?

■ For each group place the source in the centre of a large piece of paper with the heading, 'What does this source tell me?' This piece of paper stands on three pieces of paper of increasing size so that they overlap each other with the headings: 'What guesses can I make about it?' 'What does the source not tell me?' 'What other questions do I need to ask?' The children write their ideas on the appropriate piece of paper around the source. Are there more responses to one of the questions? Do some sources inspire more responses? Why? From everyone or some children?

■ Site visits. Visiting a site is not mere information collecting. Children need a genuine historical puzzle within which to root their activity. The puzzle, or enquiry, must be historically worthwhile and personally motivating and negotiated with the children. Pupils need to work on their own line of questioning. They must be prepared before the visit, so that they arrive focused and ready to go and they need to know what they have learned about historical enquiry (examples are described on pp. 61, 70, 112 and 151). How many of the pre-visit questions came from the children? How many were answered? How many of the follow-up activities were their ideas? How much of their learning were they aware of; was it process plus content? Why did they enjoy this project?

# References

Altun, A. (2001) *Aladdin's Lamp and the Art of the Anatolian Seljuks*. Yapi Kredi Kultur Sanat Yayincilic, 45.

*Anglo Saxon Chronicle* (anonymous) (2007). Teddington: The Echo Library.

Ashby, R. (2004) 'Developing a concept of historical evidence: students' ideas about testing singular factual claims', *International Journal of History Teaching Learning and Research*, 4(2), 44–55 (www.history.org.uk).

Ashby, R. and Lee, P. (2001) 'Empathy, perspective taking and rational understanding', in O.L. Davis, S. Foster and E. Yaeger (eds) *Historical Empathy and Perspective Taking in Social Studies*. Maryland and Colorado: Rowman & Littlefield.

Aydin, S. (1994) *dogu-bati arasi bir gokkusagi* [*The Seljuks: a rainbow linking East and West*]. Istanbul: Yapi Kredi Kultur Merkezi.

Bage, G. (2000) *Thinking History 4–14, Teaching, Learning, Curricula and Communities, New Directions*. Oxford: Blackwell.

Barton, K. (1996) 'Narrative simplifications in elementary students' historical thinking', in J. Brophy (ed.) *Advances in Research on Teaching, Vol. 6: teaching and learning history*. Greenwich: JAI Press, 5–83.

Bede (1990) *Ecclesiastical History of the English People*. London: Penguin Classics.

Bede (2008) McClure, J., Collins, R. and Colgrave, B. (eds) *The Ecclesiastical History of the English People*. Oxford: Oxford University Press.

Bruner, J.S. (1963) *The Process of Education*. New York: Vintage Books.

Burne, J. (1995) 'Sex change for skeleton after feminist enquiry', *Sunday Telegraph*, 15 January.

Claire, H. (1996) *Reclaiming the Past: equality and diversity*. London: Trentham Books.

Collingwood, R.G. (1939) *An Autobiography*. Oxford: Oxford University Press.

Collingwood, R.G. (1946) *The Idea of History*. Oxford: Clarendon.

Cooper, H. (1991) 'Young Children's Thinking in History', unpub. Ph.D. London University Institute of Education.

Dilek, D. and Yapici, G. (2004) 'The use of stories in the teaching of history', *International Journal of History Teaching Learning and Research*, 5(2), 61–72 (www.history.org.uk).

Donaldson, M. (1978) *Children's Minds*. London: Fontana.

Egan, K. (1988) *Teaching as Story Telling: an alternative approach to teaching and curriculum*. London: Routledge.

Elton, G.R. (1970) 'What sort of history should we teach?' in M. Ballard (ed.) *New Movements in the Study and Teaching of History*. London: Temple Smith.

Ferguson, N. (1997) (ed.) *Virtual History: alternatives and counterfactuals*. London: Macmillan, Picador.

Girling, R. (2006) 'A cemetery of secrets', *The Sunday Times*, Magazine, 14–18, 26 March (www.bbc.co.uk/timewatch).

Harlow, J. (1996) 'Found: site of forgotten battle that decided 1066 and all that', *The Sunday Times*, News, 3, 29 December.

Heaney, S. (1999) *Beowulf: a new translation*. London: Faber & Faber.

Hexter, J. (1971) *The History Primer*. New York: Basic Books.

Piaget, J. (1926) *The Language and Thought of the Child*. London: Routledge.

Piaget, J. (1928) *Judgement and Reasoning in the Child*. London: Kegan Paul.

Piaget, J. (1932) *Moral Judgement and the Child*. London: Kegan Paul.

Piaget, J. and Inhelder, B. (1951) *The Origin of the Idea of Chance in the Child*. London: Routledge.

Ryle, G. (1979) *On Thinking*. Oxford: Blackwell.

Swanton, A. (ed.) (2000) *The Anglo Saxon Chronicle*. London: Orion, Weidenfeld & Nicolson History.

Vass, P. (2004) 'Thinking skills and the learning of primary history: thinking historically through stories', History Educators' International Research Conference, St Martin's College, Ambleside, England, *International Journal of History Teaching, Learning and Research*, 4(2) (www. history.org.uk).

Vella, Y. (2004) 'Assessing history talk in a group', History Educators' International Research Conference, St Martin's College, Ambleside, England.

Vygotsky, L.S. (1962) *Thought and Language*. London: Wiley.

Vygotsky, L.S. (1978) *Mind in Society: the development of higher psychological processes*. Cambridge, MA: Harvard University Press.

Wheeler, S. (2006) 'And so the years passed . . .' *Spectator*, 48, 25 March.

Wood, E. and Holden, C. (1997) 'I can't remember doing the Romans: the development of children's understanding in history', *Teaching History*, 89, 9–11.

# 3

# Interpretations and accounts

## What are interpretations?

Interpretations of the past are accounts of a period, written in a subsequent period. To try to make sense of the past, historians combine their inferences about sources to create accounts of the past. In Chapter 2 we considered the many reasons why sources may be interpreted differently. In this chapter we shall consider why accounts may differ, but be equally valid, and also why they may be of different levels of validity.

- Sources may be incomplete but they are also numerous and wide-ranging. Historians therefore have to select the sources relevant to their accounts. Selection depends on the focus of their accounts for, as we have seen, there are many types of history, from political, social, economic to sports history, history of music or art, histories of groups or individuals, broad or in-depth.

- Historians also write from their own interests and perspectives: gender, ethnicity, politics, social class. Rowbotham (1973), Beddoe (1983), Boulding (1976; 1977; 1981) and Hill (1989; 1996; 2001) take a female perspective. Fryer (1984; 1989) writes from the perspective of a black historian and Vishram (1988) from an Indian perspective. C.V. Wedgwood's (1955) account of the English Civil War is different from that of the Marxist historian Christopher Hill (1980). Chinn (1995) takes a working-class and a female, though not necessarily feminist, perspective.

- Accounts reflect the dominant values of the time in which they were written. The Victorians, for example, focused on finding aspects of British freedoms and rights embedded in Saxon laws. In the statue of Queen Victoria and Prince Albert, in the National Portrait Gallery, London, commemorating Albert's untimely death, they are wearing Saxon costume!

## Interpretations change with time

History is dynamic. Historians challenge previous interpretations. The raids of Bomber Command in the Second World War were seen as necessary and effective for a variety of reasons until Max Hastings (1979) questioned this, saying that the raids were both ineffective and disproportionate. (As a result red paint was thrown over the statue of 'Bomber Harris'.) Anthony Grayling (2006) demonstrated the bombing to be, according to the laws obtaining at the time and subsequently, an essentially immoral activity.

*Wild Scots* (Fry 2005) challenges the dominant account of the Scottish clearances by pointing out that many Highland landlords were benevolent Tory paternalists who went to great lengths to maintain the ties that bound the people to the land. Dee Brown's *Bury My Heart at Wounded Knee* (1991) challenges the traditional image of the 'Wild West'. Niall Ferguson's *Colossus* (2002) re-examines America's dominance and argues that America really is an Empire, before going on to argue that this is something to celebrate. Churchill once said that he would ensure his place in history by writing it – but historians are still writing it.

Apparently Captain Bligh, immortalised in *Mutiny on the Bounty* as the cause of the crew's spontaneous revolt against a tyrannical captain and cast adrift by his second-in-command, Fletcher Christian, has now been found to have been a seafaring hero and a humane captain, victimised by Christian when he ran out of laudanum (Hellen 1998).

## Interpretations change with place

A letter in *The Times* (30 December 1996) from Dr Olga Ashby illustrates what she describes as 'the cultural divide between the two sides of the Iron Curtain'. She lived in Moscow during the 1980s before moving to England. She recalls how she was taught that the battle described in Tennyson's poem, 'The Charge of the Light Brigade', was lost as the result of the blunders of the British commanding officers was represented in Russia as a triumph of Russian strategy; the 'original nurse' of the Crimean War was not Florence Nightingale but Dasha Sevastopolskata.

## Children and interpretations in history books

Children can compare different written accounts at their own levels by comparing different information books on the same historical subject. As discussed above, how has the content been selected? Is the focus on everyday life of rich or poor, or on art and artefacts, on individuals or events? Are there inferences about beliefs and values, thoughts and feelings, and how are these justified? Are statements supported by evidence of why this is thought? Is a book written from the perspectives and interests of children – from different backgrounds? Do they represent and value men and women equally? Are they illustrated with artists' impressions, themselves interpretations, or with photographs of sources? What is not included? How do children's books published at different times in the past differ from those of today, in language, hidden messages, selected content?

## Examples of children's understanding of interpretations

Hoodless (2004) has analysed ten- and eleven-year-old children's understanding of the changing attitudes and values revealed in historical stories written at different times in the twentieth century. She found that they were able to identify changing styles of presentation with a subtle understanding that adults' different attitudes are transmitted through historical accounts and stories written in different periods. After reading about Boudicca in Sarson and Paine (1930) and in Deary (1994), the children commented on the way each reflected the values of its time; the earlier text avoided dwelling on death and the embarrassment of suicide. The children thought that, in the romantic style of the earlier text, Boudicca was treated with the respect due to a queen and her husband was considered to have done 'the right thing'. They were conscious that the writer's style was intended for children who were regarded differently from children today, and also of its response to the time in which it was written:

> It seems to come out of that time. It reads like it was written just after the war, all proud about how we defend ourselves.

Another child commented:

> You have an image of what other people thought of her, how she was very brave. The problem with that is that because of the time it was based in you don't know if that's what it was actually like . . . Stories change in the time they're told . . . It can completely change the image of someone.

They recognised that the first version was told as a matter of fact while in the second they were invited to decide between various possibilities. Children commented on how they preferred making their own decisions because 'people's opinions, written up in stories, might be wrong'.

Fictional stories about the past in historical settings are also reconstructions. Children can read these or write their own, identifying what is known and what is 'guessed at' to fill in the gaps.

## Interpretations through re-enactment

Accounts of the past are not made only by historians. There is now an enormous variety of forms of interpretation of past times. They may be living reconstructions such as The Black Country Museum (www.bclm.co.uk) or Beamish Museum (www.beamish.org.uk) or re-enactments of events. Kentwell Hall in Long Melford in Suffolk is the setting for a Tudor recreation for schoolchildren for three weeks each year. The surroundings of the redbrick Elizabethan manor are peopled with 400 're-enactors' at any one time, for the children to interact with: dyers, woodsmen, weavers, chandlers, alchemists, cooks, pedlars, seamstresses, musicians and gentry.

A long list of living history re-enactments is given on www.reenactor.net. Reconstructions may be static museum reconstructions, for example the prehistory galleries in the Museum of London, or reconstructions such as the Iron Age Village at Butser in the Queen Elizabeth Park, Hampshire. Such reconstructions are the product of informed historical enquiry or, as with Butser, of historical research (Reynolds 1979). Children can try to find out how such reconstructions were made (what is the evidence?) by asking questions on the site, comparing with other sources or information books, and consider why they were made and their validity.

Less academic accounts are made for different purposes and may have different levels of validity. Benjamin Britten's opera, *Gloriana*, the BBC television serial *Blackadder II* and the BBC film *The Virgin Queen* give very different interpretations of Elizabeth I that are easy for young children to identify and explain (see p. 137). Similar stark contrast is provided by a model Iceni village in Norfolk, complete with brightly painted horses' heads and skulls on poles, which is very different from the scientific reconstruction at Butser. The statue of Boudicca on the Embankment in London represents a different interpretation of the period from that in *Asterix in Britain* (Goscinny 2004). New interactive media technologies are making new kinds of historical interpretation possible. It is possible to walk through virtual museums and virtual sites. A great deal of research into virtual museums is being undertaken by Manchester Metropolitan Museum (www. doc.mmu.ac.uk/virtualmuseum). There are also BBC interactive TV adventures, for example *Pyramid: Beyond Imagination*, and interactive BBC digital programmes. I was involved as a consultant on a BBC digital history programme for three- to eight-year-olds that is intended to be used either independently or with parents to supplement work in school or playgroup. My job was to ensure that it involved the processes of historical enquiry in activities related to a prehistoric hunt, a castle and an Edwardian street. It raised some interesting problems about creating an interpretation.

## Children's accounts through re-enactments

If children can create their own interpretations through reconstructions this is not only fun but helps them to consider how interpretations are created and their validity. They may be reconstructions created through play. Play in historical contexts is discussed elsewhere (Cooper 2002; 2004) and on pages 93 and 96–7. Older children may create considered historical drama (as seen on TV!) over a longer period, researching character, place, setting, and examining a problem or an issue, considering what is based on research and what needs to be imagined based on what is known. This could link well with literacy objectives. If it were made into a film this would also have ICT objectives and the cross-curricular approach would justify the time spent. Why not add design and technology, designing sets? This would also be a way of 'communicating results of an enquiry'. Or there may be two dramas made, an interpretation from a female and male perspective. (Getting carried away now. Can't wait to get back into a school!) There are companies that provide units of history work resulting in a musical production (www. educationalmusicals.com), although I prefer the children's own creations. A range of historical costumes for Key Stages 1 and 2 can be purchased from Charlie Crow Costumes (www.charliecrow.co.uk). We once did a performance of the musical *Oliver!*

and discussed it in relation to factual enquiries about the poor in Victorian London. I have the photograph on my wall still of me dressed as a chimney sweep – because it's fun for teachers to join in too!

Interpretations created could be a series of paintings or murals, maybe as a background to a museum exhibition, depicting aspects of a period studied, based on what can be researched about different aspects of life or different key events; there are links to art here too. Any display is itself a reconstruction in which some things are selected and others neglected; models are reconstructions within a display reconstruction. Making models – Viking boats, Tudor houses, Iron Age huts – is fine as long as, in the process, children find out what they can from sources – and become aware of the problems involved in reconstructing from sources.

## Why is it important to understand 'interpretations'?

Understanding how and why accounts of the past are made has been found to be a neglected aspect of historical enquiry in primary schools, yet children enjoy thinking seriously about accounts, which can nevertheless be light-hearted and funny. They enjoy accounts made using different kinds of information technology. Since the past and heritage and family and local history are now frequently regarded as popular leisure activities and as entertainment, it is increasingly important that children can evaluate them. There are also more serious reasons for learning why there is no single view of the past and that accounts of the past are dynamic and may vary and change over time. Children are learning to challenge validity and assess validity and to recognise different motives behind creating accounts. For history is the most politically powerful subject in the curriculum and earns constant attention from politicians.

## International comparisons

The importance of allowing pupils to discuss alternative interpretations of the past is made painfully real and clear in societies where history is contested, such as Northern Ireland or South Africa. Barton and McCully (2005) emphasise how history plays a contentious role in popular discussion and community conflict in Northern Ireland and one purpose of the school curriculum is to provide alternatives to the sectarian, historical perspectives pupils encounter elsewhere. Their interviews with 253 secondary school pupils demonstrated the strong impact of community influences, especially family members, but they also revealed that pupils consciously and explicitly expected the school to provide alternatives to those influences.

Harnett (2005) analysed how the British Empire and Commonwealth Museum in Bristol attempts to construct the narrative of Empire and takes account of different interpretations and alternative viewpoints within its collection. The museum, reflecting the work of contemporary historians, revises the Victorian view of Empire, epitomised by Cecil Rhodes's remark that 'the British are the finest race in the world and the more of the world they inhabit, the better it will be for mankind' (Cannadine 2001) with contemporary interpretations that reflect current values of equality of opportunity and human rights. (The history of Britain in the nineteenth century and the first part of the twentieth century is central to the history of Empire, whether viewed from a peripheral or metropolitan perspective.) In Harnett's study primary pupils investigated the lives of different individuals and social groups within the Empire, the challenges of the early settlers, the colonisation of Australia and the experiences of a Caribbean immigrant.

Hilary Claire gives many suggestions about how to help children to understand different perspectives and references to her other excellent work (Claire 2005: 24–43).

In South Africa, Gail Weldon (2004) explains how it is the explicit aim of the revised history curriculum to identify and develop values of 'democracy, equality, human dignity and social justice'. She points out, however, that the teachers were conditioned, in varying degrees, to the attitudes and prejudices of apartheid society, and as a result projects have been set up to support teachers and learners in education for human rights and democracy through history, with Nazi Germany and Apartheid South Africa as case studies.

In 1994 Jon Nichol and I set up the History Educators' International Research Network (www.history.org.uk) through which researchers in history education could share their work. We have had a number of successful conferences. The 2005 conference on museums was about identity and citizenship. A number of the papers focused on the extent to which pupils are encouraged to understand that there may be more than one interpretation or that interpretations can change.

In a Portuguese study Barca and Pinto (2005) took children aged between ten and fourteen for a walk through the historic town of Guimaraes. They compared the large new 'castle' constructed in the days of the Salazar dictatorship with an engraving of the original, thirteenth-century castle it had replaced. The children were very articulate in comparing the two buildings, understanding why each had been built and how, and were clear about why they thought this should not have happened.

In Quebec Jocelyn Letourneau (2005) tried to contest the French Canadians' interpretation of Canadian history as a golden age until the British arrived and took it over for their own benefit. The Quebeckers are depicted in textbooks as childlike, dominated by their seigneurs and priests until the British invaders imposed commerce and progress. In 1995 nearly half of Quebeckers voted to split from Canada. Letourneau tried to set up a museum exhibition challenging the partial view of Canadian history but the challenge was not responded to. Alternative interpretations were not accepted. Other examples can be found elsewhere. In Germany there is a different interpretation of the past taught in the former East Germany and West Germany; the former teaches only about the positive values of the GDR and the latter, vice versa. Pupils are not invited to compare and discuss these interpretations. In the United States of America Rozensweig (2000) has suggested that pupils see themselves as conscripts or prisoners and teachers as drill sergeants or wardens.

Recent work on 'Doing History in elementary schools' (e.g. Levstik and Barton 2000) introduces teachers to the idea that history is about asking questions, that it is interpretive and controversial; you 'get to argue', and 'There sure aren't many facts!'

Young children may not be debating the major issues through comparing interpretations, but they are learning that there is more than one version of the past, and beginning to understand why.

# References

Barca, I. and Pinto, H. (2005) 'How children make sense of historic streets: walking through downtown Guimaraes', *International Journal of History Teaching Learning and Research*, 6, 2–9 (www.history.org.uk).

Barton, K. and McCully, A.W. (2005) 'Learning history and inheriting the past: the interaction of school and community perspectives in Northern Ireland', *International Journal of History Teaching, Learning and Research*, 5(1), 41–9 (www.history.org.uk).

Beddoe, D. (1983) *Discovering Women's History*. London: Pandora.

Boulding, E. (1976) *Handbook of International Data on Women*. Beverly Hills, CA: Sage.

Boulding, E. (1977) *Women in the Twentieth Century World*. New York: Sage.

Boulding, E. (1981) *The Underside of History*. Boulder, CO: Westview.

Brown, D. (1991) *Bury My Heart at Wounded Knee*. New York: Henry Holt.

Cannadine, D. (2001) *Ornamentalism. How the British saw their Empire*. London: Penguin.

Chinn, C. (1995) *Poverty amidst Prosperity: the urban poor in England 1834–1914*. Manchester: Manchester University Press.

Claire, H. (2005) 'Learning and teaching about citizenship through history in the early years', in *Leading Primary History*. London: The Historical Association, 24–43.

Cooper, H. (2002) *History in the Early Years*, 2nd edn. London: Routledge.

Cooper, H. (ed.) (2004) *Exploring Time and Place Through Play*. London: David Fulton.

Deary, T. (1994) *The Rotten Romans*. London: Scholastic.

Ferguson, N. (2002) *Colossus: the price of America's Empire*. New York: Penguin.

Fry, M. (2005) *Wild Scots: four hundred years of Highland history*. London: John Murray.

Fryer, P. (1984) *Staying Power*. London: Pluto.

Fryer, P. (1989) *Black People in the British Empire: an introduction*. London: Pluto.

Goscinny, R. (2004) *Asterix in Britain*. London: Orion.

Grayling, A.C. (2006) *Among the Dead Cities*. London: Bloomsbury.

Harnett, P. (2005) 'Exploring the potential for history and citizenship education with primary children' at the British Empire and Commonwealth Museum, Bristol, *International Journal of History Teaching Learning and Research*, 6, 34–9 (www.history.org.uk).

Hastings, M. (1979) *Bomber Command*. London: Michael Joseph.

Hellen, N. (1998) 'Sex and drugs drove mutiny on the Bounty', *The Sunday Times*, News, 4 January.

Hill, B. (1989) *Women, Work and Sexual Politics*. London: Routledge.

Hill, B. (1996) *Servants, English Domestics in the Eighteenth Century*. Oxford: Clarendon.

Hill, B. (2001) *Women Alone: spinsters in England 1660–1850*. London: The MIT Press.

Hill, C. (1980) *The World Turned Upside Down: radical ideas during the English Revolution*. Harmondsworth: Penguin.

Hoodless, P. (2004) 'Spotting adult agendas: investigating children's historical awareness using stories written for children in the past', *International Journal of History Teaching, Learning and Research*, 4(2), 66–74 (www.history.org.uk).

Letourneau, J. (2005) 'Museums and the (un)building of historical consciousness', QCA Symposium (www.heirnet.org).

Levstik, L.S. and Barton, K.C. (2000) *Doing History: investigating with children in elementary and middle schools*, 2nd edn. Mahwah, NJ: Laurence Erlbaum Associates.

Reynolds, P. (1979) *Butser, an Iron Age Farm*. London: British Museum Publications (www.butser.org.uk).

Rowbotham, S. (1973) *Hidden from History*. London: Pluto.

Rozensweig, R. (2000) 'How Americans use and think about the past: implications from the National Survey for the Teaching of History', in P. Stearns, P. Sexias and S. Wineburg (eds) *Knowing Teaching and Learning History: national and international perspectives*. New York and London: State University of New York Press.

Sarson, M. and Paine, M.E. (1930) *Stories from Greek, Roman and Old English History*, Piers Plowman Histories, Junior Book 11. London: George Philip & Son.

*The Times* (1996) Letters to the editor, Dr Olga Asby, 30 December.

Vishram, R. (1988) *Ayars, Lascars and Princes*. London: Pluto.

Wedgwood, C.V. (1955) *The King's Peace 1637–1641 (The Great Rebellion)*. London: Collins.

Weldon, G. (2004) 'Thinking each other's history. Can facing the past contribute to education for human rights and democracy?' *International Journal of History Teaching, Learning and Research*, 5(1), 62–70 (www.history.org.uk).

# 4

# Concepts, time and chronology

## What are historical concepts?

- Procedural concepts. Key historical concepts are concerned with the processes of historical enquiry, making deductions and inferences from sources and combing sources to create accounts that trace changes over time. These concepts include: evidence, source, cause, effect, similarity, difference, continuity, change, validity, interpretation.

- Time concepts. Other concepts central to history are concerned with the measurement of time (now, then, decade, century) or with describing periods of time (Victorian, Elizabethan).

- Concepts used in history but no longer used or used very differently today (villa, bailey, common).

- Concepts central to history but not exclusively historical. These are concepts that are at the heart of the process of tracing changes in societies, and their subordinate concepts. Examples are: agriculture (farm, field, crops, etc.); trade (buy, sell, profit, wealth); defence/attack (fight, battle, weapon).

### Learning theory and historical concepts

Vygotsky (1962) pioneered research into how we learn concepts, which has been developed subsequently. First, concepts are hierarchical. For example, if children are introduced to, and encouraged to use, the word castle, perhaps on a visit, they may associate it initially with this particular building. Through talking about the visit, the drawbridge, the moat, the mound, the battlements (level 1 concepts), they will be introduced to and use specialised concepts that are all part of an overarching concept, the castle (level 2). They will become aware, through the talk and the concrete examples, that a castle was built for defence against attack. This will give the owner power (level 3, abstract concepts). Children do not necessarily learn the most concrete concepts first.

## Learning complex concepts

Children learn new concepts by sorting into categories, at first through physically sorting pictures or artefacts into groups, using trial and error and discussion. The teacher may initially suggest the categories, for example 'old' and 'new' objects can generate a great deal of discussion among young children of what these concepts mean. Later they can sort images into categories they select. The same set of pictures about, for example, Elizabethan England, may be divided into town and country, rich and poor, adults and children, work and leisure. (They might collect pictures from books and photocopy them, or from the internet, to make the cards themselves.) This is an activity through which children can learn key concepts through images and talk. It is open ended: more able children may create categories and subcategories, country and rich/poor; town and children/adults; leisure and different types of leisure activities. They can create diagrams or lists based on the sets, or write paragraphs describing images of rich and poor children and speculate further about their lives. Perhaps they will suggest more complex categories: contemporary images or those produced later; different levels of validity, techniques and media used to create them.

I used activities base on a PowerPoint® image of *The Railway Station*, painted by William Powell Frith and first exhibited in 1862 (downloaded from www.rhul.ac.uk/visitors-guide/picture-gallery.html) to introduce an 'overarching' concept devised by historians, 'The Industrial Revolution'. Wide-ranging discussion of the image gradually led to the introduction of concepts that are central to the Industrial Revolution, such as iron, coal, steam, clock-time, mobility, middle classes.

The children then sorted images of coal mining, iron mining, industrial cities, steam power (used to power engines, ships, machines in factories). Sorting these into categories, then suggesting the connections between the categories conveyed an enormous amount of knowledge about the Industrial Revolution, generated a lot of conversation and raised many questions. Some complex and important concepts were learned without the need for any reading or writing.

If they are explicitly introduced to new vocabulary at each level and given opportunities to use it, quite young children enjoy using and experimenting with 'hard words' (Chapter 12, p. 227). Vygotsky (1962) showed how concepts are learned through trial and error, in communication with others. A visit to a castle may be followed up by research to find more examples of castles. A peel tower (farm house with defensive tower) may be rejected because it is 'only a house', which could lead to discussion about whether being fortified justifies its inclusion in 'castles'. Or claims may be made that a monastic ruin is a castle because it is built of similar materials, which would lead to further refining of the concept of castle. A Victorian folly, such as Balmoral, could extend the discussion further: what exactly is the definition of a castle?

# Concepts of time and chronology

## Similarities and differences between periods

*History for All* (Ofsted 2011) found that primary pupils had a good understanding of the topics they had studied. Indeed a study in 1997, comparing what ten-year-old children in five European countries said they knew about the past, I found that the English children were by far the most the most knowledgeable, referring to every topic in the National Curriculum (Cooper 2000). However the *History for All* (Ofsted 2011) report was critical of children's concepts of time and chronology. First, children were not able to compare similarities and differences between periods. Maybe this could be remedied by building key concepts into each study unit, for example religion, homes, leisure, transport, conflict art and music. This would give children the knowledge from which to speculate about similarities and differences and the reasons for them and the causes and effects of changes and how they interconnect.

## The big picture

Second, Ofsted (2011) found that children did not have a coherent mental map, a 'big picture' of the past or a sense of the duration of periods or of the gaps between periods or events. Blyth (1994: 154) recognised that 'the basic problem in primary history is how to combine development in children's thinking with the sweep of history itself'. This is hardly surprising, given the chronological gaps between the study units of the National Curriculum, which omits study of the Middle Ages, the seventeenth and eighteenth centuries and the early nineteenth century in primary schools. It would be difficult therefore to make reasonable hypotheses about reasons for changes across periods. What was the reason for castles and why were they abandoned? How did Tudor expansion become the British Empire? What caused the Second World War? Certainly asking questions about time and change is central to historical enquiry, yet the curriculum did not facilitate this. Hodkinson (2003) analysed the ways in which the National Curriculum failed to encourage chronological understanding: five- to seven-year-olds and less able older children were expected to use vocabulary describing the passing of time (a long time ago, now, the, before, after) yet temporal vocabulary was not mentioned in the study units or schemes of work for seven- to nine-year-olds and the learning tasks, vocabulary and use of resources in other units were, Hodkinson claims, vague and inconsistent. He finds the use of such terms as 'a long time ago' confusing since children's definition of such a term varied from a few years ago to hundreds, thousands or billions of years ago. Nevertheless it is important to remember that

> knowledge and chronology are by no means synonymous with historical sense. Teaching history involves coming to terms with particular ways of explaining time to children, which could, and sometimes do, run the risk of moulding children into preferred patterns of thinking, just as a rigid school timetable segments the day into artificial boxes.
>
> (Lello 1980: 347)

It is also important to be aware that the selection of content on timelines raises important questions about significance and to be articulate about why this is considered significant and by whom.

## Concepts of time

Concepts of time are complex. They are subjective. One study found that farm labourers in a French village, whose families had lived there for generations, had a perspective which went beyond their personal experience, whereas immigrant glass-blowers from itinerant families who moved into the village were almost without a sense of the past (Bernot and Blancard 1953). The concept of time is also cultural. The doings of Cromwell, the Act of Union and the famine of 1847 may seem more recent to an Irish person than to an English person. Teachers need to be aware of children's different personal and cultural narratives, given the enormous migration in the modern world. As Bruner has written (1996: 41) 'It is not easy, however multicultural your intentions, to help a ten-year-old create a story that includes him in the world beyond his family and neighbourhood, having been translated from Vietnam . . . Algeria . . . Anatolia . . .'.

Yet time and chronology can help children to place themselves within a temporal and cultural context and so form a sense of identity. For young children this helps them to see relationships within their own families, then wider groups – local communities, country, cultural background. Bruner continued that, 'If school, his pied-a-terre, cannot help (a child) there are alienated counter cultures that can'. Concepts of change also alter with age. I remember when 'next Summer' seemed an infinity away, four years at university seemed endless, yet now decades seem to spin by.

### Measuring time

Recently there has been a considerably increased emphasis in some quarters on the need to know dates, although the reasons for the importance of dates, in developing chronological understanding, has not been explained. Chronology is derived from the Greek meaning a study of time. It is not simply a matter of reciting the dates of the kings and queens, which in itself has little purpose. An illustrated chart of the Kings and Queens of England, recently distributed with *The Times*, accompanied the cartoon-style portrait of each monarch with particularly useless information: Athelstan (924–39) 'liked to collect relics and hunt'; Edward 1 'made the first laws to punish burglars'; Edred (946) 'had a weakness of the feet and had to spit out food he couldn't swallow'. If it is considered essential, as has recently been claimed, that children sit in rows and concentrate on key dates of Kings and Queens of England, this can be achieved quite quickly by chanting my grandma's aide memoire.

> Willi, Willi, Harry Stee,
> Harry, Dick, John, Harry Three,
> One, two, three Neds, Richard Two,
> Harrys four, five six – then who?
> Edwards four, five, Dick the Bad,
> Harrys twain, Ned six (the lad),
> Mary, Bessie, James, you ken, Then Charlie,
> Charlie, James again . . .

This will leave you ample time for learning real history! For understanding chronology involves understanding concepts of sequence, change, duration and causes and effects of changes, reasons for slow changes or rapid changes. This is central to historical enquiry and understanding. It involves asking questions and trying to answer them through calculations, and making connections between changes in different aspects of a period or periods. How do agriculture and communication systems and industry and religion and politics interact for example? Does this suggest any similarities between Elizabethan and Victorian England?

Understanding how to represent the passing of time in concrete forms varies across cultures. Ancient civilisations recorded the passing of time in cycles, in relation to seasons or planets. Some civilisations still record the passing of time as circular and cyclic. In Western Europe time has been measured in hours by clocks, in months by calendars and in years as linear, using timelines and the concept of BC and AD, or BCE and CE (Before Common Era and Common Era). The term Common Era (CE) uses non-religious terminology. The Islamic system measures time from an event in the life of Mohammed. Recording the measurement of time requires not only historical knowledge but also skills of numeracy, literacy, data handling and information processing skills.

## What chronological skills can we expect primary school children to learn and how can we teach them?

Until the later decades of the last century children's capacity for chronological understanding was thought to be limited. However, what children can achieve depends on the amount of historical knowledge they have, on the ways in which they have been taught, on their general ability and their motivation, so research findings, which vary depending on the time in which the research was undertaken, can only be regarded as a guide. Booth (1994) and others found that children's thinking about time depended not on maturation but on teaching strategies, familiarity with the material, relevant experiences and interaction with other children. Recent research (Hodkinson 2004) suggests that children remember more of what they are taught in history if they have an efficient chronological framework within which to place, store and retrieve what they have learned. Hodkinson set out to show that it is the design of the curriculum, focused teaching methods and resources that challenge and progress children's understanding of time, irrespective of such variables as intelligence, reading and mathematical ability. Hodkinson's research involved 129 eight- to ten-year-olds. Over three terms a 'treatment group' and a control group studied their locality, the Victorian era and the reasons behind invasions and settlements of Britain. 'Treatment group' pupils were encouraged to work cooperatively within activities that enabled open-ended discussion and temporal vocabulary. Activities sought to promote temporal concepts at increasingly complex levels. Historical material was also presented from time present to time past and timelines were used consistently in every lesson. Specific skills-based activities were also introduced at the beginning and end of each lesson. Although the 'treatment group' developed greater chronological understanding than the control group, Hodkinson admits that in the treatment group there was less time for developing other aspects of historical thinking.

Charlotte Mason (1864–1923) was critical of the way in which history was presented to young children as outlines of dates and facts and romantic stories, 'so that an amplified chronological table has been made to do duty for history' (1993, vol. 1: 291). She suggests that instead children should construct their own mental maps, dividing a card into centuries and adding events as they come across them. She says children at this stage do not need to bother with specific dates because the child is creating a memorable, visual, panorama.

## Sequencing

Young children's knowledge of the passing of time is measured by personal experience, recorded as sequences of days of the week, months and seasons of the year and birthdays. There has been much research into the ability of pupils from two to sixteen years old to sequence days, months and seasons (e.g. Thornton and Vukelich 1988). Young children's understanding of the passing of time also derives from conversations with family about generations, family events and 'old things', using time vocabulary (old/new; then/ now; for a long time; before/after). It can develop through stories, discussing what happened next and why, or discussing illustrations of nursery rhymes and stories about the past.

## Sequencing using timelines

Children between five and seven years old can create their own timelines and family trees, possibly illustrated by a sequence of their photographs, clothes or toys. They can compare their timelines with those of the teacher and another adult, using the same scale (see p. 100). Older children can construct their own timelines, based on information they have found out, either individually or as a class, perhaps each child writing on a card an explanatory note about a photocopied illustration and hanging these from the ceiling in chronological sequence. This is a constructivist approach that internalises the learning. The process also raises interesting questions about some events having precise dates, some changes being rapid, other developments occurring over a long and imprecise period, about causes and effects and who may or may not have affected, about the benefits or problems of changes. Groups constructing different timelines, illustrating different aspects of change, selected to raise questions about the period studied, using the same scale (perhaps events, technological, children, dress, growth of towns, food, transport, in a topic on the Victorians) could display them above each other to help to promote such discussion. Timelines should become more complex and thought provoking as children mature, using different scales and information. Bearing in mind recent criticism of children not having 'the big picture' it is important to relate timelines within periods to timelines across a continuous span of time, maybe around the school hall. This could obviate the fear expressed by Lello (1980) that time is recorded in artificial boxes. *The Sunday Times* (Gillespie 2011) celebrated the britishnewspaperarchive.co.uk going online with an illustrated article showing concerns about underage drinking, immigration and celebrity culture, with the title, 'It must be 1790'!

Time trails are a recognised activity for helping children to develop a sense of chronology through contexts within their own experience. During a walk, children identify and photograph buildings or features of buildings, then in school they can sequence the photographs and, with maturity, find out where to place them on a timeline.

## Change: causes and effects of changes

Bage (1999) explored ways in which narrative interpretations of the past can be used to develop children's historical understanding, if children are encouraged to criticise rather than copy stories. He suggests, for example, that the storyteller plans to suspend the story at points, in order to discuss motives and causes of decisions and to discuss moral issues. This makes the story motivating, forward looking and meaningful.

The CHATA project (Concepts of History and Teaching Approaches at Key Stages 2 and 3), funded by the Economic and Social Research Council (www.esrc.ac.uk/my-esrc/Grants/L208252006/read), investigated the development of children's understanding of cause and effect in detail. For example, Lee (Lee *et al.* 2000) shows how children's ideas about explanation in history depend on their understanding of the situation the person was in, on knowledge and on 'historical imagination'. People in the past sometimes appeared to do weird things and it is not part of everyday understanding to assume that these make sense. All 320 children, aged between seven and fourteen, were able to offer rational explanations of why the Roman Emperor Claudius invaded Britain. There was progression in their explanations from simply, 'because he wanted to get the gold and silver' at eight years old to a recognition of his public role as emperor at ten years old: 'He wanted more people to like him'; 'He wanted to take over other countries of the world'; 'to be better than Julius Caesar'. At eight years old nothing puzzled the children about Claudius' motives, whereas at ten years old some children argued that he could, for example, have 'stayed at home and had a better life'. By twelve years old pupils were beginning to see that his motives were not confined to personal wants or on what to do as emperor, but also considered the situation he was in. 'He was at peace and had spare soldiers; not all British tribes were friendly with the Romans'.

Since we live in a rapidly changing world it is important that children learn to consider how and why things change in order to cope with changes in the world around them now and in the future, perhaps eventually to be proactive in supporting some changes and resisting others.

## Duration

Understanding duration, how long situations or periods lasted, helps children to understand a sense of period, to see close and distant relations between events. It enables children to calculate, for example, lengths of reigns or of wars.

## Contemporaneity

Events that occur at the same time, in different localities or parts of the world can be easily represented by parallel timelines, showing that changes in different parts of the world may vary – or coincide, or occur at different rates – and raise questions about why.

## Flashback

Many books (for example Burningham 1992; Sendak 1984) and television programmes (for example *Dr Who*) involve 'playing with time', or time-travel, through flashbacks or parallel stories. These rely on a strong innate sense of chronology, which quite young children appear to have.

# Skills needed to develop chronological understanding

## Number skills

The ability to apply chronology in asking and answering historical questions depends on number skills (Hodkinson 2004). Young children need to be able to sort photographs, pictures and artefacts into sets (old/new; now/then;) and later to make Venn diagrams (old/new/could be either) in order to answer questions increasingly complex questions about time and change, similarity and difference and why they think so? At appropriate levels children need to be able to read, write and order numbers, to count on and back on a timeline, to add and subtract. Older children should understand positive and negative numbers, and BCE and CE.

## Measurement and scale

Older children need to understand scale. They might transfer census data to bar charts, spread sheets or line graphs that explore and illustrate slow, and rapid and gradual changes. They may read and interpret changes between numbered divisions on a timeline or a graph.

## Calculation skills

### Data handling and information technology

Large amounts of information, for example on census returns, can be analysed using databases. Correlation may be discovered between changes in occupations in a locality and population growth or ages of death in different areas compared, all of which can be linked to maps, newspaper information and other sources to build up an understanding of causes and effects of changes over time. Other statistics concerning change include those referring to birth and death rates, immigration and emigration, enclosure, imports and exports, height and weight (of people or cattle!)

### Information processing

Deriving information from a timeline in order to solve problems involves information processing. This is important in order to make links and connections between events and to investigate causes and motives. Levstik and Pappas (1987) argue that it is not children's historical concepts that are limited but their skills in information processing.

## Language skills

In solving problems about chronological sequence children need to understand past tenses (it was), causal connectives (because, therefore), temporal connectives (when, while, during) and probability language (perhaps, I think, maybe). Hodkinson (2003) argues that since linguistic phrases such as 'a long time ago' are subjective and can be interpreted in many different ways children should be helped to progress to more precise language (before *x*; after *y*; at the same time as *z*). Sometimes vocabulary needs to be specifically taught (duration, span, era, age, period, decade, century, millennium), if children are to be articulate about what they deduce and infer from timelines.

Children can also construct their own chronological narratives, as picture stories or chapters in a book which recreates a real story about the past or life of a real individual, possibly even writing in flashbacks or contemporaneous stories. Narratives need to be based on evidence and might be reconstructed through drama.

### Questioning and discussion

Questions, both child-initiated and teacher-initiated, are very important in enabling children to work out and to discuss their interpretations of timelines. This allows them to justify their conclusions – and maybe have them challenged – and so promotes their thinking and internalises their learning.

Because of all the variables discussed it is not possible to be precise about what we can expect of primary school children in chronology so the following figures can only be regarded as a rough guide as to what children may be expected to do by eleven years old. Table 4.1, 'What chronological understanding can we expect of older primary school children?' is based on the Historical Association E-CPD Unit, Chronology (www.history.org.uk).

## Putting it all together

The three strands of historical enquiry have been discussed in turn in the last four chapters, but they are, of course, not discrete. Nevertheless one strand may be the focus of a particular enquiry. The following chapters consider how the history curriculum may be put together in practice through whole school planning, medium-term planning and lesson planning, in ways in which assessment is an integrated part of planning and which are differentiated and cyclical in order to progress pupils' knowledge and thinking in history.

**TABLE 4.1** What understanding of chronology can we expect of older primary school children?

| Children finding chronology difficult | Most children | Particularly able children |
| --- | --- | --- |
| Use addition and subtraction facts and understand place value in reading time lines. | Can read, write, order numbers up to 1,000; see tens in decades, hundreds in centuries. Can calculate spans of time. | Count on and back in multiples of ten or a hundred. |
| Count on and back along a timeline. | Understand negative numbers (AD, BC). | Construct increasingly detailed timelines. |
| Know how many years in a century; in a decade. | Can handle data, construct bar charts, spreadsheets, line graphs (e.g. to analyse census information). | Read timelines, interpreting readings between numbered divisions. |
| Understand 'before' and 'after', 'earlier', 'later', 'next'. | | See links between events, possible connections between events. |
| Few anachronisms. | Discuss possible causes and effects of events and changes, relationships between events; use probability language. | Increasing skill in interpreting and deriving information from time lines, solve historical problems involving time; use of probability language in this context. |
| Sequence periods; identify similarities and differences between characteristics of periods. | Understand duration of periods; of time span between periods. | |
| | Use temporal connectives: e.g. when, while, during. | Understand contemporaneity (e.g. events that happened at the same time in different places or changes in different aspects of life in the same place). |
| | Understand 'ancient', 'modern', 'duration', 'span'. | |
| | Use precise time-related terminology (e.g. Medieval, timber-framed manor house). | Understand time shifts (e.g. flashbacks) within an historical novel or film. |
| | Understand how and why attitudes and beliefs change over time. | |
| | Use historical fiction as a means of understanding change over time. Create timeline for significant person. | |

## Sources for developing chronological skills

Chronology, E-PCD The Historical Association, www.history.org.uk; this resource offers many examples of strategies for teaching chronology in the primary school.

Cooper, H. (2002) *History in the Early Years*, pp. 39–63, London: Routledge.

Hoodless, P. (1998) *Children's Awareness of Time in Story and Historical Fiction in History and English in the Primary School: exploiting the links*, pp. 103–15, London: Routledge.

*Primary History* Issue 37 (2004) 'Helping students make sense of historical time'; 43 (2006) 'Time and time'. The Historical Association, www.history.org.uk

*Primary History* Issue 59 (2011) is also a special issue on chronology. The Historical Association www.history.org.uk

## References

Bage, G. (1999) *Narrative Matters: teaching and learning history through story*. London: Falmer.

Bernot, L. and Blancard, R. (1953) *Nouville, une Village Francaise*. Paris: Institut d'Ethnologie.

Blyth, J. (1994) *History 5 to 11*. London: Hodder & Stoughton.

Booth, M.B. (1994) 'Cognition in history', *Educational Psychologist*, 2(2), 61–9.

Bruner, J.S. (1996) *The Culture of Education*. Cambridge, MA: Harvard University Press.

Burningham, J. (1992) *Come Away from the Water Shirley*. London: Random Century Children's Books.

CHATA Project 'Concepts of History and Teaching Approaches at Key Stages 2 and 3' (www.esrc.ac.uk/my-esrc/Grants/L208252006/read). A project funded by the Economic and Social Science Research Council, led by Peter Lee.

Cooper, H. (2000) 'Primary school history in Europe: a staple diet or a hot potato?' in J. Arthur and R. Phillips (eds) *Issues in History Teaching*. London: Routledge.

Gillespie, J. (2011) 'Sex, drink, crime: it must be 1790', *The Sunday Times*, 4 December.

Hodkinson, A. (2003) 'National Curriculum and temporal vocabulary: the use of subjective time phrases within the National Curriculum for history and its schemes of work: effective provision or a wasted opportunity?' *Education 3–13*, 31(3), 28–34.

Hodkinson, A. (2004) 'The social context and the assimilation of historical concepts: an indicator of academic performance or an unreliable metric?' *Research in Education*, 71, 50–66.

Lee, P., Dickinson, A. and Ashby, R. (2000) '"Just Another Emperor": understanding action in the past', *International Journal of Educational Research*, 27(3), 233–44.

Lello, J. (1980) 'The concept of time, the teaching of history and school organisation', *History Teacher*, 13(3), 341–50.

Levstik, L.S. and Pappas, C. (1987) 'Exploring the development of historical understanding', *Journal of Research and Development in Education*, 21, 1–15.

Mason, C. (1993) *Charlotte Mason's Original Home Schooling Series, Vols 1–6* (www.ambleside online.org).

Ofsted (2011) (Office for Standards in Education ) *History for All: history in English schools 2007/10*. London: Ofsted (www.ofsted.gov.uk/resources/history-for-all).

Sendak, M. (1984) *Where the Wild Things Are*. London: HarperCollins.

Thornton, S.J. and Vukelich, R. (1988) 'The effects of children's understanding of time concepts on historical understanding', *Theory and Research in Social Education*, 16(1), 69–82.

*The Times* (2011) Chart distributed with 16 April edition.

Vygotsky, L.S. (1962) *Thought and Language*. London: Wiley.

# 2

# Planning for historical thinking

# 5

# What makes history enjoyable?

Part 2 explores ways in which the strands of historical thinking discussed in Part 1, which teachers have said they would like to understand better, can be put into practice as an integral part of planning and assessment. The three reports that underpin this book all found that teachers and children enjoy history and it seems important to consider first the kinds of things they enjoy, in order to embed them in the planning process. The *Cambridge Review* (Alexander 2010) found that teachers and children enjoy history because it involves activities and 'hands-on' experiences. This was endorsed by the *Primary History Survey* in which teachers said that they enjoyed site visits and museum visits, that they liked using a variety of teaching methods and drawing on the local expertise of their local communities. They said that history provides a rich and multi-faceted dimension of learning. They said that this rich diversity in pupil learning, particularly in contrasting and comparing narratives, which reflect all members of society, the role of women and ethnic diversity within our communities, is a sea change from the single British narrative. They stressed the importance of modifying the curriculum to provide a British, European and worldwide view, in order to respond to ethnic perspectives. Similarly *History for All* (Ofsted 2011) stresses the importance of local experiences and local provision in bringing history to life. This report also emphasised the value of cross-curricular approaches and of adding additional topics that respond to pupils' interests and locate the National Curriculum study units within an over-arching narrative. The *Cambridge Review* states that the dimensions of flexibility, thinking, talking and problem-solving, which require time and reflection, have been missing from the curriculum in recent years and that music, art, history, geography and the local dimension have become marginalised.

So before discussing approaches to planning it seems important to consider some dimensions of what teachers in the *Primary History Survey* said makes history enjoyable, the important areas stressed by *History for All* (Ofsted 2011) and also what the *Cambridge Review* felt was lacking, with some illustrative examples. These are just suggestions to inspire you to perhaps start planning for the history curriculum through a whole staff discussion and consider how you might include similar dimensions relevant to your school, based on your locality and the interests of your children. The headings in the following section reflect the aspects of history that teachers and pupils said that they found enjoyable and areas that *History for All* recommended developing.

## Hands-on activities

### An Egyptian day

I visited this class on the very last day of these children's time in primary school, and the culmination of a project on Ancient Egypt (Capita *et al.* 2000). The children and teacher were elaborately dressed in costumes they had made at home, by copying wall paintings or artists' illustrations in books. The girls had spent much time on exotic eye make-up; one explained how the cone on her head was designed to drop perfume throughout the day! Anubis had to remove his dog's head to speak, and a rich merchant proudly displayed his replica jewellery and his slaves. They were working in rotating groups to investigate a variety of questions about Ancient Egypt. It was multidimensional, and involved 'playing with ideas' in mathematics, language, art, science and technology. James was using 3D shapes to try to find out how pyramids were constructed; Shelley and John were making puppets of an Egyptian prince and princess in order to re-enact a story written by an Egyptian scribe 3,000 years ago, in which the son of an Egyptian king wooed and won the daughter of the King of Naharin by leaping high enough to reach her in her tall tower.

Paul and friends were playing senet. Andrea, Jack and James were designing mummy cases, looking in books to get ideas for the sort of patterns to use. Levi made a model shaduf and Jason was sitting in the sunshine grinding seeds using a quern. Laura and her friends were writing a diary account of a farming family over ten years, suggesting how their lives might have been affected each year by different levels of flooding of the Nile, which were determined by a dice game.

Another activity involved a group of girls using sources found in wall paintings, books, video and on the internet to construct an account of an Egyptian banquet, which was audio-taped for a 'radio programme' – 'Ancient Egypt'. When I met them they were discussing the myth of Isis and Osiris and, in particular, with eleven-year-old knowingness, how Isis became pregnant:

> 'After all Osiris had died – AND he was away a lot; we shall never find out.'

> 'There are different versions. In one version she turned into a kite and flew over his body. We didn't believe that one!'

I was visiting the school with a Romanian colleague who was fascinated. She later wrote:

> The English teacher's approach to teaching Ancient Egypt is quite different from classroom practice in Romania, mainly because the students are involved in the

activities. The use of drama stimulates much more discussion than debate and the use of primary sources as a basis for drama re-enactment is interesting and is able to satisfy scholars' demands. Students team up and develop a holistic approach to history. The student-centred perspective allows them to develop their own perspective on a topic. Pupils use information which is relevant to their interests and the 'abstract' character of history is avoided. The development of communication skills should, in my opinion, underpin activities.

It really is refreshing to hear, from a Romanian perspective, how Carol, the teacher, in spite of constraints, was creating thoroughly enjoyable learning activities.

## King of the Nile

One Year 4 teacher explored gender in contemporary and ancient societies, as well as spirituality, following a visit to the school by the Twisting Yarn Theatre Company, who presented *The Queen Who Would Be King*. This is the story of a working man who became a scholar and a queen who became a king. It tells the story of Senenmut, the clever son of a peasant family, who rises through his scholarship to become the royal tutor to Hatshepsut, the ambitious queen who becomes Pharaoh. Another teacher, following the visit of the company, worked on Egyptian multiplication, and made parchment scrolls and stage backdrops with her Year 5/6 class. The children became so inspired that they wrote and performed their own play, *The Eye of the Pharaoh*.

## Cross-curricular approaches

Richard Rowe, head teacher of Holy Trinity School in Guildford, has 'moved his school on' to the ethos of a topic-based curriculum, which involves working hard and having fun. His school was one of thirty-two included in the Ofsted Report, *The Curriculum in Successful Primary Schools* (Ofsted 2003). He recognises that 'this type of creativity does not just happen' but believes that any school can achieve it, but 'You have to work really hard at it' (Ward 2002). For example, all ninety-three Year 6 pupils became inventors, explorers, biologists or missionaries in their investigation of eleven countries in the former British Empire. This concluded with a recreation of the Great Exhibition of 1851 in the school hall.

Museums and historic sites are already organising visits based on cross-curricular approaches, which could be a starting point for planning a unit of study. In one scheme at Norwich Cathedral opportunities were provided for planning a visit that included history and also involved studying the different materials used in the building, the effects of chemicals and weather on stone and glass, considering how flint and limestone were formed by looking for fossils in the stonework, then making comparisons with modern materials and technologies. There is also a herb workshop in the Benedictine herb garden, English and drama activities, art and religious education, are planned appropriately for particular groups (www.cathedral.org.uk).

One of the many other examples of cross-curricular programmes that are adapted to suit teachers' requirements is the Hat Works, Stockport where children not only make felt at different levels of sophistication but observe the machinery in action, find out about the lives of factory workers in the past and try on lots of hats that reflect jobs and status in the past! The museum offers science, design and technology courses, personal, health and social education and 'literacy specials' in which storytelling and 'big book work' is linked to museum artefacts (www.hatworks.org.uk).

The Tower of London includes a programme of science options. After visiting the 'Bloody Tower' where Sir Walter Raleigh was imprisoned, children can carry out a distillation experiment, which he apparently invented while in the tower, to find out how men could survive at sea if all the fresh water ran out. 'I couldn't believe my eyes when the salt and dirty water turned into plain!' said Farzana Sulthans in Year 3. This is a lead into 'changes of state and solutions'. A replica of Henry VIII's longbow and mail armour are used as a basis for work on 'materials' at Key Stages 1–3 (www.hrp. org.uk). 'Astronomy is awesome' is offered in conjunction with the Royal Observatory Greenwich and 'Diet and disease' with the Florence Nightingale Museum. Recently schools unable to visit London have been able to book video conferences with staff in London Museums. I visited a Year 5 class, in a remote rural school in Cumbria, who were studying Tudor Exploration, while they were enjoying an interactive session with an education officer in the National Maritime Museum.

## Opportunities for using a variety of teaching methods

Teachers responding to the *Primary History Survey* questionnaire said that they enjoyed the variety of teaching methods they used in history. Here are some examples they gave:

■ using information books, critical reading of stories set in the past, of history reconstructions in drama and in museums;

■ asking questions about a variety of sources: oral sources, museum and site visits, music, art, technology, advertisements, clothes, games, toys, literature, artefacts, documents, statistics, receipts;

■ writing and analysing questionnaires;

■ using communication technologies.

The following section suggests other opportunities for using a variety of teaching methods.

## Discussion and debate

### Hot-seating in contrasting roles

For example, following some initial research two children, in turn, take the role of Francis Drake and of a sailor on board his ship. The rest of the class work in pairs to devise questions for Drake and for the sailor.

### Constructing tableaux based on an image or event, and questioning characters

Children research the background to an event shown in a painting or photograph. Then in pairs they take the role of one of the people in the picture and construct their character, motivations, feelings, thoughts. Each group in turn forms the tableau and the other group question the people in it individually. This might lead to discussion about why the two groups respond differently.

### Circle time, discuss moral dimensions and controversial issues related to a topic

Would you have hidden a Catholic priest in Elizabethan England, or a slave escaping from the south and putting other families at risk in the American Civil War? Would you have joined Ghandi on the salt marsh, or Rosa Parks sitting in a bus seat reserved for white people, or been a suffragette? Even young children can engage in these debates.

### Discuss what it might be like to be someone who lived in the past

What might it be like to be a child taken into slavery by the invading Romans? What might it be like to be a child living in Southwark during the Great Fire of London?

## Analysing changes over time, causes and effects, duration, similarities and differences between periods

In groups construct picture timelines, using the same scale, for agriculture, industry, houses, beliefs, and transport. Devise questions for others to answer. Leave suggestions in a 'postbox', or write on Post-it notes. What changed slowly, what changed rapidly and why? Did changes affect everybody? What are the connections between the timelines?

Decide to be in role as people living at this time, related to the different timelines; what did they think of the changes? Line children up in chronological order and let them explain.

## Concept development

Sort books, artefacts, pictures into sets, for example, old/new and give reasons. Does anyone disagree? Why?

Make picture cards, then sort them into categories of your choice (e.g. historical periods). What are the defining features of a period. Does everyone agree? Are they connected? If you lived in that period would your house, furniture, clothes, town be typical of the period? Why not?

Sort cards related to a period into other categories (rich/poor, town/country, adults/children, work/leisure). Do the categories overlap? Would people at the time have had a variety of perspectives depending on the combination of categories they fell into?

## Constructing accounts, comparing accounts

Having researched information, interpreted and discussed sources, considered moral issues, explored historical concepts related to a topic or enquiry, the historian combines what has been found out into an account. And since interpreting sources, analysing moral issues, explaining changes involved discussion and different perspectives children will have learned that there will be many possible and equally valid accounts.

### Written reports

Reports can be written in different ways: picture stories, historical fiction based on evidence or as word processed illustrated booklets. One group of Year 6 girls collected photographic evidence from a visit and used this to construct a fictional story based on the photographs, which were used to illustrate the book.

### Using information technologies

Accounts may be illustrated by evidence used to construct the account, selected from internet sites: paintings, photographs, census returns, maps, electronically constructed timelines, newspaper accounts. They may be made into slide shows, video or PowerPoint® presentations. One group I worked with made an electronic information board to accompany their model, with buttons to press for particular information. This included music clips. Another constructed a rotating 3D model of a castle they had visited to explain areas of weakness for attack (http://sketchup.google.com).

### Class museums

Class museums may create an interpretation of a theme or period(s) studied, illustrated by models, drawings and photographs, including explanatory labels, questions, quizzes and games designed to engage visitors in developing an understanding of the exhibits.

### Other ways on presenting accounts

A topic may be studied through researching an event or situation in some depth in order to create an account as a drama. Charlotte Mason (Mason 1993, vol. 1: 294) showed that if children draw pictures as accounts:

The drawings of the children in question are psychologically interesting, showing what various and sometimes obscure points appeal to the mind of a child and also that children have the same intellectual pleasure as persons of cultivated mind in working out new hints and suggestions.

Models based on evidence are themselves interpretations, particularly if they are informed reconstructions of ruined buildings. We may have the ground plan of a Roman villa or the post hole plan of an Iron Age hut for example. Researching what the building may have looked like and making a model can involve all the processes of historical enquiry to produce a valid interpretation. Other examples of accounts, or interpretations include writing a biography of an individual. Drama or role play based on research, paintings based on evidence or constructing diaries or newspaper accounts, based on research, which people in the past may have written are all accounts of what was found out in a historical enquiry.

## Involving local communities

### School news in the parish magazine

A recent issue of my parish magazine in Grasmere tells our community about some excellent projects in the village school, during the summer term. The upper juniors tried to understand the Thirlmere Aqueduct (created in the nineteenth century by damming a local lake to increase its capacity to supply water to Manchester), in which they learnt a great deal about science, geography and history. Andrew Leach is thanked for being 'an inspiring source of information, who came up with some great experiments to explain water pressure etc.'

The Wordsworth Trust had told the children how Wordsworth and his friends ran regattas, which led the older children to 'work on tourist guides from the period, enjoying spotting differences in the language used to advertise the Lake District "then and now"'. Instead of a Sports Day the school had a 'regatta' organised with the help of Brathay Outdoor Centre.

The parish magazine tells us that 'most of the children are studying Tudors and Stuarts in history in the autumn term, working with the Wordsworth Trust to create their own work in response to the King James Bible'. Their Christmas performance will be based on language work from medieval mystery plays and the King James Bible. It offers 'notes for your diary', 'Poetry and music by the upper juniors inspired by the King James Bible 13th December, all welcome'.

In any period working with the community may be a useful introduction to planning an enquiry. Work with the local history library to find out if there were significant local events during the period you plan to explore. These may reflect national events. Was there a time of particular change? Why? Or was there a local industry that maybe flourished and later declined? Why? What was its impact on the community? On the west coast of Cumbria, for example, children took an enormous pride in finding out about the heyday of the copper industry and published a book about it. What was going on at the same time in the farming community?

## Blurring the home/school boundaries

One group set up a travel agency complete with brochures, posters, booking forms, time changes, as part of a cross-curricular project on ancient and modern Greece. A lot of the language, mathematics and numeracy was initiated in class lessons, but continued and developed at home and in lunch hours. It is when the boundary between school and home blurs, initiated by the children, that you have evidence for your self-evaluation that they are enjoying their work! I could go on and on!

## History, personal and social education, parents, the community

In groups, throughout a topic, children made a lunch using receipts from the historical period studied, with the help of a parent. The Iron Age lunch, based on the evidence that they had wild root vegetables and Soay sheep, was a mutton stew. Guests were invited to share lunch by each group: the school nurse, the local policeman, a librarian, a school governor. This required social skills, language skills, responsibility – especially when it came to washing up.

# After school club: local military history

The forty-three members of the Stephenson Way Primary School after-school club in County Durham won an Our History, My Heritage competition organised by English Heritage, for restaging and video-recording an attack on the Durham Light Infantry, on Primrose Bridge, during the allied invasion of Sicily in 1943 (Jones 2002). They hit on the topic after a visit to the Durham Light Infantry Museum. They extended their research by reading, interviewing families and getting first-hand accounts of war from veterans of the Normandy landings and the Gulf War. Adults, including a teacher, a parent and the chair of governors, got into role and accepted the leadership of the pupil in charge. They also worked across the age range and with some pupils from the local secondary school. Watching the video helped them to see how relationships different from those in the classroom fitted together.

# Working with a local museum and the community

## Local Remembrance Day

Keyworth School in Kennington had a Reminiscence Day attended by dozens of parents and elderly relatives. After researching the bombing and rebuilding of Kennington they have designed a Second World War garden with an Anderson air-raid shelter and an allotment where they grew vegetables for the recipes their guest, Marguerite Patten, the wartime ministry of food advisor, helped them prepare. This was a National Lottery funded Heritage Initiative.

## Local heritage site

Pat Lewis, a teacher in Blaenavon in South Wales, makes clear to her pupils that their town has the same historical status as the pyramids or the Great Wall of China (Saunders 2004). Blaenavon is a Heritage site recognised for the dynamic part it played in the world's first Industrial Revolution, the powerhouse of the British Empire. It had coal, iron ore, quarries, furnaces and a primitive railway system. 'It's the part they and their families have played and are playing that makes it so special,' she said. The children have family histories, stories, photographs and artefacts. Following a cross-curricular project that included history and science (exploring types of forces and energy), art (working with an artist to produce costumes, flats for the school play and paintings of the locality), music (taking part in the Eisteddfod), citizenship (exploring regeneration plans) and language of different genres, children took part in a *son et lumière* held through the town, playing the parts of nineteenth-century children. To prepare for the event children invited historians and archaeologists into the school to help them research the history of iron and its impact on the Industrial Revolution. Useful resources about the Blaenavon iron and coal industries can be found online (www.newportsouthwales.net/revolution).

## Local dialect

Local dialect could also be an interesting starting point. Correct grammar is important, but tracing the origins of your own dialect can be fascinating. Melvyn Bragg (2003) has traced the origins of the buried words that he is proud to claim as his Cumbrian dialect: 'Aah's gaan yem.' Gaan was an Anglo Saxon word, to go, and was known to the Vikings; yem means home in Scandinavia, heim in Old Norse. As for 'laik in t beck'; leik is Old Norse for play and bekkr for stream, still beck in Cumbria. Bragg, as a child, used Anglo Saxon and Celtic words, crag, tor, pen, and some Romany from the annual gypsy fair, which harks back to an Indian dialect of Sanskrit, gadji for man and parnee for rain. One Cumbrian school started looking for Viking words in their own speech, then went on to a place-name study as the beginning of a unit on the Vikings. Books on word meanings in any local dialect can be found on the internet.

## Working with a local museum and the community

Lancaster City Museum's projects of, for example, the Vikings, bring together the museum exhibitions, historical re-enactments and visits to a specially created longhouse. These involve local schools. The school visits are preceded by a special Viking weekend, to which people of all ages are invited, in order to take education into the community. After listening to one gory tale one grandmother said, 'That's the best story anyone has told me since I was a tiddler!'

A Darby and Joan club could maybe teach children old dances and games as well as be willing interviewees, in which case you may spend a lot of time on changes in living memory. You may have children whose families are of other cultural heritages who could help select and find out about 'significant men and women' or past events from the wider world. You may be flexible enough to see where and for how long the children and their resources take the enquiry. You may discuss your options with parents, or the local history or photographic society or, for example, the Cumbrian wrestlers club.

## Working with parents

How can we ensure that children's individual interests inform how they choose to undertake a history topic? I used to tell children and their parents what the study unit on the school's long-term plan would be and discuss possibilities of what we could focus on, teaching approaches we could use, what might be particularly interesting to the children and what parents and their community contacts might be able to offer. From this it was possible to frame a group of key questions and possible ways of investigating them. This would feed into an overarching enquiry, a medium-term plan within which smaller studies by individuals and groups could contribute in different ways, concluding with some form of account, display, presentation or drama for parents and others involved. Everyone would understand and monitor the learning objectives of the medium-term plan and how these were broken down into learning objectives for the smaller studies. If the unit was taught over a number of weeks the children and adults could review and modify the medium-term plan weekly. Even if the unit was taught as a block, perhaps preparing for and following up a visit, there were constant instances of children deciding to do things differently. When they continue it at home, as previously said, you know they ARE enjoying it!

I remember one eight-year-old child who had to get herself off to school because her parents were at work, telling me that she had read her 'Beowulf Poem' to the milkman (hem), another child who had given her grandparents an impressive guided tour of Norwich Cathedral, modelled on a class visit to Canterbury, and a boy who, when told by his mother about a television programme on Maiden Castle that she had watched the previous evening, said, 'But Mum, what was the *evidence* for that?'

One example of a day that 'bridged the gaps between the generations' was a reconstruction of Breugel's 'Children's Games' (1560) in which 180 children from a small French village, who were in the last year of primary school, with their teachers and their families, recreated the painting in the town square. They walked through the town singing old French songs, rolling hoops, standing on their heads, turning somersaults, riding a hobby horse, playing with stones, sticks and barrels, and at intervals silence fell and they transformed themselves into the living image of the painting. The children had looked closely at the picture, analysed and discussed the symbolism of games as idle pursuits, carried out research on the painting, the artist and his times, learned about the games, compared them with those of today, chosen one of the people in the painting to re-enact, collaborated with the community in rehearsals, prepared costumes and props and worked on aspects of scenery. The day was a great success. Surely there are paintings, photographs, or accounts of your own area, which you could study in the same way as a community endeavour.

## Involving families

> *To forget one's ancestors is to be a brook without a source, a tree without a root.*
>
> *(Old Chinese proverb)*

Given the internet resources now available, researching family history has become very popular among adults and might become a way into a history topic for all the family. A useful website for young people is www.ffhs.org.uk/general/youngpeople.htm.

Tania Braga and Maria Auxiliadora Schmidt (Schmidt and Garcia 2004), in an ambitious experiment, 'Teaching history based on documents: a social experiment with Brazilian children', helped a primary school to write the history of their own town, using maps, family histories and photographs, which was published as a hardback book (Schmidt and Garcia 2003).

## History that encompasses different cultures

Sensitive issues need to be dealt with in an atmosphere of trust by sensitive teachers. A democratic model needs to be set up where everyone is free to speak, subject to an understood code of conduct. Draw out similarities and differences slowly, as you go, and make sure that the lessons are structured and grounded in the curriculum. Evaluate the effectiveness of the cultural diversity aspect by asking children to reflect on changes in their thinking.

Probably because of the limited resources available to support non-Anglo-centric dimensions of history they are rarely a subject of in-depth focus. Yet pupils should be taught about the social, cultural, religious and ethnic diversity of societies studied, in Britain and the wider world. Pupils should learn about change in their own area and in other parts of the world. Hilary Claire points out that the Race Relations Amendment Act of 2000 means that 'teachers must pro-actively strive in the curriculum towards inclusion of minority cultures, take responsibility and work to reduce racial tension and prejudice, paying more than lip service to a wider inclusive curriculum which challenges racism and Euro-centrism' (Claire 2002; 2003; 2005).

This means giving every child, and particularly children in mono-cultural environments, a sense of their own identity and worth, tolerance of diversity, and understanding of local, national and global connections. Children need to learn about their own, and other children's, heritage, about life in the places their families lived before, and why families move around.

### Other perspectives

The struggle to succeed has faced each generation of immigrants: Ancient Britons from central Europe (40,000 BC), Celts (7000 BC), Romans (AD 43), the Norsemen, the Normans, the 2,000 black people living and working in Elizabethan London, seventeenth-century Huguenots, nineteenth-century Irish, Russians and Jews. Perhaps we can help to make the process of assimilation easier by teaching children about their past. Bristol Museum provides a good model for exploring cultural diversity (www.bristolmuseum. co.uk).

## Insider/outsider?

The Parekh Report (2000) on the future of multicultural Britain has suggested that the position of the Irish in Britain as 'insider/outsiders' is uniquely relevant to the nature of Britain's multicultural society; the experience of 8 million citizens of Irish stock has been neglected owing to the myth of homogeneity of white Britain. This can be a particularly useful introduction to cultural diversity where there is not much cultural mix in schools.

Year 3 children can easily relate to the plight of a woman (in role) as an Irish mother during the famine and this understanding can be extrapolated to other areas of famine (O'Sullivan 2003). An Irish dimension to a Tudor study can be cross curricular at Key Stage 1 or 2, focusing on the female pirate Grace O'Malley, the battle for Ireland, Spencer's poetry on Ireland, and the bards who chronicle Gaelic history then realise that now these foreigners have come something terrible has happened. There is also Irish song and dance to incorporate.

Marcia Hutchinson, inspired by the stories of her Jamaican mother, produced a photographic exhibition of men and women who left the Caribbean to live in the UK after the Second World War (Brooks 2003). This led to her book, *The Journey*, about ten personal stories of people who settled in West Yorkshire (Hutchinson 1999), and then to *The Journey Learning Resource* (Hutchinson and Tidy 2003), which provides cross-curricular materials (history, geography, literacy, drama, personal social and health education). Hutchinson says that it is intended for all sorts of schools and has been successfully piloted in all-white schools in leafy suburbs. Other resources (www.100 greatblackbritons.com; www.everygeneration.co.uk) give a voice to an unrepresented section of society.

At Wilberforce School, Year 2 children worked with Hilary Claire and their teachers, using role play, to discuss three significant black people: the black aviator Bessie Coleman, Ruby Bridges, who went to an integrated school during the American civil rights movement, and Frederick Douglass, a slave who escaped to become an important figure in the abolition movement (Ward 2002). The older children tackled issues such as racism, with help from visitors who talked about their own childhoods. One arrived in Britain from the Caribbean in the 1950s and the other was a refugee from Nazi Germany.

## Artefacts from other cultures

The Victoria and Albert Museum and the British Museum have artefacts that can be used to illuminate rich cultures and histories: African, Asian, Indian Native American and Islamic (www.britishmuseum.co.uk). It is important to look at modern and historical works in order to avoid misrepresentation or stereotyping. However, art from non-western cultures can extend children's understanding of the purposes of art. But should we have these artefacts in British museums?

Publications for active learning about the Indus Valley at Key Stage 2 and replica artefacts can be found online (www.harapa.com/teach). Resources include cross-curricular activities such as making and testing terracotta wheeled toy carts, board games and a DVD made when Mohenjo-Daro became a world heritage site. Ilona Aronovsky (2003) also gives suggestions for teaching the Indus Valley unit.

## Gender issues

Pounce (1995) reminds us that it is important to be aware that women are still seriously under-represented in school books and when they do show women the sources are rarely interpreted from a female point of view. Osler (1995) suggests that teachers are careful to acknowledge great women alongside men of the past and also to encourage children to study the experiences of ordinary women. Children should consider why women have been invisible and undervalued and discuss how they are portrayed. The Women's History Network at the Centre for Women's Studies at Lancaster University publishes useful information relating to women's history (www.womenshistory network.org).

## Flexibility

I remember extending time planned when events went in unexpected directions, initiated by the children but still meeting my planned learning objectives. For example, after visiting the British Museum as part of a topic on Ancient Greece, one group of Year 5/6 children who had finished their work asked if they could organise a 'dig' on a waste patch of the school grounds. This led to a carefully measured archaeological excavation, which revealed numerous finds (e.g. a piece of an old beer jug, some coins, an old shoe). These were cleaned, measured and drawn, put in probable sequence of age, and displayed with labels suggesting their possible use. (Yes, they should have had tetanus jabs first but fortunately nobody needed one.) Children went on to interview a classroom support teacher who had lived in the area before the school was built and visited the library to find out more. These were entirely their own ideas, mostly carried out at lunch time, but they gave me a clear idea of what they understood about how sources are found and interpreted and communicated. There were so many examples of learning 'outside the box'.

## Starting with the children's interests

## Young children and play

Children need to have a sense of ownership of their environment. This depends on planning a rich variety of themes, play settings and experiences. Two teachers participat-ing in a project to reflect on and develop their practice (Bennett *et al.* 1997) assessed each of the National Curriculum subjects through play. They integrated play and teacher-directed activities through a topic approach, changing the topic every half term.

The children were involved in the decisions. The teachers observed links between what the children were doing in play and what they were doing with another adult. They were aiming for a curriculum model in which adults' observations inform both child- and teacher-initiated activities.

## Young children, family and folk tales

Many books young children enjoy are intrinsically concerned with the concepts of time and change. Themes that teachers might introduce include, 'When I was a baby', stories about growth and change in fictional families, oral history fairy stories and folk tales extended as play. Fairy stories and folk tales may not be literally true but they contain old features (coaches and horses, windmills, castles). They are the product of oral history and versions change with retelling. They are about a variety of types of people still to be found today (rich and poor, wicked and good, clever and stupid), and they involve sequence, cause and effect, motive. There are lots of opportunities here for meaningful, shared dialogue between children and adults, and for adults to introduce ideas that children can choose to develop or which children might introduce within the theme and adults take up and help them develop.

## History for different interests

Since history involves every aspect of life in the past we can find out a lot about a particular period from a chosen theme. Individuals or groups of children can select their own theme to research the same questions – for example, how did this change over the period? What were the causes and effects of the changes? – then combine their enquiries to draw overarching conclusions. Tracing changes in popular music and songs from 1930 will involve finding out about changes in technology and in society (e.g. the impact of the Second World War), finding out where new styles (e.g. jazz) came from and why, and making inferences about changing values and ways of life. Similarly an interest in clothes might lead to an interest in changes in dress. Here Joanne and her friend in Year 3 are discussing a wedding photograph taken during the war:

> They didn't have much money in the war. They couldn't have new dresses. She's wearing a normal dress like you'd wear to a party. She's got a small bunch of flowers and no veil. They had short dresses so they could run down the shelters.

Other themes might be cars or planes. Such themes reflect wide-ranging social changes and children make connections about how they interact, and contribute to broad patterns of change, for example, before, during and after the war.

## Let children do things 'their way'

Here is an exemplary tale, which illustrates how children, given the flexibility, will turn a teacher's plans into something that actually interests them – and still meet the teacher's objectives. I was an advisory teacher doing a local study with a Year 6 class based on four buildings in the locality, one of which was the church. 'What do we have to do this for?' two recalcitrant boys dragging along at the end of the line asked, as we trudged through the rain. 'I thought you might like to make a model,' I replied brightly. 'Nah.' Yet a few weeks later they had created a wonderful model of the church, with an indicator board that lit up and explained different parts of the church and its history, 'stained glass' windows that could be illuminated from inside, accompanied by a tape recording explaining the images and church music that played. What makes such activities part of a historical enquiry is the questions we ask – what do they tell us about the people who made and used them? – and seeking other evidence, perhaps from books, which may extend or verify our inferences.

Another way of starting with children might be Tony Robinson's *The Worst Children's Jobs in History* (Robinson 2005). As Robinson says, 'All children from 5 to 11 can enjoy these stories, those who like reading stories and those who'll just have a laugh at the wee and poo.' The book covers children's jobs throughout time and contains a selection of original primary material for the 'gifted and talented' historian. It could lead on to thinking about issues such as child labour, and give children some sense of the concept of why we are as we are and what has shaped and moulded us.

## What do the children want to know?

Southbank International School in Hampstead uses the International Baccalaureate Organisation's Primary Years Programme. This is based on a pupil profile setting out characteristics schools wish to develop and make children aware of in themselves: enquirers, thinkers, communicators, risk-takers, knowledgeable, principled, caring, well-balanced and reflective. Pupils from three to twelve play a big role in determining what and how they learn. 'You find out what they know and what they want to learn, then you can shape your unit; it's a big leap of faith sometimes', the programme co-ordinator said. 'The National Curriculum isn't looking at the bigger picture. It compartmentalises everything.' For a Year 5 unit on the Saxons, for example, children's questions are posted on a bulletin board (as in the Kendal Castle Key Stage 1 visit on pp. 150–3). What animals did they have? How did they go to the toilet? If they were wounded what did they do? Did the children go to school? From this starting point the teacher spends some time reflecting with the class on how to answer these questions, using mainly primary sources, and what further questions may arise.

### History and writing

When I showed some recent secondary postgraduate students some primary pupils' written work, in a variety of genres and for a range of purposes, which emerged through history topics they said they had never seen writing of such quality anywhere. These were not extraordinary children, so what can we infer? Enjoyment results in high standards. Amazing! It may be possible to work with a visiting historical story writer, an archaeologist or a real historian on a local project. Of course you cannot devote the entire timetable to visits and performances but some days of blocked time are important.

## History and citizenship

Citizenship, local, national and global, is not an 'add-on'. It should permeate everything we think and do. It has been found that this dimension is best taught in primary schools where the curriculum is integrated. Developing an awareness of citizenship requires us to have knowledge and understanding of social responsibility, social justice, peace and conflict and respect for diversity. It involves skills of critical thinking, the ability to argue effectively, to challenge injustice, and values that include empathy, a sense of self-esteem and identity, respecting people and things (Oxfam 1997). It is not difficult to identify ways in which to link history with discussing citizenship issues and it may be easier to discuss issues that remain today, distanced by time.

## Questions for discussion

Discussion can relate to any Key Stage 2 historical period, particularly the Tudors (protests by Thomas More at the dissolution of the monasteries, or Catholic protests in Elizabethan England), Victorian protests about bad water supplies in the big cities, for example, and the Jarrow March and similar protests in the 1930s.

At Quarry Bank cotton mill in Cheshire the National Trust staff, in role as mill owner or worker, talk about how their lives have been changed by the Industrial Revolution. Then the pupils are divided into groups: handloom weavers and spinners, mill workers and mill owners. They explore issues such as the mill owner whose profits are falling following a slump in business. Does he lower wages or sack workers? What do the weavers and spinners do, threatened by the new water technology? Do they sell up and go to the workhouse, apply for a job at the new mill or protest and break up the machinery? If they do the latter, what will happen? With no police force the army will come in as at Peterloo and they may be killed. The discussion involves questions of social responsibility, political, spiritual, moral and cultural values, empathy, debate and conflict resolution.

In Southwell Union Workhouse, recently bought by the National Trust, social change, human rights and responsibilities, employer and employee rights, conflict resolution and moral and social dilemmas are debated by the children in role as workhouse inmates. In prioritising wants and needs they need to consider where to place freedom of expression or freedom to practise their own religion. They debate issues such as child labour, adopting the role of mill owners, pauper children and social reformers. The exercise is illustrated with case studies, statistics and contemporary photographs.

It is sometimes easier to approach issues through historical fiction. There are several series that do this. Sparks series (www.wattspub.co.uk) has *Escape from Germany*, *Sid's War* and *Bodies for Sale*. Coming Alive series (www.evansbooks.co.uk) has *Dear Mum, I Miss You*, *What if the Bomb Goes off?* and *Princess Elizabeth Are You a Traitor?* My Stories series (www.scholastic.co.uk/zone) offers *Mill Girl* and *Battle of Britain*. Survivor series (www.hodderheadline.co.uk) offers *Everything to Live For*, about Northern Ireland and *Only a Matter of Time*, about Kosovo. Finally, Flashback series (www.acblack.com) has *Gunner's Boy* and *A Slip on Time*.

Claire suggests some significant events that could be explored through enquiries, concept maps, role play, letter and speech writing. Would you, without hindsight, have voted for Attlee's untried Labour government in 1945? How were the campaigns of Gandhi conducted? How did people work for the emancipation of slaves in the nineteenth century? What of the reformers who tackled the conditions of child workers such as Annie Besant and the match girls' strike in 1888? What might it have been like to be born into a poor Irish family in the 1840s? What might it have been like to be a Mexican child in Tenochtitla n when the Spanish came? Would you have hidden a Catholic priest? How do Indian galleries in the Victoria and Albert Museum illustrate the rich cultural influences of India on Elizabethan England, in clothes, buildings and garden design? What might it have been like to be a Roman soldier invading Britain? (Most of them came from the Middle East, as evidenced by artefacts in the Museum of London, the British Museum and the Temple of Mithras on Hadrian's Wall.) The Assyria and Mesopotamia study units could extend these links with the Middle East. Examples of such ideas incorporated into Claire's case studies can be found on www.citized.info by searching for Hilary Claire.

## Approaches to cross-curricular planning

*History for All* (Ofsted 2011) found that where history was taught as part of a topic, there was a danger that the thinking processes at the heart of history – discussed in Chapters 1–4 – were not rigorously planned for or assessed. However it also said that when the processes of historical enquiry were understood and planned for within a topic a cross-curricular approach was successful. Both the Rose Review of the Curriculum (DfCSF 2009) and the *Cambridge Review* recommended that the curriculum should be structured around areas of learning so this may well be a way forward to minimise curriculum overload.

There are various interpretations of cross-curricular planning. It may mean that two subjects are integrated within a history topic. This could apply, for instance, to identifying the aspects of language and literacy or of geography that can be developed through history. Or two subjects may be taught separately but be united by an overlapping theme, for example studying portraits in art might be linked to using portraits as a historical source in the period studied in history. Or aspects of a history topic may draw on another subject in a particular context. Finding out how timber frame buildings were constructed could involve experiments to investigate forces and the strength of structures, testing different ways of strengthening a roof for example. Or friction might be investigated to find out why it was difficult to move loads, particularly on clay soil but easier on water. Or mathematics might be used to investigate historical questions, for example to analyse census information or scale of maps, or journey times; this gives mathematical processes learned a practical and useful application.

## Advantages of a cross-curricular approach to history

History is an 'umbrella subject'. All societies have dimensions of art, music, literature. The history of religion and of science is integral to historical changes. In geography, for example, questions about where people settle and why, how they use the environment and change the environment in providing food, shelter, communication and trade between settlements are all an integral part of historical change. Mathematical calculation in some form has always been a societal necessity. So history embraces other subjects. A cross-curricular approach often makes a topic more meaningful, and is a more natural way of making experience holistic and seamless, particularly for young children. It is a useful context for using and applying language and mathematical skills. And it can be a way of managing time effectively. And it all involves children, whatever their subject preferences; remember the reluctant historians who were fired up by making an electronic information board for the local church (p. 69).

## Issues to consider

Combining subjects may enable teachers to share their subject expertise. But some colleagues may feel that they want control of the curriculum in their subject area. One teacher told me that she could not consider combining music, her specialism, with history. Combinations could make whole school planning that ensures balanced curriculum coverage complicated and perhaps result in lack of flexibility. And most importantly, in medium-term planning and lesson planning, it is essential that the processes of enquiry are at the heart of the learning objectives that are stated, not just for history but also for the subjects linked to history.

### Possible links with other subjects

- How are toys different from those in the past?

  **Science**: grouping materials; physical forces and motion.
  **Design and Technology**: how mechanisms make things move.

- What were homes like a long time ago?

  **Art and Design**: wallpaper, fabrics, ornaments – colour, form, texture, pattern.
  **Science**: physical processes – electricity.

- What were seaside holidays like in the past?

  **Science**: seashore, amusements.
  **Geography**: what is this place like?
  **Art**: practical work using range of materials.
  **Music**: recorded music from the time.
  **PE**: games and activities.

■ Why have people invaded and settled in Britain?

**Art**: ideas about journeys using signs and symbols in mixed media, explore tradition of making vessels and containers, explore materials – weaving, colour, texture, natural dyes.

**Geography**: investigate local area for evidence of settlement.

■ What were the differences between rich and poor in Tudor Times?

**Art**: textiles, investigating pattern, how paintings and other images communicate relationships.

**Music**: from period.

**Design and Technology**: food technology.

■ What was it like for children living in Victorian Britain?

**Art**: investigating pattern, paintings, photographs.

**Geography**: a sense of place, how and where do we spend our time?

**Design and Technology**: food technology.

**Music**: from period.

■ How has life in Britain changed since 1948?

**Art**: photographs and paintings.

**Music**: popular songs and dance.

**Communication and information technologies**: television, iPad, DVD, mobile phones.

■ How can we find out about the Indus Valley civilisation?

**Geography**: a village in India, a contrasting locality.

**Art**: textiles from other cultures.

■ What were the effects of Tudor exploration?

**Geography**: maps, voyages of discovery, trade.

**Design and Technology**: new foods.

Chapter 5 was based on teachers' and children's claims that they enjoy history. Dimensions of history that make it enjoyable have been explored: teaching strategies, working with communities, families and parents, in ways that reflect cultural and social diversity, controversial issues, and cross-curricular approaches. The next chapter will explain how this rich variety of approaches can be planned for and assessed through the processes of historical enquiry discussed in Part 1.

# References

Alexander, R. (ed.) (2010) *Children, their World, their Education: final report and recommendations of the Cambridge Primary Review*. London: Routledge.

Aronovsky, I. (2003) 'Teaching the Indus Valley Civilization in the 21st century', *Primary History*, 33, 22–3.

Bennett, N., Wood, L. and Rogers, S. (1997) *Teaching Through Play: teachers' thinking and classroom practice*. Buckingham: Open University Press.

Bragg, M. (2003) *The Adventure of English*. London: Hodder & Stoughton.

Brooks, Y. (2003) 'Finding a voice', *Times Educational Supplement*, 14 February.

Capita, L., Cooper, H. and Mogos, J. (2000) 'Children's thinking and creativity in the classroom: English and Romanian perspectives', *International Journal of Historical Learning, Teaching and Research*, 1(1), 31–8 (www.history.org.uk).

Claire, H. (2002) 'Why didn't you fight Ruby?' *Education 3–13*, June.

Claire, H. (2003) 'Dealing with controversial issues with primary teacher trainees as part of citizenship education' (www.citized.info/pdf/commarticles/hilary_claire.pdf).

Claire, H. (2005) 'Learning and teaching about citizenship through history in the primary years', *Leading Primary History*, 24–43. London: The Historical Association.

DfCSF (Department for Children Schools and Families) (2009) *Independent Review of the Primary Curriculum: final report*. London: DCFS (www.education.gov.uk/publications/ (→search publications→History for All)).

DfEE (1999) *The National Advisory Committee on Creative and Cultural Education*. London: DfEE.

Historical Association (2011) *Primary History Survey (England): history 3–11*. London: The Historical Association.

Hutchinson, M. (1999) *The Journey*. Huddersfield: Primary Colours.

Hutchinson, M. and Tidy, P. (2003) *The Journey Learning Resource*. Huddersfield: Primary Colours.

Jones, S. (2002) 'Bombs and battalions', *Times Educational Supplement*, 29 November.

Mason, C. (1993) *Charlotte Mason's Original Home Schooling Series, Vols 1–6* (www.ambleside online.org).

Ofsted (Office for Standards in Education) (2003; 2005) *The Curriculum in Successful Primary Schools* (www.ofsted.gov.uk).

Ofsted (Office for Standards in Education) (2011) *History for All: history in English schools 2007/10*. London: Ofsted (www.ofsted.gov.uk/resources/history-for-all).

Osler, A. (1995) 'Does the National Curriculum bring us any closer to a gender balanced history?' *Teaching History*, 79, 21–4.

O'Sullivan, J. (2003) 'Gael Force', *Times Educational Supplement*, 4 July.

Oxfam (1997) www.oxfam.org.uk/coolplanet/teachers/globciti.

Parekh Report (2000) 'The commission on the future of multi-ethnic Britain', Runnymede Trust.

Pounce, E. (1995) 'Ensuring continuity and understanding through teaching of gender issues in history 5–16', in R. Watts and I. Grosvenor (eds) *Crossing the Key Stages of History*. London: David Fulton Publishers.

Robinson, T. (2005) *The Worst Children's Jobs in History*. London: Macmillan.

Saunders, T. (2004) 'History on your doorstep', *Times Educational Supplement*, 12 March.

Schmidt, M.A. and Garcia, T.M.B. (2003) *Recriando historias de Campina Grande do Sul*. PR: UFPR/PMCGS.

Schmidt, M.A. and Garcia, T.M.B. (2004) 'Teaching history based on documents: a social experiment with Brazilian children', *International Journal of History Teaching, Learning and Research*, 4(2) (www.history.org.uk).

Ward, H. (2002) 'Bringing historical conflicts to life', *Times Educational Supplement*, 7 June.

# Planning for progression

## Monitoring, assessment, recording and reporting progress

The first four chapters of this book explored the processes of historical enquiry: selecting sources, interpreting sources, combining sources to create accounts or interpretations about changes over time, causes and effects of changes and similarities and differences between past times. Chapter 5 explored the reasons why teachers and children in the three reports that underpin this book said that they enjoy teaching history. The intention was to encourage you to develop your own imaginative ideas about how to use the resources and expertise available in your locality, community and school, in ways which you, the children and their families will find meaningful, worthwhile and engaging.

This chapter will consider how you can structure your initial ideas about the kind of history you want to teach so that the processes of historical enquiry are integrated into the activities you plan. It will examine some of the decisions you have to make. This will enable you be articulate in explaining, to children, parents and others, the skills as well as the content the children are learning and why this is important. It will enable you to plan for, monitor, assess and report on children's progress. It will also help you to reflect on, evaluate and develop your own practice with confidence. This is an area in which teachers have said they would welcome further guidance.

## Whole school planning to lesson planning

Figure 6.1 illustrates the planning process from whole school to lesson planning, which is discussed below.

### School philosophy, values and ethos

Curriculum planning starts with the ethos of the school. The *Cambridge Review* and *History for All* (Ofsted 2011) outlined a rich selection of value-laden reasons why history is important (pp. 2–3). Integrating these values into planning and practice requires

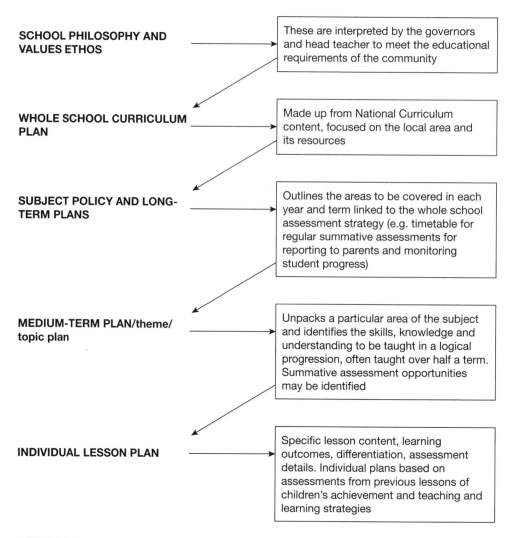

**SCHOOL PHILOSOPHY AND VALUES ETHOS** → These are interpreted by the governors and head teacher to meet the educational requirements of the community

**WHOLE SCHOOL CURRICULUM PLAN** → Made up from National Curriculum content, focused on the local area and its resources

**SUBJECT POLICY AND LONG-TERM PLANS** → Outlines the areas to be covered in each year and term linked to the whole school assessment strategy (e.g. timetable for regular summative assessments for reporting to parents and monitoring student progress)

**MEDIUM-TERM PLAN/theme/ topic plan** → Unpacks a particular area of the subject and identifies the skills, knowledge and understanding to be taught in a logical progression, often taught over half a term. Summative assessment opportunities may be identified

**INDIVIDUAL LESSON PLAN** → Specific lesson content, learning outcomes, differentiation, assessment details. Individual plans based on assessments from previous lessons of children's achievement and teaching and learning strategies

**FIGURE 6.1** From whole curriculum to lesson plans.

teachers' shared understanding of the aims of education and of how children are thought to learn. If, for example, the teachers in a school share a view that significant aims of education across the curriculum should be to respect individual differences, to promote social cohesion and to acquire interests, skills, understandings and values that are satisfying to the child and continue to develop into adult life, they will create experiences in history that involve parents and the local community and environment. If they believe that children learn best through observing and interacting with the environment and with others, gradually building their own mental maps of the past and of different perspectives, if they think that young children are able to rationally consider controversial issues, then these teachers will encourage children to discuss artefacts, values different from their own, to compare and construct different accounts of the past. Their philosophy of education will inform the way they teach history.

This does not of course preclude learning facts, dates and chronology; indeed it has been pointed out that both are central to historical enquiry, but chronology also involves discussion of causes and effects and an imaginative and sometimes value laden discussion of how situations or events were caused and of their impact on people. Facts need to be imbued with meaning, and selected for significance.

Biggs (2003: 41–3) describes a curriculum that analyses the way we tackle challenges and look at life and compares this with rote learning without understanding or with knowing what comes next in a sequence without knowing why.

## Reflecting statutory requirements into the whole school plan

Statutory requirements, which also stem from a particular view of the aims, purposes and methods of education, must be interpreted and embedded in planning at whole school, medium-term and short-term planning levels, in ways that reflect the philosophy and needs of each school and the professional experience of the teachers, based on their understanding of professional literature, their experience and their personal values. For, as Pollard says,

> Professional ideologies are always likely to remain strong among teachers – they represent commitments, ideals *and* interests. Reflective teachers should be open-minded enough to constructively critique their own beliefs, as well as those of others.
>
> (Pollard 2008: 94)

## Cross-curricular or single subjects?

Whole school decisions must be made about cross-curricular approaches, teaching subjects discretely, subjects grouped as 'areas of learning' or a combination of these approaches. Schools also need to decide whether the same approach is appropriate for all age groups. Some teachers responding to the *Primary History Survey* said that they taught history through a cross-curricular approach at Key Stage 1 but not at Key Stage 2. The *Cambridge Review* suggested that single subject teaching by specialist teachers might best suit the needs of Years 5 and 6.

Teachers must also have informed ideas about the values of subjects. Are literacy and numeracy skills best learned if they are made a curriculum priority or might this demotivate many children. If literacy skills are integrated into other subjects, and history lends itself particularly well to this, are children motivated to develop these skills more rapidly? Examples of planning for history topics through blocks of time, in a cross-curricular way, at Key Stage 1 and at Key Stage 2, and the rationales for doing so can be found at www.sagepub.co.uk/rowlewyandcooper with further examples in the related book (Rowley and Cooper 2009).

## Blocks of time?

Decisions also need to be made about whether time should be blocked, to focus intensely on a particular subject or theme for perhaps a week, then not revisiting it for maybe a term. This enables children to get really involved in a topic but perhaps it does not facilitate gradual progress over a period of time.

## Subject policy and long-term plan

The sequence of units of study throughout the school is a whole school planning decision. This may depend on listing the local resources and expertise available and the ages of the children most likely to benefit. Nichol and Guyver (2005) suggest different focuses, so that different aspects of history can be taught. One unit of history may be based on biography, perhaps learning about Henry VIII or Elizabeth I. Another unit may be studied from the perspective of a local historian. We could move between depth and breadth studies. Different study units could focus on learning different strands of historical enquiry or different methods of presenting interpretations. There needs to be some rationale for sequencing units; some have suggested that 'the big picture' is best understood by sequencing units chronologically. Why might this be controversial?

## Medium-term plans (theme or topic plan)

Once it has been agreed which study units will be taught in which year groups and decisions have been made about 'blocks of time' or weekly lessons it is possible for teachers to construct their medium-term plans. This may take some time initially but it is essential, in order to ensure that, exciting though the activities you plan may be, they enable children to progress in their historical understanding and the teacher to monitor this.

The first step is to work out how many sessions (if this is to be a block of time) or weekly lessons are available and how long each is. Then, assuming you have done your own reading and research about the topic, identify some key questions related to the theme, which will involve children in historical enquiry.

## Identifying key questions

It is important to liaise with colleagues teaching each year group in identifying key questions, to ensure that there is some progression in the kinds of questions being asked. However, there are many variables influencing progression in history and children do not necessarily progress at the same rate through each strand of historical thinking. There is little research on progression so this is not a precise art.

It must be clear how questions selected reflect any statutory requirements. Given the considerable opportunities for teachers to interpret the curriculum in their own ways, it must nevertheless reflect any national requirements, which aim to ensure equal opportunities. The National Curriculum (DfEE/QCA 1999) also referred to the knowledge and enquiry skills, needed to investigate a question. The newly devised Australian Curriculum (www.acara.edu.au→search→curriculum history) is given here as an example for reflection and discussion, not as a blueprint. It is interesting that there is little emphasis on chronology. For progression in chronological understanding see Table 4.1, page 50. The new Australian history curriculum at Key Stage 2, shown below, focuses on progression in posing questions. It suggests the progressively independent role of pupils in contributing to identifying questions to investigate.

## Historical questions and research

Y4    Pose a range of questions about the past.
Y4    Locate relevant historical information from sources provided.
Y4    Identify traces of the past in the present.
Y5/6  Develop questions to inform an enquiry.

The Australian national curriculum for history suggests the following progression in the use of sources, in understanding different perspectives and in communicating findings.

## Analysis and use of sources

Y4    Compare aspects of the past with the present using sources provided.
Y5/6  Identify relevant historical sources and locate information related to questions.
Y5/6  Identify a variety of primary and secondary sources.
Y5/6  Locate and record historical information from a variety of sources.

## Perspectives and interpretations

Y4    Identify different points of view.
Y5    Compare key ideas and information in a range of sources.
Y6    Compare key ideas and information in a range of sources.

## Comprehension and communication

Y4    Sequence historical people and events.
Y4    Use historical terms.
Y4    Develop historical texts, particularly narratives.
Y4    Use a range of communication forms (oral, graphic, written and technologies).
Y5    Develop historical texts, particularly as narratives and descriptions that incorporate evidence.
Y5/6  Perspectives and interpretations: identify points of view, values and attitudes in historical sources.
Y5/6  Sequence historical events.
Y5/6  Use historical terms and concepts.
Y5/6  Use a range of communication forms (oral, graphic, written and technologies).

By contrast the French national curriculum simply requires six- to eight-year-olds to work on 'discovering the world', which involves 'understanding the local environment, time and the natural world'. Eight- to eleven-year-olds study 'humanities', described as 'history and geography, arts including history of art and music' (www.inca.org.uk). These examples of other statutory curricula are given to encourage critical thinking about curriculum planning.

## Constructing a medium-term plan

A grid of rows and columns for constructing a medium term plan can be created in several ways but it is essential that it contains:

- a sequence of sessions, each with clear and very specific learning objectives, which are sequential and are referenced to the national curriculum;

- information about how learning objectives may be differentiated;

- plans for how children's achievement of the learning objectives will be assessed.

This provides a framework for planning each week and lesson.

If the planning is cross curricular it is necessary to indicate where other subjects are included in the history topic and to construct separate medium-term plans for each subject, to ensure that the enquiry processes at the heart of each discipline are planned for, with references to statutory requirements. If the project is planned over a block of time the same planning process is required with sessions planned for rather than lessons, although these may involve concurrent group activities.

An example of a medium-term plan is shown in Table 6.1. This is developed from *Films, History and Alexander the Great* (Brown *et al.* n.d.), a Historical Association scheme of work (www.history.org.uk).

## Monitoring and assessment of learning in history

*History for All* (Ofsted 2011) and the *Primary History Survey* found that, probably because teachers were unsure how to integrate learning processes into planning, teachers rarely assessed children's learning in history. When they did this was at the end of each term or year. This suggests that they were assessing content covered rather than progress in historical thinking. Yet assessment in history need not be a burden. It is a waste of time filling in innumerable boxes as required by the original national curriculum. Assessment must be an integrated part of learning. First it is necessary to consider the purposes of assessment and appropriate types of assessment for different purposes and audiences.

**TABLE 6.1** Example of a medium-term plan.

| Wk | Key question(s) | NC links | Key knowledge | Key skills of historical enquiry | Differentiation | Assessment methods | Cross curricular links |
|----|-----------------|----------|---------------|----------------------------------|-----------------|--------------------|------------------------|
| 1 | Who was Alexander the Great? | | Historians' accounts of Alexander the Great and events of his life. | Compare similarities and differences in accounts | Level 1: Make notes on 1 simple account; Level 2: On 2/3 simple accounts; Level 3: Compare similarities and differences in 3 accounts. | Formative (questioning, observation) + product. | |
| 2 | What does Oliver Stone's film say about Alexander the Great? | | An examination of a detailed interpretation of Alexander the Great. | Record details of life of Alexander the Great as shown in this film. | Level 1: List: events in film; Level 2/3: List events and other information. | As above. | |
| 3 | What do historians say about Alexander the Great? | | How does the film compare with historians' accounts? | List similarities and differences between historians' accounts and the film. | Level 1: List differences in accounts of events; Level 2: Causes and consequences of events; Level 3: On personality of Alexander the Great. | As above. | |
| 4 | So why do historians and film makers say different things about Alexander the Great? | | Why do the interpretations differ? | Discuss reasons why the accounts are different. | Discuss in mixed ability groups. In groups construct PowerPoint® presentations explaining the reasons. | Summative: observation, questioning, product. | |

# Types and purposes of assessment

## Formative assessment

Formative assessment is the assessment of the extent to which children in the class have achieved the learning objectives for a lesson. It is ongoing. Most teachers have intuitively carried out continuous intuitive assessments; there is little point in teaching if children are not achieving the learning objectives you set out to teach. But learning objectives need to be differentiated to make them attainable by each of the pupils.

For example, in a Year 2 class working on the history of their locality some children may be able to place photographs of buildings in a local street in chronological sequence, others may be able to retell a visitor's account of changes in the street in sequence and some may be able to place the photographs on the timeline in sequence and explain the sequence using time vocabulary.

In Year 6 some children may identify similarities and differences between transport in Tudor times, in Victorian times and today. Some may be able to calculate how long horse-drawn carriages were used and how long steam trains were used and the overlap between them, using a timeline to calculate. Others may be able to construct timelines and maps showing increases in the distribution of goods caused by rail travel. But it is important not to put children into assumed ability groupings in history but rather to let them work at the levels they choose within a shared topic. For thinking in history is complex and not rigidly hierarchical. Children who may be thought the least able may make thoughtful and original suggestions about sources (see pp. 24 and 94) or respond beyond their expected level.

## Processes of formative assessment

Evidence about what children are learning can be gathered in three ways: by observing what they are doing and how they are interacting; by questioning; and by what is demonstrated in the products they produce. Often this involves a combination of all three.

### Observing what children are doing

What suggestions are children making to each other about how the Roman villa they are modelling may have been built, how might the rooms have been used, who might have lived there and based on what evidence? How did the model windmill work? Why has this town increased in size as shown on maps of different periods? Can we find out from the census evidence? Why did people come to live here? What evidence and reasoning are children using to construct their role in a drama or tableau? Where on the map might they have lived? What, given the Parish records, might they be called? What might their occupation be and their family size? How do they decide to respond to a crisis in the community, an outbreak of the plague, the proposal for a railway?

## Questioning

Questioning may well be initiating such questions and listening to resulting discussion, cueing and asking for reasons. It may be questioning the group or a discussion with an individual. This kind of questioning, particularly if it is a genuine question to which the adult does not necessarily know the answer, is far better than 'question time' at the end of the lesson because it reveals more and deeper insights about more children and also takes their learning further. Or questioning may be more formal, taking turns to answer other children's questions when hot seating, as different characters in different situations. Closed questions may be used sometimes, to ascertain whether information given has been learned but open questions, requiring opinions or hypotheses will encourage discussion and thought.

## Products

Products have the advantage of providing more permanent evidence of children's knowledge and thinking; they may also be the result of previous discussion and questioning in the process of making them. They may involve reading and writing, perhaps for some children who choose to record findings in this way (e.g. the children who decided to rewrite the castle information board so that it was easier for children to understand; Figure 10.4, page 153). Or it may be a story set in the past, based on evidence, a timeline, a 'newspaper account', a diary, a maid's diary compared with the diary of her mistress, a review of a historical novel . But a product may also be a picture illustrating an event, a quiz, a labelled plan, a model with explanatory information, cooking using an old receipt, designing a typical outfit of a given period based on paintings and research in information books.

## Pupils' self-assessment

If it has been clearly explained to children what the key learning objectives of an activity are they should be encouraged to assess what they have learned, or did not understand or find easy themselves, through conversation with other children and with adults. This is both powerful and motivating.

Given these combined opportunities to monitor what children are learning and thinking only brief Post-it notes, or annotations on a lesson plan need to be made of information that is particularly significant about individual children, a surprising insight or skill from a particular child, what motivates another, who needs some extra support.

## Purposes of formative assessment

Clearly the teacher needs to know what children can do in order to provide the next step, to support some and challenge others. The children too need to be articulate about the purposes of activities and what they have learned. Often this is how parents make sense of some apparently bizarre account of the day. 'Why were you making "hard tack" and eating it?' (ships' biscuits made of hard baked flour and water). 'Because we were imagining we were on a Tudor ship sailing around the world. We read part of a sailor's diary and he said the hard tack had got weevils in. We wondered what it was and why he ate it – and why he was going on this journey anyhow . . .'

## Summative assessment

Summative assessment 'sums up' what a child has achieved at the end of a unit of study in relation to the learning objectives. The teacher makes a note of what each child has achieved. But this is not an 'add-on' exercise. It is a synopsis of all that has been done and learned through all the formative observations. It may be that the unit of study has been leading up to creating an account or a variety of accounts or interpretations (see pp. 42, 46, 60–1, 68 and 173) to which everyone has contributed. If the focus of the study was on interpreting evidence this may be a museum display to which everyone has contributed a model, a drawing of an event or artefact, a piece of writing, each with an explanatory label, saying what it is, the evidence we have about it, what might not be known, how it may have been made and used and the effects it may have had on the people who made and used it (see pp. 17–18). I remember one museum display resulting from a visit to Butser Iron Age village. It contained, among other things, a hand-made leather shoe, a model of an Iron Age kiln, a receipt for Iron Age stew based on what we knew of their agriculture and husbandry (lamb, carrots, onions and celery), wool died with natural dyes, woven on a miniature Iron Age loom, a model Iron Age hut and village, a review of *The Changeling*, a story by Rosemary Sutcliff (1986), a poem about Caesar's invasion and maps of a local Iron Age site. All had detailed notes on how they were made and used, evidence for this and further questions and speculations. (I remember it clearly because one of Her Majesty's Inspectors spent some time in my classroom and was mightily impressed!)

A learning objective concerning time measurement and change may relate the display to a timeline. Or summative assessment of each child's interpretation of evidence may be assessing the character they have created for a role play. It may be a video or slide show or PowerPoint® presentation made to an audience, other children, parents or visitors to the school. (I remember, after doing a village study, inviting village residents who had been involved to tea and cake – made by the children of course – in order to see the display of their work. One very elderly gentleman came into the room and stared at a gravestone rubbing. The children had chosen it because it was recent and nice and sharp. 'That's my sister', he said . . . Fortunately he felt honoured and happy to see it.)

## The planning and assessment cycle

Planning and assessment are part of an iterative process that underpins progression in learning. This is shown in Figure 6.2.

## Examples of assessment in history

There are some excellent examples of assessment and of resources for assessment for learning at Key Stages 1 and 2 on the Historical Association website, in the resources section (www.history.org.uk). There is also a good continuing professional development unit on progression in historical learning on this website (Cooper and Nichol 2010).

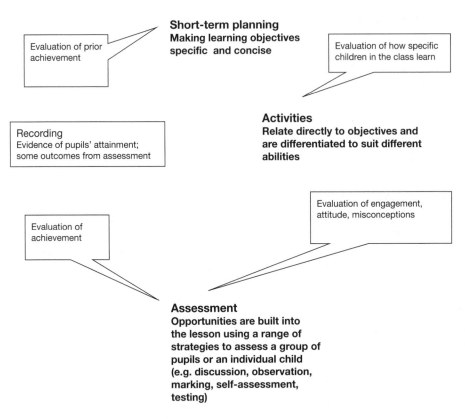

**FIGURE 6.2** Planning and assessment cycle.

## Reporting progress

Teachers are required to write reports for parents on children's progress in each subject. This should be about development in their thinking skills, the ways in which children find out about and construct accounts of the past in history, and compare the accounts of others, explaining why they may be different (see Chapters 1–4). This may not make much sense to most parents so I used to invite them into school each half term to explain what, why and how we would be studying and to invite them to participate – accompanying visits, or helping with pottery, model making or cooking. So they too became involved in, and understood the purpose of what we were doing. School inspectors also have a right to evaluate history teaching in schools and to write reports that are informed by observation but also by teachers' plans and summative assessments. And of course teachers need to know what new classes of children have achieved in order to plan for progression.

## Weekly plans

Weekly plans are taken from the medium-term plan, adjusted, if the children are progressing through the plan more – or less – quickly than expected. From weekly plans an individual lesson plan can be constructed. Weekly plans consist of a timetable for the week. These are necessary to ensure that all areas of the curriculum are taught effectively and in adequate depth. Although weekly plans are meant to outline specific activities and sessions throughout the week they also need to be flexible, so that you can respond to changes, in order to extend – or revisit – children's learning.

## Lesson plans

Detailed lesson plans are derived from the medium-term plan, modified by the weekly plan, depending on how fast, or otherwise, children are progressing (Figure 6.3). It is essential that the learning objectives are simple, manageable, attainable, realistic and time-related (SMART). Children will probably learn many aspects of historical understanding in a lesson so it is important to be clear what are the two or three specific, historical learning objectives of a lesson. Then it is essential that these are at the core of the activities planned for the lesson. Lesson plans may vary in format but they must include the following:

- Year group: references to statutory curriculum.
- Intended learning outcomes.
- Activity(ies) planned to enable children to achieve the intended learning outcomes.
- Differentiation: this will include learning, social, emotional, and any physical needs. In any class of children there will be a range of abilities. This may be linked with understanding of concepts, skill levels or factual knowledge. For example, there may be children for whom English is an additional language (EAL), or who have physical, social or emotional barriers to learning.
- Assessment opportunities.
- Timings of each section of lesson.
- Groupings: these may be based on partners, friendship or ability groups. There are good reasons for any of these groupings but it is essential to be clear about why you have chosen a particular grouping for a particular activity and do not keep the same groups all the time.
- Key vocabulary.
- Key questions.
- Possible misconceptions.
- Resources, including staff (other adults).
- Plenary to correct misunderstandings, consolidate learning, or introduce next learning steps.

| Date | Duration | Year group | Class size |
|---|---|---|---|
| Activity: Interpretations of Alexander the Great Lesson 1/4 | | | Links to statutory curriculum |
| Links to previous learning: Compared interpretations in portraits of Elizabeth 1; Ancient Greeks | | | |
| Learning objectives: 1. Overview of life of Alexander the Great; 2. Understand people can be represented in different ways. | | | |
| Assessment: 1. Observe how well sequence of life events is constructed; 2. Question reasons for/extent of 'greatness' | | | |
| Times | Introduction, activities, key vocabulary, groupings | | |
| 10 min. | Ask, 'What does "great" mean?' Ask which definitions apply to the 3 images. | | |
| 30 min. | Each group given A1 sheet: Explain horizontal line represents Alexander's life and top of vertical represents highest degree of greatness. Invite children to put cards in chronological order on horizontal line then position them on vertical axis to show 'degree of greatness' event represents. Class discussion of reasons for placements. | | |
| 10 min. | Explain found evidence of greatness and decided how far facts of his life reflect 'greatness'. But did first 3 images show all aspects of his greatness? Why did they show different aspects? | | |
| 20 min. | Divide class into groups: 2 film makers filming A's life; 2 writers of children's books; 2 Arab chroniclers. Each group has to create a tableau showing a scene from A's life (using event card). Rest of class guess which event is represented in each tableau. | | |
| Resources | 1. Colin Farrel still (fierce warrior); contemporary coin (horned god), romantic painting, Alexander enters Babylon. 4 sets adjective cards (butcher, hero etc)<br>2. List of definitions of 'great' 'living graph', 4 sheets sugar paper, 4 sets chronology cards representing events in Alexander's life. | | |
| Evaluation of teaching | | | |
| Assessment of pupils' learning | | | |
| Notes for next lesson based on evaluation of teaching and learning | | | |

**FIGURE 6.3** Example of a lesson plan derived from the medium-term plan in Figure 6.1.

Although detailed lesson plans underpin the quality of teaching and learning it is also important to allow the children to make their own suggestions about an investigation, sometimes even in the middle of the lesson. If their idea meets appropriate learning objectives that is fine. I am thinking, for example, of the Year 5/6 children who were making a reconstruction of a timber frame building they had visited built in an area of heavy clay soil with roof tiles made in a local brickworks in the sixteenth century. 'Can we dig up some soil on the school field and make some tiles?' a group of children asked. They did, rolled it out and cut it into tiny oblongs, each with a hole made with a pin to attach it to the roof spars, then put these in the school kiln. I shared the amazement and excitement when, after being fired, small friable pottery tiles emerged. This met the learning objective – deduce how things were made and used in the past – and doubtless science and technology objectives too.

## Evaluating, monitoring and developing your own practice

In order to be responsible for your own professional development it is important to record briefly, probably on the lesson plan, to what extent you think that children achieved the learning objective, who did not, and why not. This is linked to the effectiveness of your teaching. So, what went well in the lesson, what went not so well (risk-taking is an important part of professional development so do not be afraid of taking risks), and what will you do in response to your evaluation of children's learning and of your teaching. If this is recorded on the subsequent lesson plan, perhaps by highlighting, you will be recording your own professional development. Pedagogy, teaching and learning, is not learned once and for all. Children and society change and you interact with these changes and your professional expertise grows and remains up to date.

## References

Alexander, R. (ed.) (2010) *Children, their World, their Education: final report and recommendations of the Cambridge Primary Review*. London: Routledge.

Biggs, J.B. (2003) *Teaching for Quality Learning at University: what the student does*. Buckingham: SHRE and Open University Press.

Brown, G., Morel, D. and Tournham, M. (n.d.) *Films, History and Alexander the Great*, The Historical Association (www.history.org.uk).

Cooper, H. and Nichol, J. (2010) *Progression in Historical Learning*, E-CPD unit, The Historical Association (www.history.org.uk).

DfEE/QCA (1999) *National Curriculum for England and Wales: handbook for primary teachers in England*. London: DfEE/QCA.

Historical Association (2011) *Primary History Survey (England): history 3–11*. London: The Historical Association.

Nichol, J. and Guyver, R. (2005) 'In my view: the debate upon the English national Curriculum for History', *Primary History*, 42, 8–10.

Ofsted (Office for Standards in Education) (2011) *History for All: history in English schools 2007/10*. London: Ofsted (www.ofsted.gov.uk/resources/history-for-all).

Pollard, A. (2008) *Reflective Teaching, 3rd edn.* London: Continuum.

Rowley, C. and Cooper, H. (eds) (2009) *Cross-curricular Approaches to Teaching and Learning*. London: Sage.

Sutcliff, R. (1986) *The Changeling*. London: Penguin Books.

# 3

# Examples of planning and assessment in practice

**7**

# Planning at Key Stage 1

## Time: why should we regard time as so important?

Adults working with young children have always helped them to explore the past and the passing of time, although they may not call this history. We talk to children about changes in their own lives and in the lives of their families, why things change and their implications – moving house, a new baby. We help them to tell us about events in their lives, to sequence and explain them. We talk about ways in which the past was different – when you were a baby, when granny was little. We help children to measure the passing of time: birthdays, seasons, months, weeks, days. The language of time is integral to such talk: before, after; then, now; yesterday, tomorrow, next week. Witherington and Neate (2003) show how children's own stories can extend to finding out more about grandparents and great-grandparents.

### Time and change in stories

Everyone loves a story and stories have always been at the heart of early years education. Indeed, Bage (2003) suggests that the whole curriculum should be organised around stories. Children can relate their own experiences of time to stories in picture. We can only find out about the past through developing communication skills. This requires interacting with others, enjoying listening to spoken language – stories, rhymes, music, songs from past times – and using language to recreate roles and stories in play; exploring new words (haystack, tuffet, piper; then, now, until).

### Books about children and families

Kingsbury (1998) lists a variety of such books. Children can also relate to the many fictional stories about growth and change: *When I Was a Baby* (Anholt 1998), *Grandpa* (Burningham 1984), *The Old, Old Man and the Very Little Boy* (Franklin 1992). Woodhouse (2002), Barkham (2002) and Rogers (1995) show how children's personal biographies and those of people they meet can be used as a starting point for exploring the past through their direct experience.

## Stories about the more distant past

Stories are inevitably concerned with sequencing events over time, with discussing causes and effects of events and with motives, why people behaved as they did: 'because, so . . .' Young children can engage with true stories from the past. Salter (1996) describes how, in role as Grace Darling, she told her reception class the story of the brave daughter of a Victorian lighthouse keeper, which they were able to retell two weeks later to a 'reporter'.

## Fairy stories, folk tales, myths and legends

A myth is part of a jigsaw of tales in which gods and goddesses mirror the activities of the cultures that create them. They speak of social behaviour and our spiritual longings. In a fairy story human beings and supernatural beings meet; human beings are often rewarded or punished for disrespect. Folk tales illustrate our day-to-day lives, with all their hopes, fears, small challenges, rewards, punishments, dangers and absurdities. Legends are mixtures of history, memory, fact and fiction. Myths and legends help children to decode the mysterious and sometimes threatening life they are growing into.

Traditional stories are derived from oral history. They tell us how there have always been wise and foolish people, good and evil, rich and poor, in all societies. They tell us of ways in which life in the past was similar to ours: people bought and sold things, went on journeys, had celebrations, had hopes, fears and disappointments. And we see how things were different, in a world of chimney sweeps, cobblers, woodcutters, goose girls, baronial feasts, of castles and windmills. Woodhouse (2001) suggests ways in which nursery rhymes can be used to develop historical skills and understanding.

The same myths, legends and folk tales have spread throughout the world. They give insights into how people lived long ago in many places and their shared human characteristics. The Welsh tale of King March who had enormous ears, which he could not keep a secret from his barber, is thought to be linked to the horned helmet of Alexander the Great and to the ancient Greek tale of King Midas; other versions are found as far apart as Ireland and Africa. This story reflects the common human difficulty in keeping a secret. *The Barefoot Book of Fairy Tales* (Doyle 2006) contains a broad selection of stories from around the world. Recurrent themes and characters promote universal understanding.

Fairy tales, myths and legends also link the generations more precisely in a continuity of experience. They are the stories of our grandparents and the stories of our grandchildren. Traditional tales help children to develop logic and predictive thought, to consider cause and consequence. They also tell us that we are in many ways all the same but also show us how different we all are, because we are individuals from different ethnic groups, religions, cultures and geographical areas. Children are able to extract the moral in folk tales from other cultures and times and translate it into their own experiences – continuity and change – and personal and social education (Cooper and Ditchburn 2009: 58–70; Cooper 2010: 25–35).

## Stories about the past and identity

Developing an awareness of the past, in the context of our own lives and through stories about the more distant past, is important in understanding who we are and how we relate to others. It enables us to consider why people behave as they do, to infer from their actions how they may feel and think, why things happen. Such discussion involves core values. Bracey (2003) says that it is essential that, from the very beginning, children learn to discuss stories critically. He quotes Ben Okri (1996): 'Stories are the secret reservoir of values: change the stories individuals and nations live by and tell themselves and you change the individuals and nations.' It also develops imagination, an aspect of children's developing thinking that is sometimes ignored (Meadows 1993). Langley-Hamel (2002) shows how, from reception to Year 2, children are increasingly able to retell and modify traditional stories in ways which integrate their own experiences; this helps them to make sense of their lives as part of a continuum of human experience.

Finding out about past times, then, makes an important contribution to personal, social and emotional development. It helps children to respect cultures, be aware of their own needs and feelings and those of others, discuss what is right and wrong and consider consequences of actions.

## Planning for historical enquiry at Key Stage 1

### Planning for play

Play needs to be planned for in terms of groupings and learning objectives, and time (for adults to observe, interact and assess learning), while remaining open-ended and integrated with the curriculum. Bennett (Bennett *et al.* 1997) describes how one teacher used a 'plan, do, review' model to discuss planned play, encouraged children to make links and connections, to experiment, initiate and follow up ideas, which fed into the teacher's curriculum plans. Shefatya (1990: 153) has shown that many children also need to learn how to play: how to say what their role is, how to use objects as symbols, how to create elaborate situations and co-operate.

Meadows and Cashdan (1988: 39), Vygotsky (1978) and Bruner (1987) all consider that social interaction with adults can enhance the quality of play, although most teachers would agree that it is important to enable children to have a sense of ownership and to explore and make choices and take risks in their play.

### Measuring time

Measuring time involves counting (candles on birthday cakes, months of the year, a long/short time), ordering events in sequence, solving number problems (how much older are you than your sister?). Time measurement may provide an ideal context for working with parents. To find out about the sequence of events in their personal time requires finding out from parents. This of course requires talk. In the example of

Key Stage 1 history (Figure 7.3, p. 107) Kirstie devised a questionnaire for her mother, who answered the questions, then helped her to put them on a timeline. The children in the class shared their timelines, which required them to explain them and communicate them to others, to compare similarities and differences. The teacher's timeline and the head teacher's timeline, illustrated with pictures and artefacts, were compared not just by the children but also discussed with genuine interest by colleagues and parents.

An explicit awareness of the types of questions to ask and of how they may be answered makes it possible to maximise children's ownership of their learning, yet to intervene appropriately to extend their thinking, to engage with them in sustained shared thinking (Siraj-Blatchford *et al.* 2002). Young children implicitly develop concepts of time. Wendy Scott (2005) has explained that a wealth of brain research shows that from birth young children construct a world of time, change and sequence. She recognised evidence of this working with children from the age of two in the Fortune Park Day Centre in Islington. Children keep profile books of photographs and are able to articulate differences between the time when a photograph was taken and the present.

Finding out about the past involves making inferences (good guesses) about sources, that is, traces of the past that remain. Sources may be visual: photographs or paintings, advertisements. They may be music: songs, dances, games from past times – whether pop groups from granny's youth or Victorian street cries. They may be oral: 'When auntie lived in Lancaster . . .' 'The lollipop lady said . . .' Rogers (1995) suggests voluntary organisations that may be contacted to liaise with older people. Sources may be things that were made in the past, ranging from buttons to castles, found at home or in museums. They may be written; for very young children these include baby tags, birthday cards, old picture books, names on statues and memorials.

## Creating meaning from sources

To create meaning from sources we need to ask questions about what they are made of, who made them, why, how were they used, what did they mean to the people who made and used them, are there others?

Since sources cannot give us a complete picture of the past because only some remain and we cannot know the thoughts and feelings of those who made and used them, our responses to these questions must be hypotheses, reasonable guesses based on what we know of human nature and past times. With maturity and greater knowledge children's guesses become more likely to be valid, in line with what is known and likely. But it is important to embark on the process of offering a variety of possible ideas from the beginning, to engage imaginatively in 'what if' thinking, which will be refined with maturity. This is an ideal context for learning to develop an argument and explain a point of view ('I think . . . because'), to learn to listen to the views of others, to accept that they may be equally valid ('perhaps', 'maybe'), and that often a question has no single 'right' answer. It is a context in which everyone, including the adults, can engage in genuine shared thinking – and sometimes, in my experience, children's suggestions that appeared improbable have been endorsed by academics. (The shells that children thought were money were indeed used as currency!)

## Sequencing sources

Historians sequence sources in order to trace the causes and effects of changes over time; to understand how and why past times were different from and similar to today. Young children love to put their own photographs in order, to put them on a timeline, to explain the sequence and to compare them with their friends' sequences. They can link the photographs to relevant artefacts that remain – baby clothes, old toys, birthday cards, books and family stories. Linked to adults' timelines the process has endless extensions and interest. Or children might sequence pictures of, for example, clothes or houses, over a long or a short period, or sort into age categories. It is fascinating to listen to the children's often surprisingly complex reasoning about sequences or categories, and their responses to challenges.

## Historical concepts

Discussion about changes over time extends time vocabulary, and the process of making reasoned guesses about sources develops syntax and the language of viewpoint, argument, hypothesis and probability: I think; if . . . then; because; perhaps. Discussing sources, whether artefacts (button hook, castle, oil lamp) or written or oral sources (stories written a long time ago, fairy and folk tales, old rhymes that describe activities familiar in the past), introduces words no longer in everyday use: Mrs Tiggy-Winkle the *washerwoman* was an excellent clear *starcher*. The miller is *grinding* the corn into flour . . . Jack took the cow to *market* . . . Wind the *bobbin* up . . . Concepts often change over time (market, queen) or have several meanings (ball, coach), so that children may have a different image of market from an adult, although they may both think they are sharing meaning. Children often accept the unfamiliar without question (Donaldson 1978). Therefore it is important for adults to discuss meanings with children, to use words in a variety of contexts, to provide visual illustrations, to give children opportunities to use new words themselves in their own contexts.

Learning new vocabulary is an active process. If we see several pictures of different types of castle, or windmill or carriage, we can work out what their shared characteristics are: what their essential meaning is. This involves trial and error, risking using new words in retelling stories and in play, seeing which fit.

## Interpretations: creating and comparing accounts of the past

There is no single 'correct' account of the past. Historians select from, piece together and interpret sources that remain. The accounts they write depend on their own interests. Are they interested in kings and queens or the lives of ordinary people; in the distant or recent past, in powerful women or helplessness; in clothes or how things work, in explaining good and evil, fairness and injustice; in the history of their own country or of others. As new evidence comes to light, and with experience, accounts of the past change. Accounts vary too depending on the time in which they were made.

Young children's exploration of the past can reflect each of these dimensions. They can look for similarities and differences in different versions of folk tales, myths and legends, explore the aspects that are different and suggest why. *The Magic Lands of Britain and Ireland* (Crossley-Holland 2001) is a collection of lesser-known versions of folk tales, while *Fairy Tales* (Doherty 1999) goes back to early versions of the tales so that even Cinderella and Sleeping Beauty have surprising elements. *The Barefoot Book of Fairy Tales* (Doyle 2006) also contains a selection of stories from around the world. Three is often seen as a magic number in folk tales; how many stories can children remember where things happen in threes?

The stories children reconstruct through retelling or act out in play may appear fanciful, with imagination only loosely linked to what is known, but it is the process of understanding why versions may differ and change that matters fundamentally. Only in closed societies is there one true story of a country's past and this is politically contrived, open to manipulation and denies individual identity.

## Interpretations and illustrations

Young children can compare artists' illustrations of stories set in the past. They may differ because of the times in which they were made – a Kate Greenaway illustration (1991) and a contemporary one, for example. Or they may both be contemporary but differ because the styles of the artists express different ideas and feelings; children can discuss how they do this through colour, line and shape, which they prefer and why.

Or the story in the text may tell a different story from the pictures. Thomas (1993) found that nursery children were able to recognise and suggest reasons for this and Hoodless (2004) found that three-year-olds could explain the difference between a story of a child's experiences in imaginary time and a parallel story of the parents' experiences told in real time.

*Fairy Catalogue* (Gardner 2000) works on the premise that children can make up their own versions of fairy stories by choosing the ingredients and categories from a selection of pumpkins, spinning wheels and wicked witches.

## Interpretations and story

There are many versions of traditional fairy stories, often across cultures. Of course white mice do not turn into coachmen or wolves dress up as grandmas. However, it was argued above that these stories are rooted in the oral tradition. They therefore introduce the idea of past times and of continuity and provide contexts for discussing motives, causes and effects, values. Since there are so many versions they also help children to identify the common features and to discuss reasons for differences: why gender roles are inverted in modern versions (e.g. Little Red Riding Hood, Wilson 1998; the Paper Bag Princess, Munsch 1988) or why the story is told from the perspective of the villain, or set in a contemporary context. And there is evidence that by discussing such interpretations children learn to differentiate between fact and fiction.

## Interpretations and 'living history' reconstructions

Very young children may need help in understanding the concept of a 'living history' reconstruction. One group of nursery children found the Beamish Open Air Museum fascinating but needed the concept of 'in role' explained; they thought what they saw was 'real'. Older children need to be encouraged to ask questions such as 'How did they know?', 'Are there others?', 'What might it have felt like when . . .?' They can engage with the notion of how a reconstruction is made and that some may be more accurate than others.

## Interpretations and oral history

Talking to more than one adult about the same aspect of the past (their schools, games they played, food they ate, celebrations) provides rich opportunities for considering how and why adults' accounts may be different. Is it because they lived in different parts of the country, or of the world? Did they do different jobs, are they different ages, in spite of having children or grandchildren the same age?

Reconstructing stories through play provides an ideal opportunity to engage with and make sense of the past. Imaginative play frees children from the constraints of the immediate environment and allows them to form new aspirations in role as a fictitious person. In play children behave beyond their age. Play begins with situations close to the real one but gradually children consciously realise the purpose of play and creating imaginary situations as a means of developing abstract thought (Vygotsky 1978). Tough (1976: 79) believes that imaginative play enables children to think in a historical way, to consider alternative possibilities about how the past may have been, to consider 'what if?' and 'as if' scenarios.

## Interpretations through play

Play, long cherished by educators as the richest and most powerful vehicle for early learning, provides a splendid opportunity for children to engage with past times. Winnicot (in Bruce 1991: 71) suggested that adults are able to relate to powerful events, hero figures, music and paintings if they have related to them and merged with what is important through play. Erikson (1965) found that if children are encouraged to reconstruct exciting scenes from folk tales through 'let's pretend play' they serve as metaphors for their lives, concerns and interests and help them to engage with the mainstream of human emotions in other times and places. Bruce (1991) describes how a group of five-year-olds heard stories about the Black Prince and King Arthur, which led to extensive play about princes and princesses, how Hannah, five and Tom, three, used a rough script based on St George and the dragon as a basis for play and how a teacher added wings to a child's toy pony to retell the story of Pegasus. Garvey (1977) emphasised the importance of play that reconstructs stories about other times and places since it involves experimental dialogue and allows children to explore emotions, relationships and situations, times and places outside their experience. Woodhouse and Lomas (2002) describe how a play area can be organised to develop historical thinking in a Year 1 class. An integrated approach, with play at its centre, can be the foundation for good practice at Key Stage 1.

An interesting starting point could be to support a traditional fantasy play area about pirates, then to challenge this by introducing the true story of Grace O'Malley, a real pirate – and a woman (Kirkland and Wykes 2003). In a different approach, Barnsdale-Paddock and Harnett (2002) give detailed ideas for developing a museum as a focus for play.

Practitioners, then, need to be aware of the interweaving strands of historical enquiry and of the capabilities of the children they teach and to apply their teaching and creative skills to devise exciting activities that they and the children will enjoy: a shared ownership of engagement with and reflection on learning.

# Some professional development activities

The workshops outlined below aim to raise practitioners' awareness of ways in which they can implicitly help children explore the past, to encourage them to experience some of the processes of historical enquiry at their own levels, to devise related activities which reflect their experience at appropriate levels for the children they teach, and so to develop collaborative action research approaches, which are dynamic and in which practitioners take the initiatives.

## Teaching about time

- In pairs, write on cards all the contexts in which concepts of time have arisen in your teaching in the past three (?) weeks.

- Whole group collates on flip-chart.

- Group into aspects of historical enquiry: measuring time, sequencing, changes over time, continuity/change, similarity/difference.

- Discuss why these activities occurred; why they were important.

## Using photographs

Bring a collection of photographs of you taken over time.

- In pairs, try to sequence each other's photographs. How do you work out the sequence? Is it correct? If not, why not? Is it easier with more/fewer photos, longer time intervals? Is there evidence of changes over time (in clothes, people, and activities)? Rapid or slow?

- Tell the other person's story from the photograph evidence. How true is it? What do you not know? Why?

- How valid is the story (e.g. are photos posed or snaps)? What sorts of occasions do they depict? How typical (e.g. are people dressed up, always smiling)? Would others in the photos tell the same story? Why not? Can you find out? Does the age of the photo (e.g. black and white) influence inferences?

## Using artefacts

■ Each person brings an interesting 'old thing' important to them. No one discusses their artefact. Artefacts are displayed as in a museum. In pairs, write explanatory labels saying: what it is, how it was made. Why? How old? How used? How did it impact on the lives of those who used it? Differentiate between what you know, what you can 'guess' and what you do not know.

■ In turn, correct the label on your artefact. Reasons why incorrect? Could you find out more? How?

## Oral history

Why are accounts of the past different?

Colleagues volunteer, in turn, to tell the group something about their childhood, based on the same theme: my favourite game, food, clothes. What did all the stories have in common? What were the differences? Why (e.g. different places, ages, gender)?

## Planning for continuity

■ Try out, initially, one of the workshop ideas, in a simplified form suitable for children. Carry out the activity across different age groups of children. Keep records on (some) individual children's responses in each age group.

■ Collate for each age group in sequence. Is there progression? In what ways? If not, why not? Were there any surprises about some children's level of response?

And in conclusion, here is one of my favourite quotations.

If one respects the ways of thought of the growing child, if one is courteous enough to translate material into its logical forms, and challenging enough to tempt him to advance, then it is possible to introduce, at an early age, ideas and styles that, in later life will make him an educated man.

(Bruner 1966)

This is already a historical text! What about an educated woman?!

## 'Me', Years 1 and 2 – Key Stage 1

This topic is about changes in the everyday lives of the children and in the lives of familiar adults. The fourth focus, 'Stories', could be extended to include stories about famous men and women and famous events; this would allow opportunities to discuss why people did things and why events happened. However, it is not necessary to include all aspects of historical enquiry in one topic. A topic in the following year might focus on a period in the distant past, and involve stories about people and events through a theme such as 'castles'.

Years 1 and 2 worked on the theme 'Me' with a history focus. Year 1 concentrated on their own timelines for six years, which recorded their own experiences of change over time. They brought in their own baby clothes, and toys they had had over the previous five years, sequenced socks and mittens to illustrate growth, sequenced their photographs and recounted memories. They interviewed one of the parents about a new baby who was brought into school, weighed, measured and compared with them. They listed their achievements since they were babies: talking, throwing and catching balls, and so on. The children were also paired with Year 6 children as part of the Year 6 work on 'human development'. Each pair worked on a cross-curricular theme planned by the older child for a week, at their own level. One pair, for instance, studied an old oil lamp, wrote about it, painted it and found out about it, each in their own way, then they put the resulting work in a book and discussed similarities and differences of the five-year-old and ten-year-old approaches. Both the Year 1 and Year 6 children enjoyed this, and it enabled the younger children to predict what they may be like and able to do when they are 'twice as old as now'.

The Year 1 teacher and the head teacher also participated 'at their own level'. The Year 1 teacher made her own timeline illustrated with photographs of her family and key events in her life, concluding with her graduation day and her wedding.

## Examples of planning and assessment at Key Stage 1

Since she was twenty-five, the teacher's was a very long one, and allowed the children to discuss their life span in relation to hers, and to compare different scales for recording time. The teacher displayed her own collection of books and toys, surrounding her wedding dress on a stand in the middle of the room and invited her own grandma to come to school! Gran, teacher and children all enjoyed exchanging memories. Meanwhile, in the foyer, the head teacher, who was new to the school, took the opportunity both to introduce herself and to support the history project, by making her timeline. This was very long indeed because she was nearly fifty years old. She was able to show us photographs of her father leaving home to go to war and other very personal records – a long swathe of her golden hair, cut when she was five, her (nearly) fifty-year-old teddy, her first mitten. She told us, in one assembly, a moving story of how she had found these things hidden in a secret box in her parents' home on their death. In other assemblies, she read to us moral tales from her parents' Sunday school prizes. This infant project developed excellent interpersonal understandings and insights throughout the whole-school community. Figures 7.1 and 7.2, and Table 7.1 show aspects of the planning process.

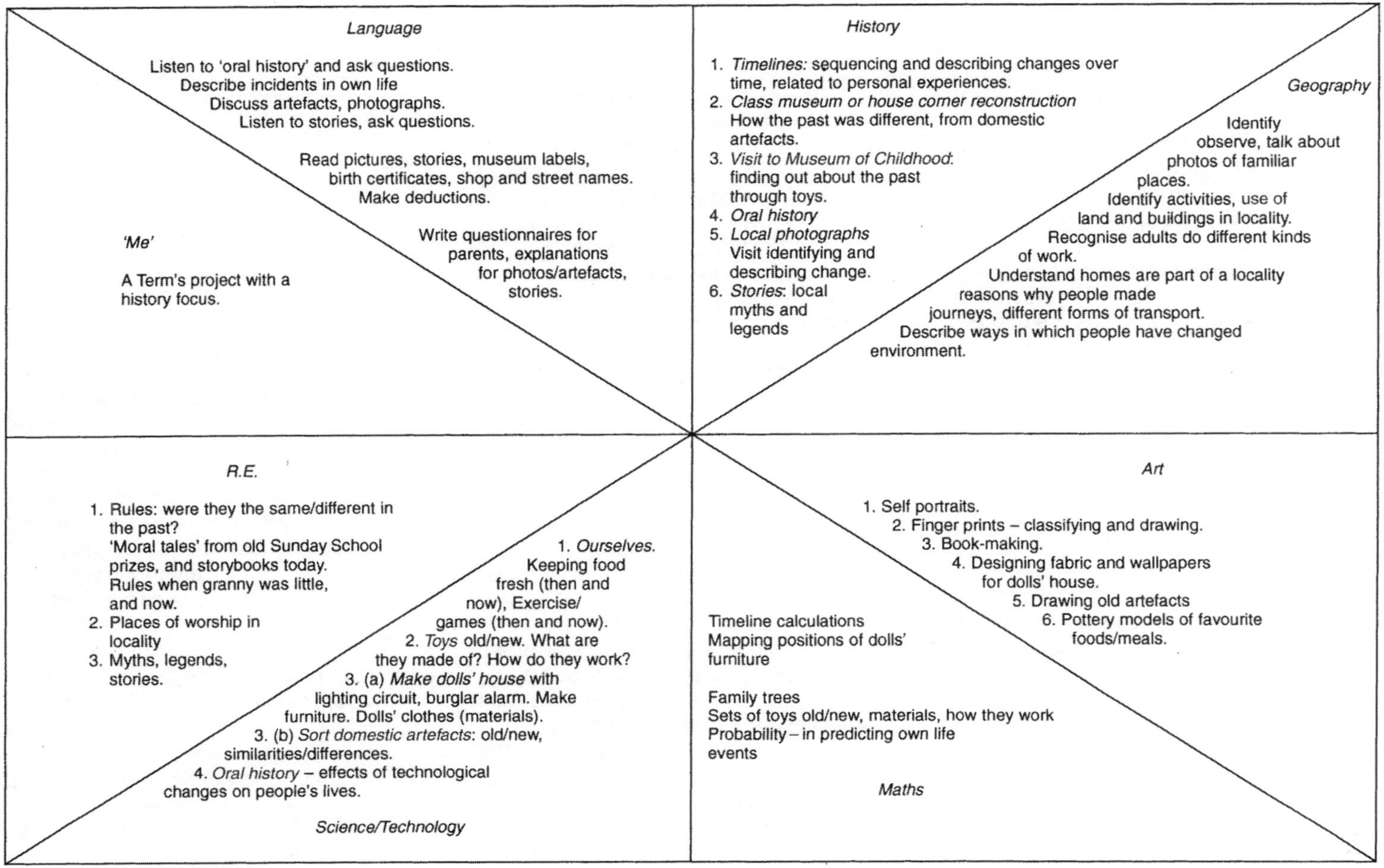

**History**

1. *Timelines*: sequencing and describing changes over time, related to personal experiences.
2. *Class museum or house corner reconstruction.* How the past was different, from domestic artefacts.
3. *Visit to Museum of Childhood*: finding out about the past through toys.
4. *Oral history.*
5. *Local photographs.* Visit identifying and describing change.
6. *Stories*: local myths and legends

**Geography**

Identify observe, talk about photos of familiar places.

Identify activities, use of land and buildings in locality.

Recognise adults do different kinds of work.

Understand homes are part of a locality reasons why people made journeys, different forms of transport.

Describe ways in which people have changed environment.

**Language**

Listen to 'oral history' and ask questions.

Describe incidents in own life

Discuss artefacts, photographs.

Listen to stories, ask questions.

Read pictures, stories, museum labels, birth certificates, shop and street names. Make deductions.

Write questionnaires for parents, explanations for photos/artefacts, stories.

'Me'

A Term's project with a history focus.

**R.E.**

1. Rules: were they the same/different in the past? 'Moral tales' from old Sunday School prizes, and storybooks today. Rules when granny was little, and now.

2. Places of worship in locality

3. Myths, legends, stories.

**Science/Technology**

1. *Ourselves.* Keeping food fresh (then and now), Exercise/ games (then and now).
2. *Toys old/new. What are they made of? How do they work?*
3. (a) *Make dolls' house with* lighting circuit, burglar alarm. Make furniture. Dolls' clothes (materials).
3. (b) *Sort domestic artefacts*: old/new, similarities/differences.
4. *Oral history* – effects of technological changes on people's lives.

**Art**

1. Self portraits.
2. Finger prints – classifying and drawing.
3. Book-making.
4. Designing fabric and wallpapers for dolls' house.
5. Drawing old artefacts
6. Pottery models of favourite foods/meals.

**Maths**

Timeline calculations
Mapping positions of dolls' furniture

Family trees
Sets of toys old/new, materials, how they work
Probability – in predicting own life events

**FIGURE 7.1** Cross-curricular approach.

**TABLE 7.1** 'Me' history grid.

| What I want children to learn | What I want children to do | Assessment opportunities |
|---|---|---|
| To communicate awareness and understanding of history in the following ways:<br>(i) sequencing objects and events in order to develop a sense of chronology | Timelines<br>Make own timeline 0–7<br>(i) place photographs of themselves in sequence on timeline<br>(ii) compare with timeline for teacher; use words such as then, now | Level 1<br>Can sequence photographs, events.<br>Can recognise the distinction between past and present in their lives; in teacher's life: can use language such as now, then, next, before, after.<br>Can use questionnaire to answer questions about their own lives |
| (ii) using words and phrases relating to the passing of time<br>(iii) finding out about aspects of the past through learning to ask and answer questions which help to identify<br>(a) differences between past and present<br>(b) different ways in which the past is represented using artefacts | (i) bring in 'old things' for house corner role play/class museum<br>Draw them; attach (by Velcro, which allows rearrangement) to a sequence line with categories (very old/old/new).<br>(ii) Visit Museum of Childhood.<br>Handling session – old toys<br>What were they?<br>What are they?<br>How did they work? | Level 1 Beginning to find out about the past from sources of information and to recognise a distinction between past and present<br>Level 2 Also beginning to identify some of the different ways in which the past is represented, and to answer questions about the past from sources of information through making books or presentation for grandparents, or tape or video recordings for 'Children's TV or radio' can: |
| Oral sources | (i) write questionnaire for granny, grandad, or older person about life when they were little, or tape-record interview at home | Level 1 recognise distinction between past and present, in other people's lives |

**TABLE 7.1** *continued.*

| What I want children to learn | What I want children to do | Assessment opportunities |
|---|---|---|
| | (ii) invite several older people who were brought up in different parts of the world and in different circumstances to tell children about their early years, to show photographs of themselves in the past and of their treasured possessions. | *Level 2* identify some of the different ways in which the past is represented<br>*Level 1* ask and answer questions about photographs which recognise similarities and differences using concepts of time<br>*Level 2* also demonstrate factual knowledge about events or people beyond living memory, related to photographs |
| Photographs | Collect and display selected old photographs of locality; take photographs of/visit same sites today | |
| Stories | (i) invite someone from a local history society to tell 'true stories' about locality which children can retell, draw, act out<br><br>(ii) myths and legends from different cultures | *Level 1* can sequence events and use time vocabulary in retelling stories<br>*Level 2* also can begin to explain why people acted as they did, demonstrate factual knowledge learned from 'true stories' and ask and answer questions about the past, based on the stories |

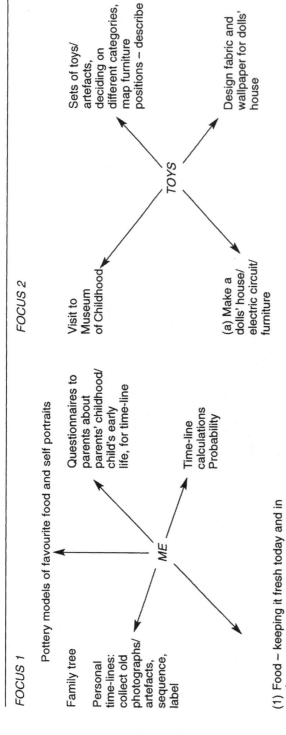

FOCUS 1

Pottery models of favourite food and self portraits

Family tree

Personal
time-lines:
collect old
photographs/
artefacts,
sequence,
label

Questionnaires to
parents about
parents' childhood/
child's early
life, for time-line

Time-line
calculations
Probability

ME

(1) Food – keeping it fresh today and in
the past
(2) Keeping healthy today and in the past
(3) Exercise/games today and in the past
(4) Fingerprint classification
(5) The senses: smelling, tasting

FOCUS 2

Visit to
Museum
of Childhood

Sets of toys/
artefacts,
deciding on
different categories,
map furniture
positions – describe

TOYS

Design fabric and
wallpaper for dolls'
house

(a) Make a
dolls' house/
electric circuit/
furniture

(b) Toys
old/new
similarities/
differences in materials,
in how they work

FIGURE 7.2 Plan for the term showing how work was organised around four focuses, each lasting several weeks.

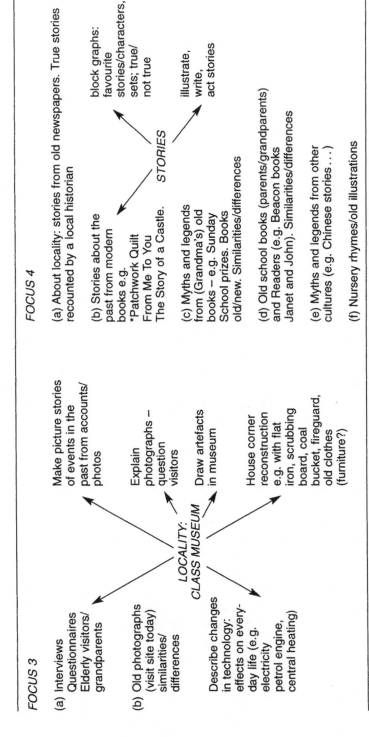

FOCUS 3

(a) Interviews
Questionnaires
Elderly visitors/
grandparents

Make picture stories
of events in the
past from accounts/
photos

(b) Old photographs
(visit site today)
similarities/
differences

Explain
photographs –
question
visitors

Draw artefacts
in museum

*LOCALITY:*
*CLASS MUSEUM*

Describe changes
in technology:
effects on every-
day life (e.g.
electricity
petrol engine,
central heating)

House corner
reconstruction
e.g. with flat
iron, scrubbing
board, coal
bucket, fireguard,
old clothes
(furniture?)

FOCUS 4

(a) About locality: stories from old newspapers. True stories
recounted by a local historian

(b) Stories about the
past from modern
books e.g.
*Patchwork Quilt
From Me To You
The Story of a Castle.*

*STORIES*

block graphs:
favourite
stories/characters,
sets; true/
not true

illustrate,
write,
act stories

(c) Myths and legends
from (Grandma's) old
books – e.g. Sunday
School prizes. Books
old/new. Similarities/differences

(d) Old school books (parents/grandparents)
and Readers (e.g. Beacon books
Janet and John). Similarities/differences

(e) Myths and legends from other
cultures (e.g. Chinese stories . . .)

(f) Nursery rhymes/old illustrations

Note: * V. Flournoy (1987) *The Patchwork Quilt.* Puffin.
    P. Rogers (1987) *From Me To You.* Orchard Books.
    J. S. Goodall (1986) *The Story of a Castle.* Andre Deutsch.

**FIGURE 7.2** *continued.*

The Year 2 extension of the theme was originally going to be 'when granny was little', but since grannies ranged in age from mid-thirties to about sixty, this was not a very useful title, and certainly did not go back to pre-electricity and horse-drawn carts. So they stuck to an extended version of 'me'. This was not a multicultural school, but a Chinese boy had recently joined the class. He spoke little English and did not adjust easily. The class teacher seized this opportunity to develop his work on 'when Mummy was little' into a rich subtheme on what it was like to grow up in Shanghai, with the help of the boy's mother. The class went to the Chinese exhibition, and went to see the Chinese New Year festivities in Soho. This led to work on old Chinese tales, with big collages and models of dragons and of the 'willow pattern' plate, work on Chinese paintings, experiments in writing with a Chinese brush in ink, and Chinese calendars and counting systems. The term concluded with a Chinese meal, which Mrs Chan showed the children how to prepare, then they compared old China with what Mrs Chan told them about life in China today, and how life in Shanghai is different from and similar to life in Croydon! The Chinese work gave the project a far richer dimension and also led to greater personal understandings for all those involved.

## Children's work

Some children's questionnaires for their parents ask about the arrival of cats, dogs, goldfish, brothers and sisters, about holidays, cuts and bruises, or moving home. This six-year-old, however, is already preoccupied with self-assessment and monitoring her progress! The information from the questionnaire was transferred to the timeline (Figure 7.3). There were great opportunities here for transactional writing and for parental involvement. Parental understanding and support is particularly important in family history, which can be a sensitive area. The family tree was optional and done with help at home (Figure 7.4).

The children were very interested to use the information in their timelines, photographs and collections of toys to make deductions about the past, and about changes over time. These were certainly 'interactive' displays.

The account of the visit to the Museum of Childhood is a piece of shared writing (Figure 7.5). It refers, in a very sanguine way, to the initial excitement of the day, when the coach driver deposited the children outside Burlington Arcade, telling the teacher, 'It's just up the road love' (assuming they were going to the Museum of Mankind!). Although she had made a preliminary visit, the teacher assumed that this was another entrance. The novelty of the tube journey from Piccadilly Circus to Bethnal Green was so exciting that James had a nosebleed before they were able to discuss such concepts as continuity and change, similarity and difference, during the 'handling session' led by the museum staff. Later, they wrote a book explaining how the toys in the past were sometimes different from theirs, and why (Figure 7.6).

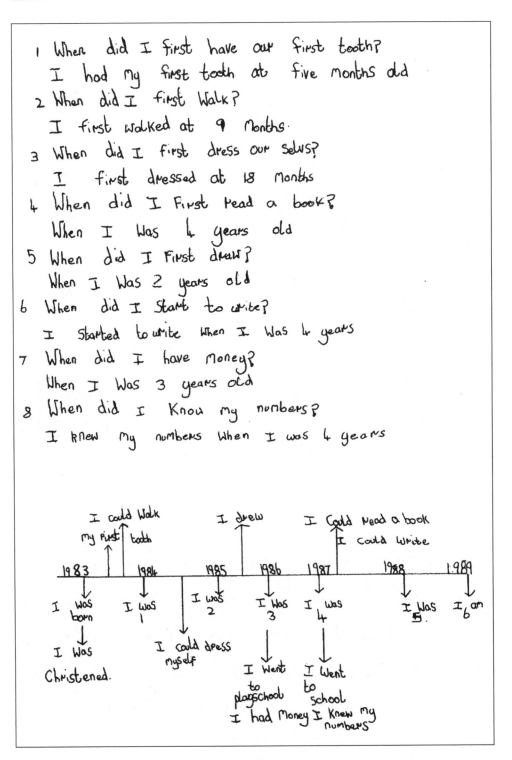

1 When did I first have our first tooth?
  I had my first tooth at five months old
2 When did I first Walk?
  I first walked at 9 months.
3 When did I first dress our selves?
  I first dressed at 18 months
4 When did I First read a book?
  When I Was 4 years old
5 When did I First draw?
  When I Was 2 years old
6 When did I Start to write?
  I Started to write when I Was 4 years
7 When did I have money?
  When I Was 3 years old
8 When did I Know my numbers?
  I knew my numbers When I was 4 years

I could Walk
my first tooth

I drew

I Could read a book
I Could Write

1983    1984    1985    1986    1987    1988    1989

I was
born

I was
1

I was
2

I Was
3

I was
4

I Was
5.

I am
6

I Was
Christened.

I could dress
myself

I Went
to
playschool

I Went
to
school

I had Money I Knew my
numbers

**FIGURE 7.3** How a questionnaire for parents was used to make a timeline.

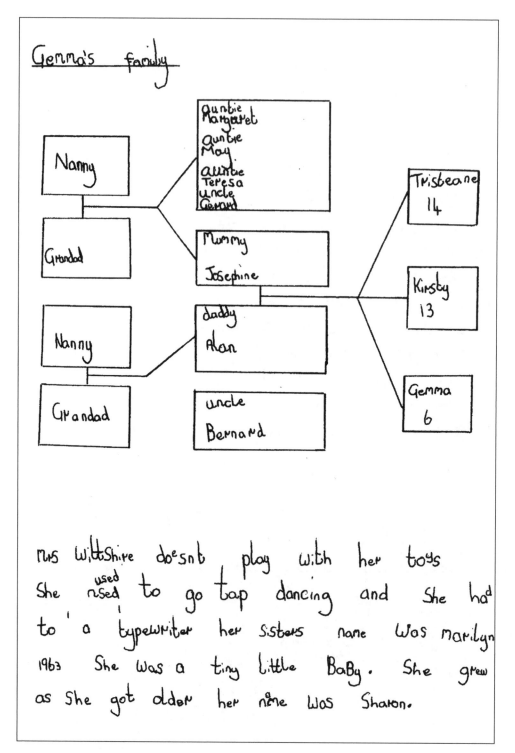

**FIGURE 7.4** Gemma's family tree.

# OUR TRIP TO BETHNAL GREEN
## TOY MUSEUM.

On Wednesday, 14th June, we went on the coach to the toy museum.
The coach driver took us to the wrong museum. We had to go on the underground
When we got to the toy museum James had a nosebleed.
In the museum we saw old toys:
Trains, cars, dolls, games, soldiers, puppets, doll's houses, boats, teddy bears, horses and theatres.
We found out that old toys were made from wood and our new toys are made from plastic.
WE found out that dolls were made out of wood, wax, china, clay, paper and plastic lots of old dolls had real hair.
We had a talk about old toys—it was very interesting.
We were tired when we got home.

A Story by Class 7.

Gemma

Toys

my grandprents would have played with hoops and ropes

**FIGURE 7.5** Report on visit to a toy museum.

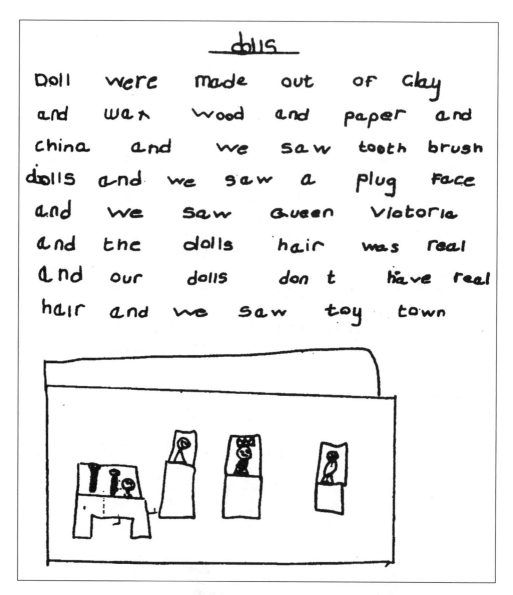

**dolls**

Doll were made out of clay and wax wood and paper and china and we saw tooth brush dolls and we saw a plug face and we saw Queen Victoria and the dolls hair was real and our dolls don t have real hair and we saw toy town

**FIGURE 7.6** Report on information about dolls learned at the toy museum.

# Reconstruction of a ball at Belvoir Castle in 1814

I was asked to organise a workshop at Belvoir Castle for Key Stage 1 teachers, considering how the castle could be used as a historical source to plan a visit, and preparation and follow-up activities. The aim was to help them to be more flexible and imaginative in planning history and less dependent on published schemes and to plan for blocks of time and cross-curricular activities. I was surprised at the challenge this would be for them, indicated by some initial remarks.

'We have to download schemes in my school.'

'We are only allowed to do Florence Nightingale.'

'We have to fit into the timetable.'

'As a music co-ordinator, I should not want to mix music up with anything else.'

Yet they all said they had come to 'get some creative ideas'.

## Aims of the workshop

- to consider how to help Key Stage 1 children to 'reconstruct' an interpretation of a banquet at Belvoir in 1814, using primary and secondary sources;

- to link knowledge, skills and historical thinking with other subjects when appropriate;

- to consider how a visit to Belvoir and preparatory and follow-up activities could be applied to other castles and stately homes.

## The workshop

Tables 7.2–7.7 below are some of the suggestions made, as the teachers moved through the rooms of the castle, about how children could select, carefully observe and record aspects of the castle for a purpose – to imagine and act out what a ball might have been like at Belvoir Castle at a particular date in the past, 1814. This involved all aspects of historical enquiry. (Of course this case study could be modified to apply to a large house or stately home near you.)

The enquiry would have a purpose, for children and teachers: to select, discuss and record sources (the building, the paintings, furniture, kitchen equipment, written evidence of who lived in the castle in 1814), in order to create and communicate their account (given the children's immaturity) of what the ball may have been like.

However, I think that teachers also need to see an enquiry as valid and interesting and worthwhile at their own level, if they are to generate enthusiasm in children. I modelled my own research so far, before visiting the castle. I read an extract from *War and Peace*, describing the ball at the Rostovs', typical of balls across Europe at the time.

**TABLE 7.2** Reconstruction of a ball at Belvoir Castle in 1814: before the visit.

| Activity | History | Literacy |
|---|---|---|
| What do you know about castles?<br><br>Make a 'concept map'; draw and label a picture of your idea of a castle and tell us about it.<br>Look at pictures of different kinds of castles: How are they the same? Different? What is 'a castle'?<br>(Could be modified as 'a great house') | 1b a long time ago; now/then<br>2b identify differences between now and then | 1.1.4 write captions<br>1.2.22 labels for drawings and diagrams<br>1.3.21 explain and describe |
| Who has been to a party? Why? What did you do?<br><br>Introduce idea of balls and banquets, a long time ago. For example, read/retell (different versions of) Cinderella. Anyone got other stories and pictures of balls?<br>Explain there used to be grand balls at Belvoir Castle a long time ago. Shall we pretend to have a grand ball? Shall we go to Belvoir to find out what it might have been like? What shall we need to find out?<br>General discussion; group questions around key points.<br>• How would they dress?<br>• What would the rooms/ furniture be like?<br>• What dances?<br>• What would they eat?<br>• How might it be cooked?<br>• How would it be cooked? | 3 identify different ways in which the past is represented<br>4b ask and answer questions about the past | 1.1.1; 1.2.4; 1.3.5 read and retell familiar stories<br>2.1.4 understand time and sequence in stories<br>2.2.5 discuss story settings |

**TABLE 7.3** During the visit to Belvoir: the state dining room.

| Activity | History | Literacy | Other subjects |
|---|---|---|---|
| Take slides of room and of details, as before.<br>How many words can we think of to describe the room? (Tape-record or list.)<br>How is it different from the room where you eat?<br>Why? | 2b identify differences between life at different times | English speaking and listening 1b use words with precision | ICT 1a gather and retrieve info from variety of sources |

**TABLE 7.4** During the visit to Belvoir: the ballroom.

| Activity | History | Literacy | Other subjects |
|---|---|---|---|
| • Between ballroom and Elizabeth saloon, in the Chinese dressing room, look at family picture of children of the fifth Duke. Who are they? How old? What are they wearing? Draw/write notes about one of them. | 4a find out about past from sources (e.g. historic buildings, pictures) 4b ask and answer questions abut past | 1.1.4 captions, notes 1.1.5 describe story settings and relate them to their own experience and that of others | ICT 2a use images to develop their ideas |
| • Take slides. These can be projected in school to recreate ballroom during role play or details of furniture, fireplaces can be recorded to use later in making 'props'. | As above | 1.1.14 write captions 1.1.15 lists for planning and reminding 1.1.6 write and draw simple instructions and labels, e.g. for use in role play | Art and design 1a record from first-hand observation |
| • Draw statue of the Duchess. What is she wearing? How is it made? What sort of material do you think? Why do you think that? Make notes on/draw her hairstyle.<br><br>• Look at portraits of the fifth Duke and Duchess and their children. Does the Duchess in the painting look different from the statue? How? Why? Do the children look different from the portrait in the Chinese room? Describe each of them: their clothes, what do you think they were like? Why? Who are they?<br><br>• What sort of dances would they have done? Guess. Why do you think that? Do we know? How can we find out for our pretend ball? | 3 identify different ways in which the past is represented<br><br>4a, b | | 4c work of artists and crafts people (e.g. sculptors) |

**TABLE 7.5** During the visit to Belvoir: the old kitchen.

| Activity | History | Literacy | Other subjects |
|---|---|---|---|
| • Find the two ranges. What were they for? How long would it take to get them hot? How do you think the cradle spit worked? How could you boil water, vegetables, puddings? What was the hood for? What did the big tray collect? Why were the walls painted brown?<br><br>• In groups find three kitchen utensils. Draw, label; what were they for?<br><br>• In groups find a chopping board, pestle and mortar, fish kettles, water boilers, bench with revolving top; draw and label.<br><br>• Can you see anything made of: iron? copper? brass? wood? Differences? Why?<br><br>• Imagine the kitchen preparing for a banquet. What sounds would you hear? What smells? What might they be cooking? How can we find out more? | 1b use words relating to time<br>2a recognise why people did things<br>2b identify differences between life at different times<br>4a find out about the past from artefacts and historic buildings<br>4b ask and answer questions about the past | 1.1.16 write and draw simple labels<br>1.2.23 extended captions<br>1.2.25 assemble info from their own experience<br>1.2.22 and labels or pictures | Science<br>1a use senses to recognise similarities between materials<br>1b sort into groups on basis of material properties<br>1c recognise and name common materials<br>1d Find out uses of materials and why they are chosen for different uses<br><br>Art 1a record from observation |

**TABLE 7.6** During the visit to Belvoir: the nursery/schoolroom.

| Activity | History | Literacy | Other subjects |
|---|---|---|---|
| • Can you remember the children who lived here in 1814? I wonder what they were like? How might they have spent their time?<br><br>• What games might they have played with? Are they different from yours?<br><br>• What lessons do you think they had?<br><br>• Do you think they might have made up stories like you do? What about? Why do you think that? | 4 find out about the past from artefacts; ask and answer questions about the past<br>2b find out about differences in life at different times | 2.3.14 describe character descriptions<br>1.1.5 describe story settings and incidents and relate them to own experience, and that of others<br>1.2.10 identify and compare basic story elements<br>2.1. 5 identify and discuss reasons for events in stories | Physical education 7c play simple games.<br><br>Music 1b, 2b sing songs, play tunes and untuned instruments |

**TABLE 7.7** After the visit: planning a pretend ball at Belvoir Castle.

| Activity | History | Literacy | Other subjects |
|---|---|---|---|
| • Write invitations to the banquet, (modelled on party invitation). | 5 | 1.2.13 substitute and extend patterns from reading through language play | ICT 3a make invitation cards |
| • Find out more about banquets and balls from non-fiction text and story illustrations (e.g. what to wear, food). | 4 find out about past from range of sources 2b identify similarities and differences between life at different times 1a, b time vocabulary; place objects in order | 1.2.18 1.3.17 2.1.14 2.3.14–18 non-fiction reading 1.3.22 2.3.19 read and record info | ICT 1b enter and store information |
| • Create the 'ballroom' and the 'dining room'. Project slides of parts on wall; discuss shapes, materials, colours. Paint on lining paper. Add 3D stucco, gold paint, velvet scraps, brocade, etc. | 2b similarity/ difference 4a, 5 find out about past from sources and communicate 3 different ways in which the past is represented | | Art and design 1a record from experience and imagination 1c collect visual and other info to help develop ideas, combine visual and tactile, and match to purpose of work 4 visual and tactile – colour, pattern, texture 4c roles and purposes of crafts people in different times D&T 1–4 |
| • Make models from drawings/ photos, slides, of selected detail (e.g. gilded chair back, clock, dining plates) | as above | | |
| • Design dress or aspect of dress, e.g. brooch, necklace, necktie, tie pin, noted during visit or in book research or download illustrations from internet, e.g. http://hal.edu.~cathy/re/rd.html or http://locutus.ucr.edu/cathy/ reg3.html. Make an eighteenth-century fashion book. | as above | | D&T 1–4 |

**TABLE 7.7** *continued.*

| | | | |
|---|---|---|---|
| • Listen to music for ball (see resources). Make up and practise dances suitable for the ball. Draw and label diagrams to record dance patterns. | 2b similarity/ difference 4a ask and answer questions about the past 5 communicate findings | Read and record info (as above) 1.1.16 write simple instructions and labels 1.2.22,1.3.21 record in labels and drawings 2.1.17 use diagram as part of instructions 2.2.21 to explain a process | Music explore and express feelings about music using movement, dance and expressive and musical language 5c, d work in groups, as class; a range of recorded music from different times. PE 6a use move- ment imaginatively responding to dance music 6d create and perform dances using simple movement patterns including from different times |
| • Plan banquet. Use sources of information to design menu. (See resources; see also http://homepages.ihug.co.nz/ ~awoodley/Regency.html# recipes.) | 2b (sim/diff) 4a, b ask questions about sources 5 communicate findings | simple lists 1.1.15 organise lists 1.2.25 read and record 1.3.22 | D&T passim |
| • Make models of/draw and cut out, selected items for role play. | 2b, 4a, b, 5 | Use models (e.g. of food for each course) to organise sequentially, make simple notes from non- fiction texts | |
| • Write schedule for work in the kitchen to prepare banquet. (See resources; see also Woodhouse, M. (1992) *Scrub- a-dub Nellie*, The National Trust, for picture story of a day in the life of a kitchen maid.) | 1b time vocab 4a use range of sources 5 communicate in variety of ways | 1.1.15 make simple lists 2.1.16 use models from reading to organise points in order (see resources) | D&T passim |
| • Write recipe and cook small dish for banquet (see resources). | | 1.1.13, 16, 2.1.15 read and follow simple instructions | |

**TABLE 7.7** *continued.*

| | | | |
|---|---|---|---|
| • Pretend you are in the school room. Which one of the children are you? Rewrite a traditional story, pretending it happened at Belvoir. Describe things you saw at Belvoir and put them into the story. Draw them in your illustrations. | | 1.1.10 use patterned stories as models using basic conventions 1.2.14 represent outlines of story plots 1.2.14 write stories based on reading 2.1.11 use the language of time 2.3.10 use the language of story | |
| ...And now you can go to the ball... | | | |

I played Regency ball music and read to the group about a day in the life of Careme, the great chef of the period who travelled around great houses catering for grand balls. I had found this and the music resources, and also information about dance steps, and wonderful Regency fashion plates on the internet. The websites are given below. Yes, this took some time, but I became genuinely interested and hoped that I could communicate this to the group. (Not sure that I was successful in every case.)

A ball was agreed to be a good idea, because of children's familiarity with parties in their own lives, and with castles and balls in folk and fairy stories, and their enjoyment in dressing up, in order to try to 'get into the skin' of other people, living in different times. Tables 7.2 to 7.7 outline the activities planned before the visit to the castle, during the visit and following the visit in the first column. For each of the activities in column one the second column indicates the learning objectives in history, the third column shows literacy learning objectives and the fourth column shows links to other subjects.

Pupils should be taught to select from their knowledge of history and communicate it in a variety of ways (for example, talking, writing, drawing) and to identify different ways in which the past is represented).

# Resource notes

I include the resources I researched in detail, partly because you may wish to plan the visit to a 'great house' and use some of them, but also to illustrate the extent to which I became interested in the project at my own level and wanted to share this with the workshop participants, in this case, and with children, if I were their teacher. To me equal child/adult involvement and research is essential to good teaching. It enables us then to engage in what is called in the REPEY study (Siraj-Blatchford *et al.* 2002) 'sustained, shared dialogue'. The adult may know a little more than the children but they are both involved in the process of finding out together. Without this approach I should find teaching very boring! So the results of my researches are given in some detail below.

The research informed the planning for the preparation to the visit (Table 7.2), during the visit (Tables 7.3–7.6) and the follow-up of the visit (Table 7.7).

## The ball

Video of ball scenes in Jane Austen's *Pride and Prejudice* (*Pride and Prejudice*, DVD, BBC) give the flavour. In spite of the *War and Peace* extract, dances were often walked, in a stately fashion, in time to the music. There are so many versions of a dance that it would be quite appropriate for children to make up their own dances to the music, using traditional country dance figures based on some traditional country dance patterns:

- to 'lead' – partners move up and down the set with joined hands;

- to 'cast off' – turn outwards and proceed around the other line of dancers;

- to 'cast one' – adjacent couples change positions at the end of a movement;

- to 'cross hands' – right/left hands of partners joined – or both hands crossed behind backs;

- 'hands across' – opposite couples join right hands and move clockwise in circle;

- 'bows and curtseys'.

If you are interested, at your own level, there is a great deal of information on the internet:

- www.cam.ac.uk/societies/round/dances

- www.earthlydelights.com.au/english3.htm

- Dance, dress, music: BBC – DVD/video, *Pride and Prejudice* (Jane Austen)

- Ball music: CD, *The Pride and Prejudice Collection: A Selection of Dances Popular in the 18th and 19th Centuries*, the Pemberley Players, available from Fain Music, 8 Pensall Drive, Heswall, CH61 6XP (www.fainmusic.co.uk).

## Clothes

For clothes: very good, large images can be found on www.pemberley.com/janeinfo/ppbrokil.html

## The banquet

Famous French chefs were hired whenever possible (see Kelly 2004 for some of his recipes).

## A day in the life of Antonin Careme

The evening menu consisted of seven services, rather than courses, offering eighteen choices of dish. Nearly all the food was presented on the table at the start of the meal with only the soups and entrees 'making an entrance hot'.

- *6 a.m.* Stoves stoked and sauces set on hobs. Oranges hollowed. Cochineal added to orange jelly to fill half shells; blancmange into half shells. During day alternate layers built up.

- *7 a.m.* Careme explained the menu to the staff: pastry chefs, underchefs, kitchen hands, table deckers and footmen.

> Soups
>
> Fish: bass and cod
>
> Lamb garnished with quails
>
> Entrées: filets of beef; chicken; rabbit
>
> Roasts
>
> Chicken; pigeon
>
> Nectarine ice cream; oranges with marbled jellies
>
> Centrepiece: the castle made in sugar.

- *11 a.m.* Quails, rabbits, pigeons, partridges, chicken in rows on table. Lamb boiled.

- *Midday* Work begun on making spun sugar for centrepiece – made in two copper pans and poured into mould.

- *Mid-afternoon* Make fish soup, garnished with oysters, crayfish, truffles.

- *4 p.m.* Roasts on spit and cauldrons for boiling meat and fish (fowl, game, 45-pound beef, 35-pound veal).

- *6 p.m.* Table deckers in dining room covered table with cloth. Each place had flat tablespoon, facing down. Napkins folded like water lilies. Centrepiece put in place.

- *6.15 p.m.* Oranges cut in quarters to reveal layers of jelly and blancmange and arranged with laurel leaves in two pyramids.

- *6.45 p.m.* Guests enter dining room. Footmen enter with two silver tureens. Roasts already on table. Host carves roasts. Beef fillets and rabbits brought in on silver salvers.

(Taken from Kelly 2004)

## Similar reconstructions

In Cooper (2002), a variety of role-play interpretations in Key Stage 1 classes are described (pp. 24–32, 79–94). The rationale for learning about the past through play is explored in *Exploring Time and Place Through Play* (Cooper 2004: 5–11, 16–23, exemplified in case studies, 24–6).

## People probably living in Belvoir Castle in 1814

These included John Manners (35), the fifth Duke of Rutland; his wife, Elizabeth Manners (34); his children, Elizabeth Manners (12), Emmeline (8), Katherine (6), Adeliza (3) and Charles, Marquess of Granby (baby).

Staff close to the family were Susanna Gooding, governess; Mary Hanby, lady's maid to Elizabeth and Emmeline; Mrs Griffiths, nurse to Katherine and Adeliza; Maria Holland and Elizabeth Howard, nurses to Charles; Anne Keeling, house keeper; Molly (13), tweeny; and Mary Brewin, housemaid.

Visitors to the castle included the Duke of Wellington, the Prince of Wales, Sir John Thornton, vicar.

### A word of thanks

Finally I should like to thank Rhi Clarke, the education officer at Belvoir Castle, for her help, in particular for her information about the inhabitants of the castle in 1814 and about the use of the kitchen. Of course, a ball could be recreated at a different level by Key Stage 2 children. Nonsuch History and Dance Company think that Year 6 children are the perfect age for their Tudor dance workshops (www.nonsuch-history-and-dance.org.uk). This is an excellent opportunity for linking the dance and history curriculum.

## References

Anholt, C. (1988) *When I Was a Baby*. London: Heinemann.

Bage, G. (2003) 'In my view: revolting subjects?' *Primary History*, 33, 5–6.

Barkham, J. (2002) 'History book for the literacy hour: *A Street Through Time*', *Primary History*, 30, 16–17.

Barnsdale-Paddock, L. and Harnett, P. (2002) 'Promoting play in the classroom: children as curators in a classroom museum', *Primary History*, 30, 19–21.

Bennett, N., Wood, E. and Rogers, S. (1997) *Teaching Through Play: teachers' thinking and classroom practice*. Buckingham: Open University Press.

Bracey, P. (2003) 'In my view: enjoying a good story', *Primary History*, 34, 6–8.

Bruce, T. (1991) *Time to Play in Early Childhood Education*. Sevenoaks: Hodder & Stoughton.

Bruner, J.S. (1966) *Towards a Theory of Instruction*. Cambridge, MA: Harvard University Press.

Bruner, J.S. (1987) *Making Sense: the child's construction of the world*. London: Methuen.

Burningham, J. (1984) *Grandpa*. London: Jonathan Cape.

Cooper, H. (2002) *History in the Early Years*, 2nd edn. London: Routledge Falmer.

Cooper, H. (2004) (ed.) *Exploring Time and Place Through Play*. London: David Fulton Publishers.

Cooper, H. (2010) 'Contemporary English versions of traditional Russian folk tales', *International Journal of History Teaching Learning and Research*, 9, 1 (www.history.org.uk).

Cooper, H. and Ditchburn, E. (2009) 'Folk Tales: universal values, individual differences', *International Journal of History Teaching Learning and Research*, 8(1), 58–71.

Crossley-Holland, K. (2001) *The Magic Lands of Britain and Ireland*. London: Orion.

Doherty, B. (1999) *Fairy Tales*. London: Walker Books.

Donaldson, M. (1978) *Children's Minds*. London: Fontana.

Doyle, M. (2006) *The Barefoot Book of Fairy Tales*. Bath: Barefoot Books.

Erikson, E.H. (1965) *Childhood and Society*. London: Penguin.

Franklin, I.L. (1992) *The Old, Old Man and the Very Little Boy*. New York: Simon & Schuster.

Gardner, S. (2000) *Fairy Catalogue*. London: Orion.

Garvey, C. (1977) *Play: the developing child*. London: Collins Fontana.

Greenaway, K. (1991) *Nursery Rhymes Classic*. London: Cresset Press.

Hoodless, P. (2004) 'Potting the adult agendas: investigating primary school children's understanding of changing attitudes and values through stories written for children in the past', *International Journal of History Teaching Learning and Research*, 4(2), 66–75 (www.history.org.uk).

Kelly, I. (2004) *Cooking for Kings: a day in the life of Antonin Careme, the first celebrity chef*. London: Walker.

Kingsbury, B. (1998) 'Picture books for teaching history', *Primary History*, 20, 17–18.

Kirkland, S. and Wykes, M. (2003) 'Grace O'Malley, alias Granaile, pirate and politician, c.1530–1603', *Primary History*, 34, 34–6.

Langley-Hamel, K. (2002) 'Traditional stories and rhymes: Goldilocks, don't you do owt!' in H. Cooper and C. Sixsmith (eds) *Teaching Across the Early Years 3–7: curriculum coherence and continuity*. London: Routledge, 46–55.

Meadows, S. (1993) *The Child as Thinker: the development and acquisition of cognition in childhood*. London: Routledge.

Meadows, S. and Cashdan, A. (1988) *Teaching Styles in Nursery Education: final report to SSRC*. Sheffield: Sheffield City Polytechnic.

Munsch, R. (1988) *The Paper Bag Princess*. London: Hippo Scholastic.

Okri, B. (1996) *Birds of Heaven*. London: Phoenix.

Rogers, P. (1995) '"Silver linings": using the elderly as a resource', *Primary History*, 10, 14–15.

Salter, K. (1996) 'Grace Darling and Reception children', *Primary History*, 14, 18–19.

Scott, W. (2005) 'When we were very young: emerging historical awareness in the earliest years', *Primary History*, 39, 14–17.

Shefatya, L. (1990) 'Socio-economic status and ethnic differences in socio dramatic play: theoretical and practical implications', in E. Klugman and S. Smilansky (eds) *Children's Play and Learning: perspectives and policy implications*. New York: Teachers College Press.

Siraj-Blatchford, I., Sylva, K., Muttock, S., Gilden, R. and Bell, D. (2002) *Researching Effective Pedagogy in the Early Years*, Research Report 356. Annesley: DfES.

Thomas, E. (1993) 'Irony Age Infants', *Times Educational Supplement*, 23 April.

Tough, J. (1976) *Listening to Children Talking*. London: Ward Lock.

Vygotsky, L.S. (1978) *Mind in Society: the development of higher psychological processes*. Cambridge, MA: Harvard University Press.

Wilson, H. (1998) *There's a Wolf in My Pudding*. London: Pan Macmillan.

Witherington, A. and Neate, B. (2003) 'Book for the literacy hour: what babies used to wear', *Primary History*, 34, 30–1.

Woodhouse, J. (2001) 'Teaching history through nursery rhymes at the Foundation Stage', *Primary History*, 27, 17–18.

Woodhouse, J. (2002) 'History coordinators' dilemmas', *Primary History*, 31, 8–9.

Woodhouse, J. and Lomas, T. (2002) 'History coordinators' dilemmas', *Primary History*, 32, 9.

# 8

# Planning at Key Stage 2

## Life in Tudor times, Years 5 and 6

The unit on life in Tudor times began with an initial overview of the period: Henry VIII and the break with Rome, followed by rivalry with Spain over religion and trade in the 'New World', which led to the Armada of 1588. Key events were located on a class timeline. Two focuses were selected within this topic, one on 'Houses' and one on 'Ships'. These focuses were chosen because they allowed children to explore aspects of Tudor history that represent complex underlying changes, in ways that they could understand. 'Houses' included both a visit to Hampton Court, the showpiece of Henry VIII's new style of government, and also to a nearby timber-frame Elizabethan house representing the increasing wealth of the new 'gentry'. 'Ships' began with a visit to the *Mary Rose*, which represented the beginnings of British sea power under Henry VIII, created as a defence after the break from Catholic Europe, and which led, in Elizabethan times, to exploration, an increase in trade and the emergence of a new class of merchants and 'gentry'. Rivalry with Spain in the 'New World' over trade resulted in the Armada of 1588, an event about which loyal British Roman Catholics felt ambivalent and which reflected conflicting loyalties and rivalries throughout Europe.

This unit allows children many opportunities to consider non-Eurocentric and non-Anglocentric perspectives. First, the competition between Britain and Spain to find new routes to India and the East Indies, and the ensuing conflict in Central America and the West Indies allows children to use sources that reflect both cross-cultural influences and cultural conflict. Children can discover from Indian miniatures (in the Victoria and Albert Museum) the rich cultural influences of India on Elizabethan England, by comparing clothes, buildings and garden design.

Often, sources that challenge Eurocentric perspectives can be selected from books for older children. In Roberts (1992: 22–5) there are excellent Mughal pictures of the rejoicing at the birth of Jahangir, son of Akbar the Great in 1569. The relief at the birth of an heir and also the idealistic representation of this event suggests similarities both between portraits of Elizabeth and her succession problems. Figures 8.1 and 8.2, and Table 8.1 show aspects of the planning process.

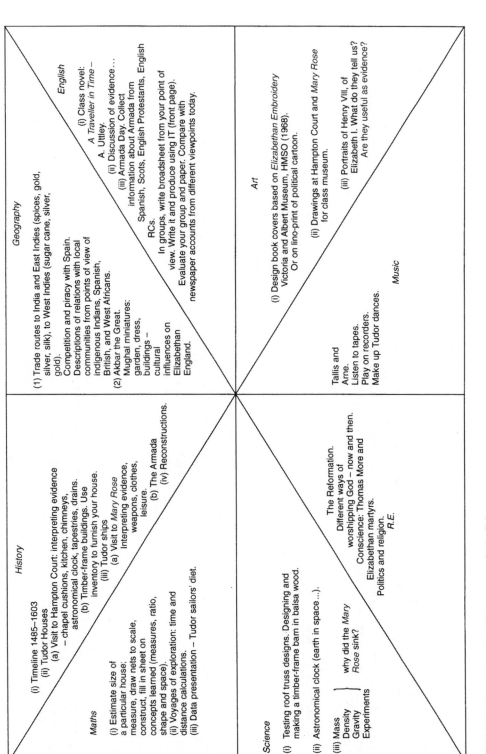

**FIGURE 8.1** Tudor times: possible cross-curricular links.

**TABLE 8.1** Study unit 2: life in Tudor times.

| What I want children to learn: key elements | What I want children to do | Assessment opportunities |
|---|---|---|
| • To place events, people, changes within a chronological framework<br>• To use dates and terms relating to the passing of time (e.g. century, decade, Tudor, Elizabethan, court, monarch, civilisations, trade)<br>To explain to others:<br>  Reasons for and results of events, situations, changes and to make links between events and situations | (i) Make a class timeline 1485–1603, put on key events learned through class lessons and reference work (e.g. related to Reformation, voyages of exploration, Armada, Monarchs) | *Level 3* Give a presentation to an audience, explaining the timeline with some explanation of causes and effect of events shown (e.g. of Reformation or of Drake's voyages to central America, or of Armada)<br><br>*Level 4* Can use more factual information and more detailed explanations to play a 'chaining game' which involves (orally or through devising clue cards) thinking of all possible effects of an event<br><br>*Level 5* Can devise a game involving selecting 'cause' or 'consequence' cards for a situation and explain what links there are between them (scoring based on number of reasonable causes/consequences identified) |
| • To select, organise and communicate historical information<br>• To identify characteristic features of the Tudor period: buildings, clothes, music, drama | (ii) In groups, use variety of resource materials to collect pictures and other information and make a book (or display) on one of the following, in Tudor times: homes of different kinds; work; leisure (including theatres and music); health; trade | *Level 4* Can explain overarching and characteristic features of one of the group books |
| • Have some understanding of diversity of political and religious ideas, beliefs and attitudes of men and women in Tudor times<br>• Describe and identify reasons for and results of Armada | Collect information about the Armada ('press releases' can be pre-selected by teacher)<br>In groups (English Protestants, English Catholics, Dutch, Scottish, Spanish, French) write a broadsheet account from one of these perspectives | *Level 3* Can show a restricted perspective in broadsheet article<br><br>*Level 4* Can try to explain a given perspective in a broadsheet article |

• Give reasons for different ways in which the past is represented and interpreted

• Have some understanding of the reasons for the symbolism of and attitudes and values represented in portraits of Henry VIII and of Elizabeth I

1. Ask questions and make deductions and inferences about life in Tudor Times from a variety of sources:
(a) at Hampton Court: e.g. tennis court (leisure)
chapel (beliefs)
furniture, kitchens, cellars (food, daily life)
paintings, images of Henry VIII; the Field of the Cloth of Gold
astronomical clock (understanding of time and space)
(b) in Mary Rose Museum: e.g. the ship and its contents (clothes, tools, leisure, weapons, medicine)
2. Organise findings, record and communicate to audience

Look at postcards of portraits from National Gallery of (a) Henry VIII (b) Elizabeth I
(i) Discuss to what extent they tell what the person was really like, and what else (symbolism) they represent
(ii) Compare with written sources describing Henry VIII and Elizabeth I

1. Visit Hampton Court. Drawings and photographs used in school as clues to find out what they may tell us about Henry VIII and his court

2. Visit Mary Rose and Museum, Portsmouth. Use drawings and photographs as clues to find out about life on board a Tudor ship

Present information in poster or book or as a video or audio tape for an audience

*Level 5* Can suggest reasons why events and personalities in broadsheets are portrayed differently

*Level 3* Can explain why the portraits are idealised images

*Level 4* Can describe differences between written sources and portrait

*Level 5* Can explain why portraits and written sources tell different story

*Level 3* Can make inferences from selected sources; and write explanatory label

*Level 4* Can combine inferences from several sources to write a poster, possibly using one piece of evidence to answer a question raised by another, e.g. how was the gun (on *Mary Rose*) fired?; use dates and special vocabulary where appropriate (e.g. court, monarch)

*Level 5* Can select and evaluate sources using them in a structured way to make a book or a video investigating an historical question (e.g. who were the people on board the *Mary Rose*? Why did the *Mary Rose* sink?)

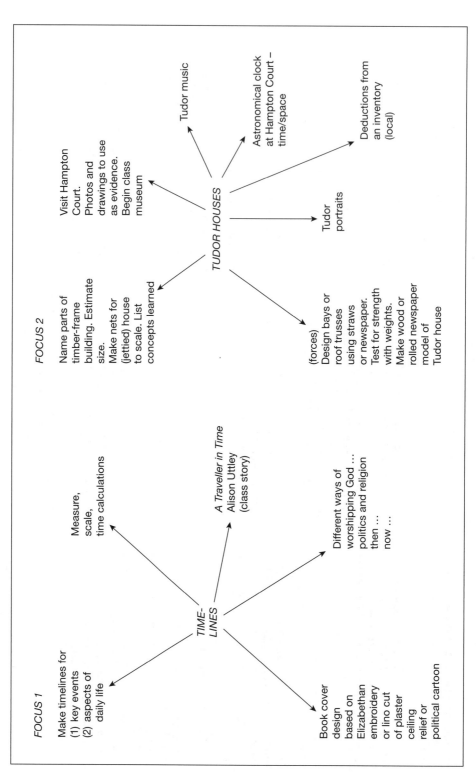

**FIGURE 8.2** Plan showing how work for the term was organised around three focuses.

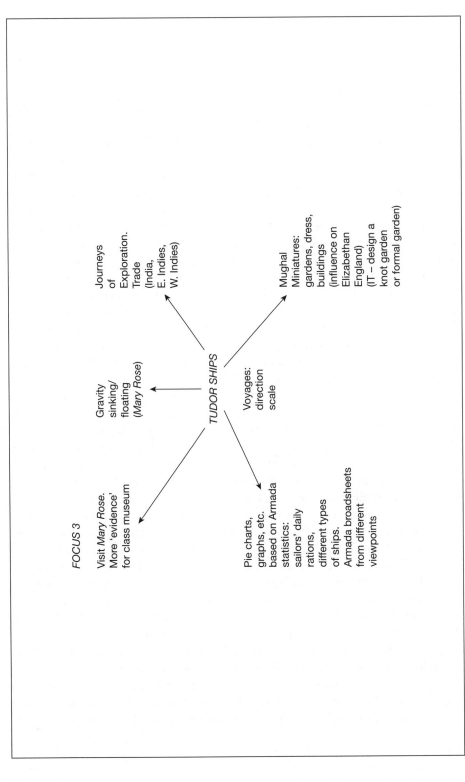

*FOCUS 3*

Visit *Mary Rose*.
More 'evidence'
for class museum

Gravity
sinking/
floating
(*Mary Rose*)

Journeys
of
Exploration.
Trade
(India,
E. Indies,
W. Indies)

*TUDOR SHIPS*

Voyages:
direction
scale

Mughal
Miniatures:
gardens, dress,
buildings
(influence on
Elizabethan
England)
(IT – design a
knot garden
or formal garden)

Pie charts,
graphs, etc.
based on Armada
statistics:
sailors' daily
rations,
different types
of ships.
Armada broadsheets
from different
viewpoints

**FIGURE 8.2** *continued.*

It is interesting too that when Sir James Ross arrived at the Court of Jahangir, the Emperor thought most of the gifts from Europe were poor but he did like an English miniature portrait of a lady (a result of Indian influence on European art), and a map of India that he was given. However, Jahangir was not really interested in foreign rulers as he saw them as subordinates.

The Benin Empire was also at its peak at the same time as the Tudors were ruling England, which is when the British first arrived there. Sources related to the Benin Kingdom can be found in the British Museum (www.britishmuseum.org→research→ 'search the collection database'→benin). They invite comparisons and contrasts with Tudor England; the mother of an Oba, or ruler, was of great importance, for example, and had her own palace and political power. Benin contained craft guilds of leather workers, weavers and blacksmiths. Written sources record its richly decorated palaces and houses. Extensive trade with Europe from the end of the fifteenth century included slaves. Sir John Hawkins, a successful English slave-trader of the sixteenth century, designed a crest for himself and which depicts a defiant, captured African.

Similarly Green (1992) offers a picture of what life was like for the native peoples of the Americas when Europeans first arrived and of how they perceived each other. For example, George Best – who sailed with Martin Frobisher to North America – wrote a detailed diary, which is quoted, and there is also a contemporary painting of Frobisher's fight with an Inuit in 1577. From knowledge of such sources, children can develop a less Eurocentric and a more questioning attitude to life in Tudor times and view it from a range of perspectives.

As part of the focus on ships, both Year 5 and Year 6 spent two weeks finding out about the Armada. The competition between Britain and Spain to find new routes to India and the East Indies, and the ensuing conflict in Central America and the West Indies, underlined by religious differences, was explained in class lessons. The viewpoints of different groups were discussed. How would the English Protestants feel, the English Catholics, the French, the Dutch, the Spanish? Why might the Scots be ambivalent? Children then worked in groups or individually to find out all they could about the daily progress of the Armada, making charts, maps and diaries. They made a display of daily rations for a Spanish and an English sailor, pie charts of the estimated food needed on a ship, and graphs showing ships of different kinds. Finally, each class worked in six groups together with the advisory teachers for ICT; by the end of a day, each group succeeded in producing a 'broadsheet' giving news of the Armada from the standpoint of a particular group. The French produced 'La Grenouille', the Spanish 'L'Escorial', the English Protestants 'The Golden Hind', the English Catholics 'The Priesthole', the Scots 'The Record' and the Dutch 'The Orange' (Figures 8.3–8.5).

Later, they evaluated the extent to which they had reflected different attitudes. These examples show that children are considering the reasons for behaviour and events.

The extracts from broadsheets representing different points of view were written on 'Armada Day'. They are based on 'press releases' and information in simulated teletext using 'Simtex', prepared by the Croydon humanities advisor, Don Garman.

**TABLE 8.2** Child's self-evaluation of mathematical concepts learned in making a model of a Tudor house.

Mathematics
I learned Making
Tudor House Models.

| length estimate measure | metres centimetre | I estimated the height of my house as 4m. |
|---|---|---|
| Scale | 1:100 | The lenght of my house in real life would be 12m and on my model it is 12cm |
| Convert from one unit to another. | metres to cm cm to mm (to nearest m) | The width of my house is 6m which on my model would be 6cm it could also be 6mm. 6m=600cm =6000mm |
| area rectangle triangle | cm² m² | the area of my first rectangle is 72cm². The area of my roof is 16cm² |
| Volume of cuboid | cm² m² | The volume of my 2nd cuboid is 252cm³. |
| Properties of solid shapes Cuboid | faces edges angles | On a cuboid there is 6 faces 12 edges 24 angles |
| △ based prism | faces edges angles | 5 faces 9 edges 12 angles |
| measuring angles right angle | | the right angle on my roof is 90°. the rightangle on the side of my roof is 90° |
| acute angle | | there are 4 acute angle on my house. the acute angles are 45° |
| obtuse angle | | there are 0 obtuse angles on my house. |

# LA GRENOUILLE

6f

## 10/7/1588

## STAY OR DIE

The Duke of Madina Sidonia commented that if any Spanish Captain fails to maintain his position the penalty would be death, by hanging.

Soon the English are expected to run out of ammunition and surrender to the Spanish and the noble king Philip II is once more going to demonstrate his enormous power. We are all behind hm in the forthcoming final few battles at the sea.

# THE PRIESTHOLE

1d

## 11th August 1588

## SAIL AWAY, SAIL AWAY, SAIL AWAY

9 July 1588 6.0pm Captain Fleming of the Golden Hind has signalled the sighting of the Spanish fleet off the Lizard.

The tide will not allow the English fleet at Plymouth under Admiral Lord Howard of Effingham to put to sea till 9.0pm.

4 vessels of the English fleet managed to use their boats and anchors to warp out of Plymouth harbour before 9.0pm.

July 30 3.0pm Armada sighted by the English fleet to the south of Eddystone Lighthouse.

Beacons are reported to have been lit from Cornwall to London, local militia being organised to defend the English coastline.

July 31st the English pinnace Disdain opened fire off Plymouth at the rata encoranda.

At 9.0am this morning the Spanish flagship raised her national flag to signal the beginning.

After a four hour battle the Armada continues eastwood with the English in pursuit. Medina Sadonya gives the order for the fleet to form a cresent with the more heavily armed ships positioned at the horns. Drake reported to have left fleet during the night to investigate sails to the south.

**FIGURE 8.3** Extracts from the French and English Catholic newspapers describing the Armada.

# L'ESCORIAL

2D

JULY 1588

## HE MUCKED UP OUR – INVASION PLAN

He Duke of Palma mucked up our invasion plan because he was not ready in Dunkruk to sail.

Philip II was very angry when he found out. On the other hand Philip was pleased with The Duke of Medina Sidenia because he had reached Calais but losing too many ships and not having a sea battle with Englande.

After this achievement, How did the Duke of Palma dare to say that his 17,000 men, 1000 cavalry, 170 ships would not be ready to 2 weeks.

# THE GOLDEN HIND

1gr

1st August 1588

## ARMADA SIGHTED

It was two weeks ago at south of Eddy-stone Lighthouse that the Armada was spotted by the English Fleet. 1 week ago the English Fleet positioned themselves behind the Spanish Fleet and had the advantage of being windward. A couple of days ago the prize ship. "San Salvardor" arrived at Weymouth badly damaged. We think that there was an explosion below decks. There were quite a few smoke blackened corpses on board.

## Fight for Elizabeth

—She is our Queen—

### FIRE SHIPS

A plan to send out some fire ships to Calais harbour in France is still to be decided on for Queen Elizabeth is not sure whether it is a good idea.

**FIGURE 8.4** Extracts from the Spanish and English newspapers describing the Armada.

# THE ORANGE
## AUG 1589

# THE DUTCH LURE

We have been looking at our reports and they say that England ae going to win. We do hope so, when we went to interview Lord Effingham he said they have a good chance of winning. Spains ships are sinking by the hour and about 150 men have been killed. We will continue this story next week.

# THE RECORD
4D
## AUGUST 14

# THE ARMADA

PHILIP OR ELIZABETH There has been months of conflict between England and Spain. Does it really matter to us Scots ? Our contacts inform us that defences have been set up in England, because rumours of the invasion, beacons have been set up in selected areas.

Rumours of Philips invasion plan have leeked out of Spain, he plans to make Elizabeth 1 pay for the invasion 2 stop helping the Dutch 3 stop killing catholics.

**FIGURE 8.5** Extracts from the Dutch and Scottish newspapers describing the Armada.

Models of Tudor timber-frame houses, based on particular examples, involved a range of mathematical concepts: measure, scale, properties of solid shapes. Table 8.2 shows part of a child's self-evaluation sheet, made when he had finished his model, to explain the mathematics he thought he had learned in making it.

A good case study of Year 5 children studying Tudor exploration can be found in Ager (2009).

## Britain and the wider world in Tudor times

The revised title of the study unit on life in Tudor times reflects recent scholarship that has done much to change perceptions of Elizabethan England. The study of the Armada from various perspectives could now include an Islamic perspective. For Matar (1999) has shown how the English were so afraid of 'popery' and of the Spanish that they became close allies with the forces of Islam. Indeed there was a permanent Muslim community in London and large numbers of Englishmen could be found in the Middle East and North Africa. The English were close military allies of the Moroccans and the Ottoman Turks: for example there was a joint Anglo-Moroccan attack on Cadiz in 1596.

In 1603 Ahmad al-Manser, the King of Morocco, proposed to Elizabeth I that England should help the Moors to expel their hated Spanish enemies from America and keep the land under joint dominion for ever. He suggested the colonists should be mainly Moroccan, 'in respect of the great heat of the clymat'. Such a proposal, which although finally rejected by Her Majesty, raised few eyebrows at the time, would have completely changed the history of the modern world.

## Interpretations of Queen Elizabeth I

The Year 5/6 case study on Life in Tudor Times, outlined above, did not explore children's understanding of why the past is represented in different ways, in subsequent periods. Yet this is central to understanding and participating in the process of historical enquiry that underpins this book. The reasons why accounts and reconstructions of the past vary were discussed in Chapter 3. Historians' accounts may be different but be equally valid. But accounts of the past are constructed by people other than academic historians, for a variety of reasons. If young children compare and contrast accounts that are markedly different and consider why, they are learning, in an embryonic way, that accounts of the past are constantly reinterpreted for different reasons.

I visited a school where the Year 3/4 class were studying a unit on the Tudors. Their teacher allowed me to plan and teach an afternoon session with them. I decided to see, first, how they thought people who write books about history find out about the past, then to what extent they could identify ways in which three video clips of Elizabeth I were different and why, and finally, to let them make brief video recordings in three groups to reveal how their own interpretations of an event would also be different. While each group made their video in another room, the rest of the class wrote 'advertisements' for the video clips they had seen, showing in another way how and why they differed.

## The lesson: how do we find out about the past?

One child said, when asked how people could find out about Queen Elizabeth I, 'there may not be sufficient evidence'. An encouraging start. Some things we cannot know. Others suggested looking at paintings. I showed them the Ditchingham portrait and asked them if that gave us some idea of what Elizabeth I looked like. There were interesting responses: 'You can't paint every tiny detail', 'Different people paint people in different ways', 'She can't have had a waist THAT small. It is trying to make her look beautiful and powerful.' I explained that Elizabeth had censored pictures of her and the reasons why, then went on to talk about the symbolism of Elizabeth standing on a map of England, dispelling the storm clouds and ushering in the sunshine. 'Was that after she won the Armada?' someone wondered. Someone else suggested that things get left behind or buried, which give us clues about the past. Another child had a clear understanding of oral history: 'Someone tells their children and they tell their children and it goes on and on.' 'That is like the Bible,' someone else explained. 'Certainly these children understand something about "historical enquiry",' I thought. The lesson plan is shown in Table 8.3.

## Three video clips

The three five-minute clips I selected were from *Blackadder II* (carefully avoiding innuendo which might have upset parents!), *The Virgin Queen* (BBC) and Benjamin Britten's *Gloriana* (ambitious!). The children's adjectives describing the Queen in each clip are collated in Table 8.4. They clearly describe the differences in the three portrayals of her personality. They also identify certain similarities: When asked why *Blackadder* was made, one child immediately said, 'To make money and to make you laugh!' *The Virgin Queen* was probably made 'to help history teachers with their lessons'. *Gloriana* was 'a musical, like *Joseph and the Amazing Technicolor Dreamcoat* – which we are doing for our concert'.

## The children's three interpretations

I read from *Our Island Story* (Marshall 1905) about Sir Walter Raleigh throwing down his cloak for the Queen to step on to avoid a puddle, and, since we were examining interpretations, showed the accompanying illustration. The children were noticeably unimpressed by the quality of the picture – and I had forgotten how bland and patronising the prose is!

They enjoyed making the videos, in which everyone took part as courtiers, cheering crowds or the hooves of the approaching horses. We had a 'quiet, calm, gracious Queen', a 'funny Queen', and a silent movie from the group too overawed to speak. The 'funny Queen' included some interesting jokes. For example, when the Queen was considering turning back, to the disappointment of the roaring crowd, a courtier suggested she might cross on a great big bird, 'since aeroplanes haven't been invented yet'. The following week I showed the class the videos and discuss with them why they made the interpretations they did.

**TABLE 8.3** Lesson plan: comparing interpretations of Elizabeth I.

| Date | Duration | Year Group | Class size |
|---|---|---|---|
| 27.02.06 | 1.00 p.m.–3.00 p.m. | Y3/4 | |
| **Activity**<br><br>Understanding why Queen Elizabeth I is represented in different ways; identifying differences in way she is represented and reasons for different interpretations. | | | National Curriculum Programme(s) of Study: History KS2, ksu 3, historical interpretation |

**Learning Objectives**

Children will have some understanding of why the past is represented in different ways (incomplete evidence; sources often made for a particular purpose); accounts made by 'filling in the gaps'; accounts are made for different purposes.

**Assessment**

- Discussion of how accurate a representation of Elizabeth I is in Ditchingham portrait; reasons it was painted.
- Children's adjectives describing Elizabeth I in 3 different video clips (product).
- Children's explanations of different reasons why videos made (questioning + product – write TV advert flagging each programme).
- Children make own videos of Queen Elizabeth and Walter Raleigh in groups then compare similarities and differences.

| Times | Introduction, activities, conclusion |
|---|---|
| 1.00–1.15 | • Whole-class discussion of Ditchingham portrait<br>1. Who is it?<br>2. Explain official, censored image; explain symbols (map, cloud, etc.).<br>3. How much does it tell us of what she was really like?<br>4. What do people do when they want to make a film about e.g. Elizabeth I and they don't know everything about her? |
| 1.15–1.30 | 1. Explain going to watch a clip of one interpretation of Elizabeth I: *Blackadder*.<br>2. Ask children to remember how Elizabeth looks; behaves.<br>3. Show clip.<br>4. Children asked in groups of 4 to discuss and write words describing how she looked, behaved on red cards (6 cards per table); list cards on board using Blu-tack. |
| 1.30–1.45 | Repeat above activity, using clip of *Gloriana*, recording adjectives on blue cards and making separate list on board. |
| 1.45–2.00 | Repeat activity using *The Virgin Queen* clip and green cards. Form third list on board. |
| 2.00–2.10 | 1. Whole class compare lists; identify similarities and differences.<br>2. Why is Elizabeth different in each video (audience, purpose, validity)? |
| 2.10–2.25 | Read story of Sir Walter Raleigh putting his cloak on ground for Elizabeth to walk from *Our Island Story*. Explain this is old book written for children. Discuss illustration; interpretation; purpose. |
| 2.25–3.00 | Three groups. Each group, with adult support, writes flier to advertise one of the videos as a TV programme. Each group taken out in turn to make a video of the Walter Raleigh story (10 minutes each group) in separate room. Next lesson watch and compare videos, recapping on what children learned about why interpretations are different. |

Resources: video recorder, Hi8 and video tape, Ditchingham portrait
Cards in 3 colours and felt tips, H.E. Marshall (1905) *Our Island Story*
Blu-tack, clips put onto CD for showing on interactive whiteboard

**TABLE 8.4** Adjectives used by Year 3/4 children to describe Queen Elizabeth I.

| Blackadder | The Virgin Queen | Gloriana |
|---|---|---|
| excitable | unhappy | excited |
| very giddy | grumpy | big voice |
| sneaky | thoughtful | powerful |
| very noisy | nervous | serious |
| greedy (wanted to go to the feast) | powerful | important |
| very girly | sad (at end of last clip) | old |
| happy | cross | in charge |
| bossy | extremely cross | theatrical |
| laughs a lot | rude | strict |
| bold | annoyed | sad |
| joyful | like she wanted to run away | bossy |
| funny | angry | |
| mean (she tricked them in the game) | worried | |
| strict | furious | |
| crazy | moody | |
| good fun | selfish (she wanted to marry who she wanted) | |
| | scared | |
| | a bit bossy | |
| | powerful | |
| | upset | |
| | posh | |
| | making a fuss | |
| | moody | |
| | bossy | |
| | not pleased | |
| | nervous of all the powerful people | |
| | bad tempered | |
| | ratty | |
| | not nice to the old Spanish king | |
| | silly (cos if the Spanish King is old he may be wise) | |
| | arguing | |
| | gloomy | |
| | in a paddy | |
| | cool | |
| | bored | |
| | in a bad mood | |
| | tired | |
| | happy (because she got a ruby) | |
| | sad (because she couldn't marry Essex) | |
| | frustrated | |
| | hot | |
| | frowny | |
| | ungrateful | |
| | unconvincing | |
| | rude (at end of last clip) | |
| | powerful | |
| | very loud | |
| | horrible | |
| | weird and strange as well | |
| | insane | |

## Television previews

The previews written to advertise television showings of each of the video clips the children had seen reinforced their previous understanding that the different interpretations were made for different audiences (Figures 8.6–8.8).

Elizabeth

Come and See this exeliant movie adout Queen Eliza beth and it's realy funny it will take your sox of with laghtter. TVchannel4 on at 4 30.

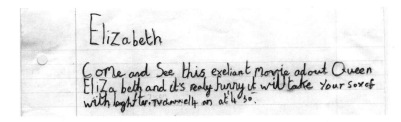

**FIGURE 8.6** Television preview of *Blackadder II.*

Eliz abeth

It is very funny! halerese
Very loud.
It was very Sloppy.
Elizabeth has to get marrid to the king of Spain She doesen't want too because She has seen another man
it is for 5 - 9 year olds

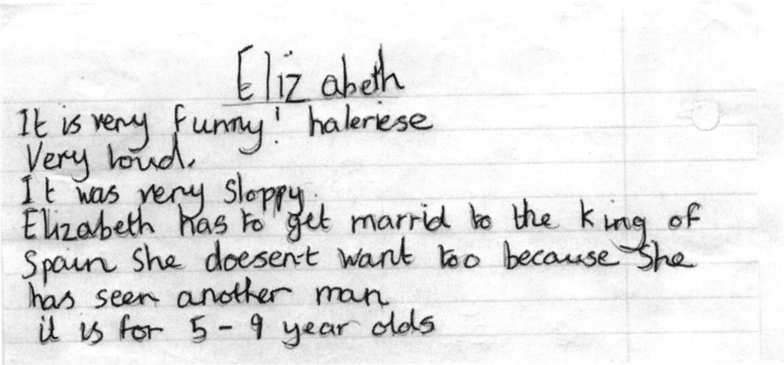

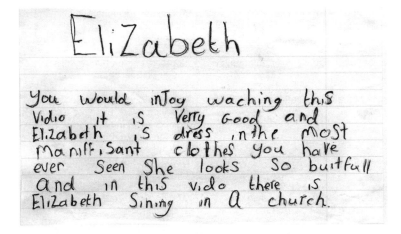

**FIGURE 8.7** Television preview of *The Virgin Queen* (BBC).

EliZabeth

You would inJoy waching this Vidio it is Verry Good and ElIzabeth is dress in the most maniff, Sant clothes you have ever Seen She looks So buitfull and in this vido there is Elizabeth Sining in a church.

**FIGURE 8.8** Television preview of Benjamin Britten's opera *Gloriana.*

**TABLE 8.5** Checklist to support observations: what makes a good history lesson?

| Checklist | Notes |
|---|---|
| *Planning* | |
| • Is confident in constructing imaginative schemes of work. | Imaginative lesson ✓ |
| • Takes into account the varied requirements of the National Curriculum. | NC links ✓ |
| • Has clear objectives for lessons but may also seize opportunities to go beyond these objectives. | e.g. utilised 'aeroplane fixation' of child with Asperger's syndrome to develop anachronistic joke ✓ |
| • Is able to accommodate the varied experiences of all pupils. | Drew on children's experiences of 'musicals' and of TV to discuss reasons for interpretations. |
| *Development of skills* | |
| • Has high expectations based on pupils' previous learning. | Drew out what children already understood of 'how we find out about past'. |
| • Uses personal knowledge to inspire and challenge pupils. | Included relevant 'stories', e.g. Elizabeth and Essex; Elizabeth's quarrel with Ditchingham. |
| • Utilises a range of interactive strategies designed to promote pupils' historical skills and conceptual understanding. | Discuss: how 'true' is Ditchingham portrait? Videos: list adjectives through group discussion. Write advertisement. Video-record role play. |
| • Bases these strategies, where possible, on evidence-based tasks. | Use of primary and secondary sources. |
| • Is able to pick up on pupils' misconceptions to develop understanding. | Addressed misunderstanding that Elizabeth in *Gloriana* actually was Queen Elizabeth! |
| • Uses historical language fluently and appropriately. | Sources, interpretations, bias, symbol; courtiers; Elizabethan. |
| • Conveys a sense of the drama and emotion inherent in the subject. | In 'love story' – Elizabeth could not marry for love – engaged everyone's point of view; in narration of Sir Walter Raleigh story. |
| • Is able to use analogy to relate the present to the past. | Comparison of Elizabeth I and Elizabeth II. |
| • Is able to utilise pupils' own person/family experiences to develop their historical understanding. | ?? |

**TABLE 8.5** *continued.*

| *Assessment and Evaluation* | |
|---|---|
| • Is able to adjust and modify tasks to ensure all children are challenged. | Advert – extended prose or picture and captions. Level of narrator's input in role play varied. ✓ |
| • Identifies tasks appropriate for assessment purposes. | Evidence in video! |
| • Encourages children by providing constructive and positive responses. | Periods of time: drew on previous knowledge of 'Tudors'. |
| • Demonstrates knowledge of level descriptors and can apply appropriately. | Identify different ways past represented. |

## A good history lesson?

Much later, I was looking through my lesson observation guide for tutors in school and college, which was designed by history tutors to be used for formative assessment of students' lessons. I decided to see how my lesson reflected the checklist for 'what makes a good history lesson?' I had not used this before and had certainly not used it as a checklist for my planning. My completed checklist is shown in Table 8.5. What I found interesting was the extent to which, however well a lesson may be planned, the checklist requires responses to an ongoing interactive situation: 'goes beyond the objectives'; 'accommodates the varied experiences of the pupils'; 'uses personal knowledge to challenge and inspire'; 'picks up on misconceptions'; 'conveys a sense of drama and emotion'; 'uses analogy; utilises pupils' personal and family experiences'; 'adjusts and modifies tasks'. We expect student teachers to have good subject knowledge and good knowledge of the individual pupils and to weave a web between the two. And they generally do! Good for them.

## References

Ager, J. (2009) 'Comparing life today with someone's in the past', in C. Rowley and H. Cooper (eds) *Cross-curricular Approaches to Teaching and Learning*. London: Sage, 109–19.

Green, J. (1992) *Native Peoples of the Americas*. Oxford: Oxford University Press.

Marshall, H.E. (1905, reprinted 2005) *Our Island Story*. Cranbrook: Galore Park.

Matar, N. (1999) *Turks, Moors and Englishmen in the Age of Discovery*. New York: Columbia University Press.

Roberts, F. (1992) *India 1521–1800*. London: Hodder & Stoughton.

# 9

# Transition from primary to secondary school

I hope that you will forgive another anecdote! Many years ago I was invited to apply for a post as a Local Educational Authority advisory teacher for history. I was unsuccessful. I was told that I was 'by far the best candidate but that secondary colleagues would not take advice from a primary school teacher'. Fair enough. However I was offered a part-time post to develop primary secondary liaison in history.

Unsurprisingly I did not change the world; the lack of continuity between Key Stages 2 and 3 is still regarded as problematic. The *Primary History Survey* found that there was practically no communication in history between primary and secondary schools and the *Cambridge Review* found that links between primary and secondary schools were weak. There are many reasons for this.

## Why is transition in history problematic?

As primary secondary liaison teacher I found that, because of the structure of the school day in secondary schools, into hour long lessons of discrete subjects, teachers said that it was very difficult to arrange out of school visits. A whole day visit would mean that they could not teach their timetable for that day and nor could their colleagues. Colleagues teaching complementary subjects find it very difficult to plan cross-curricular work because of timetables and subject-specific schemes of work. Pupils join a large secondary school from a range of primary schools, having studied historical periods at different times during their primary education and primary teachers have different levels of expertise in teaching the processes of historical enquiry. So many Key Stage 3 history teachers decide that it is best to start 'with a blank sheet'.

And often history at Key Stage 3 does not involve the rich variety of hands-on approaches a pupil may have been experienced in primary school. Recently I met a young lawyer I had taught as child in primary school and who had been passionately interested in history. He told me that he had dropped history at secondary school 'because it was so boring' but had taken history at A level and achieved a first-class degree in history at university.

And I remember a Friday afternoon lesson I taught, as part of my primary secondary liaison brief, in quite a demanding secondary school. I asked the students to discuss newspaper cuttings, letters and photographs about when their school was evacuated during the Second World War – a typical primary school activity. Yet they were able to bring much more complex questions and observations to the discussion of 'Was the evacuation a good thing?' Later I was told that they had never been so quiet on a Friday afternoon!

## Suggestions for a smoother transition

The lack of smooth primary secondary transition is a problem for many reasons. So what can be done about it? *History for All* (Ofsted 2011) suggests that formal and informal networks, clusters and federations should be developed to provide more secondary school specialist support to non-specialists in primary schools. Networks and clusters seem a good idea but sensitivity is necessary if they are to succeed. I was at a conference recently where it was intended to set up the initial organisation of such networks; it became apparent that the primary teachers had an enormous variety of successful teaching strategies to share with the history 'specialists', who were genuinely amazed at the quality of the primary children's work they were shown, even saying that they could hardly believe it was produced by primary school children. On the other hand it has been seen that primary teachers agreed that they needed to know more about the processes of historical enquiry. More experience of Year 6 and Year 7 teachers planning and working together on cross-phase projects might be the solution.

## Some case study examples

### A shared visit

A project in which a Year 6 class and a Year 7 class visited a local medieval castle is described by Cooper and West (2009). Given the secondary school timetable constraints the pupils had introductory sessions in their respective schools, in which they planned questions to investigate, the evidence they would need to look for and how they would record it when they visited the site. It was possible to organise mixed groups of two Year 6 and two Year 7 pupils during the visit since the teachers had met previously to collate the enquiries. It is not possible to claim that the primary and secondary pupils in the groups worked closely together; this was not unreasonable since they had not met before. On the visit the Year 6 girls gasped at the sight of 'boys' and some of the older boys slunk sheepishly off on their own. However on the third week of the project both year groups met in the hall of the secondary school to share each group's findings. This resulted in an impressive variety of tableaux with explanations, role play, posters, PowerPoint® presentations and historical fiction based on evidence shown in accompanying photographs.

# A shared topic

A primary school teacher and a colleague who taught history to a first-year class in a nearby secondary school worked together to devise a task involving historical reasoning for Years 3–9.

All the children heard a recording one of the teachers had made, telling the story of the murder of Thomas à Becket in Canterbury Cathedral. The story was constructed in such a way that it was possible create a 'case for the prosecution' or a 'case for the defence' for each group of protagonists:

■ The knights who killed Becket unnecessarily brutally; the king had said, 'Who will rid me of this turbulent priest?' but said nothing about murder.

■ The monks who witnessed the murder and did not intervene.

■ Becket himself, because he returned to Canterbury from France, knowing he would put his life at risk if he did so.

■ The Pope, Alexander III, because he had sought Becket's help in the quarrel with the king over allowing Church courts to continue, yet had urged Becket to be cautious.

■ The king who had appointed Becket as Archbishop of Canterbury although Becket had told him that if he did so he would support the church against the king.

The two teachers analysed the historical thinking involved in answering the question 'Who was responsible for the murder of Thomas à Becket?' It required the ability to reason about and weigh evidence for and against the five protagonists. The range and variety of answers was impressive. This is represented by the three responses below. Of course there was a wide range of reasoning ability both within and between the classes. Table 9.1 opposite shows the A1 answer sheet the pupils were given to support their thinking.

This task involved the teachers in working together and in discussing thinking in history. It raised many interesting questions about different levels of thinking and how to assess them and about the range of levels of thinking across the primary/secondary divide and how to provide for them. Here is an example of different levels of response to cases for and against, the knights.

## The knights: case for prosecution

Year 7: 'They were headstrong and impetuous and rushed off to kill Becket, just because the king let slip a chance remark. They probably knew if they had actually thought about it, that the king did not really want anyone to murder the Archbishop, but they were too eager to obey Henry's every word. One reason for the keenness may have been a desire for wealth and power and large rewards. However they must have felt guilty rather than proud afterwards because they slipped away so surreptitiously. It was also wrong of them to murder Becket in a Cathedral.'

**TABLE 9.1** A1 answer sheet pupils were given to analyse the case for and against the protagonists in the murder of Thomas à Becket, from five perspectives.

| Suspect | Case for prosecution | Case for defence |
|---|---|---|
| Knights | | |
| Monks | | |
| Becket | | |
| Pope | | |
| King Henry II | | |
| Summing up | | |

## Case for the defence of the knights

Some responses saw only one perspective for one group.

Year 6: 'They were only doing their duty to the king. When they murdered Becket they may have been blinded by their desire to serve Henry. They did try to drag Becket out of the cathedral before murdering him and they had previously tried to make him obey the king. But then it only took one impetuous knight to strike the final blow.'

A Year 5 response said that, 'I think they shouldn't have jumped to conclusions. But I suppose they did the right thing. Becket was a nuisance. I think he deserved it.'

At a lower level response, Year 4, there was only one point of view: 'The knights were nasty people!'

The lowest level of response, Year 3, was based on an illogical misunderstanding. 'I think that the knights were responsible for the murder of Thomas à Becket, because they were paid to guard Becket.'

There was a continuum of increasing complexity between these polarised responses.

### Case for the defence and the prosecution of each group

At the highest level of response, some Year 9 pupils were able to make a case for the prosecution and the defence of each of the groups, weigh their hypotheses, synthesise all the reasons for the points they made and reach a conclusion:

> Henry and the knights seem to have most of the facts in the prosecution and the least defence. I think Henry was more responsible than the knights because, after all it was he who 'ordered' Becket to be killed (by a casual remark, which may have been a Freudian slip). The Pope was not really involved at all and it was not directly to do with him. The monks just happened to be there and most people would probably have fled in their positions; at least two stayed, for a while anyway, to try to save their Archbishop. Becket could have been more co-operative with Henry but as Archbishop he felt that his loyalties lay towards the church. He was a holy man, quick tempered though he may have been, and his murder was a great tragedy.

At a lower level of response, children did not take account of all the evidence or produce a synthesised conclusion and the evidence given was not weighed or rational. A Year 4 response was: 'I think the culprits were the knights. The knights were a bit hasty. The king, well, he was getting too big for his boots as well. You can't expect everyone to do what you say, even if you are a king!'

## A shared exhibition

At the end of my year as primary secondary liaison teacher for history, all the schools I had worked with had exchanged visits with their partner schools to share ideas and their pupils' work. I had worked with some on joint projects. For example the children in one Year 7 class, who had been studying the local church, revisited it with their partner Year 6 class, working in pairs of a Year 6 and a Year 7 child. The Year 7 children explained what they had learned and the Year 6 children took photographs as a basis for developing the work themselves. At the end of the year all the pairs of classes in the project contributed to a large exhibition of work, which extended interest in the project to a wider audience.

## The way forward

These examples show that it is possible to develop mutually useful networks and collaborations of different kinds, between primary and secondary schools in which teachers discuss expectations and share expertise and pupils work together. However it is essential that these collaborations and networks are long term and evolve, and are based on mutual respect, if they are to be of any real benefit.

### Historical Association Key Stage 2/3 transition project

This 2005 project, which can be found on the Historical Association website (www.history.org.uk) in the resources section, describes five training sessions in which secondary teachers worked collaboratively with three colleagues from feeder primary schools to create nine schemes of work for Year 6 classes that aimed to extend work already done and to focus on interpretation. Contrary to the findings of *History for All* (Ofsted 2011) and the *Primary History Survey*, this project claimed that primary pupils in Cambridgeshire had found history irrelevant and boring. Examples of the work include pupils providing commentary to accompany extracts from films about Victorian England, a consideration of why Boudicca's reputation changed over time and interpretations of evacuation to the countryside in the Second World War. Pupils studied feature films, television documentaries, newsreels, paintings and photographs.

The teachers spent some time designing suitable questions for the enquiries, beginning with a starter activity that 'hooked' children's interest, followed by a sequence of subordinate questions and activities to explore the questions, building up to a culminating task that would help the children to answer the initial question. The project also explored links between history and ICT. This project is well worth reading and could serve as a useful model for developing networks and collaboration.

## References

Alexander, R. (ed.) (2010) *Children, their World, their Education: final report and recommendations of the Cambridge Primary Review*. London: Routledge.

Cooper, H. and West, L. (2009) 'Year 5/6 and Year 7 historians visit Brougham Castle', in H. Cooper and A. Chapman (eds) *Constructing History*. London: Sage, 9–32.

Historical Association (2011) *Primary History Survey (England): history 3–11*. London: The Historical Association.

Ofsted (Office for Standards in Education) (2011) *History for All: history in English schools 2007/10*. London: Ofsted (www.ofsted.gov.uk/resources/history-for-all).

# 10

# Generic learning across the history curriculum

The *Cambridge Review* stated that an overcrowded primary curriculum had eliminated opportunities for activities that involved thought, talk, problem-solving, and meaningful and rewarding in-depth studies, across the curriculum. This chapter explores ways in which investigations that involve history activities can also involve thinking in literacy, mathematics and information and communication technologies and so allow time for thought, talk and problem-solving across these areas. There is also a section on history and art, which a reviewer suggested would be a welcome addition.

## History and literacy

### A sequence of Key Stage 2 sessions with shared history and literacy objectives culminating in an exhibition

Conferences were organised in York and in London to model for teacher trainers how literacy objectives could be applied to a range of subjects. I was invited to write materials for literacy and art, based on work I had recently published (Cooper and Twiselton 2000). Our intention had been to develop a sequence of literacy sessions on the theme of 'The Impressionists', linked to practical work in art that would conclude with an exhibition of work in an 'art gallery', created by Year 4 children. I have modified this project to focus on an exhibition of historical sources that could lead towards a class museum exhibition. This would be most suitable for work on the Victorians or more recent Britain because artefacts and photographs are available. For other periods it might be an exhibition of relevant art for an art gallery exhibition. Visitors to the school could be given plans, information leaflets, guided tours, audio tape recordings. The extensions to the suggested activities are endless. Of course, other history and literacy would flow outside this sequence as well.

## PLAN 1  Making inferences about artefacts

### OBJECTIVES

*History*

To understand that opinions about artefacts differ; to form and express opinions.

*Literacy*

To define familiar vocabulary in own words.

To understand and use the term 'opinion'.

To identify use of voice and of headlines.

### OUTLINE

1  **Discuss an obscure artefact**: How was it made, used, what was its effect on people who made and used it.

2  **Groups**: Using different Victorian artefacts and a writing frame if necessary, write labels stating what the object is made of, opinion(s) about how it may have been used and why they think so.

3  **Focus group**: Write short article, possibly for audio tape recording.

4  **Plenary**: List opinions on flip chart; rephrase those that are not opinions.

## PLAN 2  Describe key features of a Victorian artefact, painting, photograph

### OBJECTIVES

*History*

To understand features and diversity of the period.

To find out from sources and select and record information relevant to an enquiry.

*Literacy*

To use alternative words and expressions that are more interesting or accurate than obvious choices.

To revise and extend work on adjectives, constructing adjectival phrases.

To make short notes, abbreviating ideas, selecting keywords, recording in diagrammatic form.

## PLAN 2 *continued*

### OUTLINE

1 Explain that we are going to look at a painting in detail and write brief notes recording what information in the picture tells us about what Victorian life was like, using adjectives to describe things.

2 Make spidergram around picture, indicating place in picture with ruled lines and arrows. 3 Groups: use Victorian paintings or photographs showing different aspects of Victorian life by attaching postcard images on A3 paper.

3 Underline adjectives.

   **Focus group**: Write in continuous prose.

4 **Plenary**: Share, evaluate.

## PLAN 3 Instructions for Victorian activities

### OBJECTIVES

#### History

To understand about people in the past.

To ask and answer questions about sources.

To communicate knowledge and understanding in a variety of ways.

#### Literacy

To revise work on verbs.

To identify features of instructional text, including noting intended outcome at the beginning, listing materials, clearly setting out sequential stages, language of command, imperative verbs.

This could focus on creating instructions about how to do anything in the period studied: a dance, learning a song, cooking a recipe, using an old artefact such as a washboard, riding a penny-farthing.

### OUTLINE

1 Model creating instructional text, emphasising verbs, imperatives, sequence, using children to carry out, then evaluate and change instructions.

2 **Groups**: Write instructions for other activities using differentiated historical sources.

3 **Plenary**: Try to carry out instructions; evaluate, correct.

## PLAN 4  Writing captions for the exhibition

### OBJECTIVES

*History*

Recognise that the past is represented in different ways and give reasons for this.

*Literacy*

Reread own writing and check for grammatical accuracy; identify errors; suggest alternative constructions.

Identify features of non-fiction text (e.g. headings, captions, which support the reader in gaining information efficiently).

### OUTLINE

1  Children collect (photocopy) different interpretations of Victorian period, e.g. Villainous Victorians (Deary 2004), old children's textbook, cartoon, a video clip, picture of reconstruction in a museum or living history reconstruction.

2  Where do we find captions? (Museums, galleries, illustrated books.) Who are they written for? What purpose do they serve?

3  Read caption. What does it tell us? (Fact, some background information, intended to be read in conjunction with the interpretation.)

4  Conclude, purpose to inform and interest reader, help to understand a little more; note economical language, headings, quick to read limited information.

5  Model creating a caption for one of the interpretations, using writing frame if necessary (title, name of creator, where found, description, purpose in making it, how valid as information about period?).

6  **Groups**: Write captions for other interpretations.

7  **Focus group**: Devise catalogue to record categories of information, using ICT so that entries can be word processed for exhibition.

## PLAN 5  Advertising the exhibition

### OBJECTIVES

*History*

Organisation and communication.

*Literacy*

To understand fact and opinion.

To investigate how style and vocabulary are used to convince.

**PLAN 5** *continued*

> To evaluate advertisements and their impact, appeal, honesty.
>
> To design an advertisement.
>
> **OUTLINE**
>
> 1 What information is on a poster? What is it for? What is main heading, subheading? Which text is trying to persuade us? Are there reviews quoted? (speech marks and opinions).
>
> 2 Is it brief, informal, colourful? Identify need to create poster with title, factual information (price, time, place, transport). Are there persuasive text reviews? Make best copy using word processing (variety, different fonts, colours, digital photographs).

These sessions require children to access information in books and on the internet, record information in note form, evaluate, form opinions, and discuss and record them. It is only possible to give a flavour of the session plans, which can be developed in relation to particular history topics.

## Kendal Castle

In order to define precise links between learning objectives for history and for English, five student teachers worked intensively for three days with a Year 1/2 class in Stramongate School, Kendal. Children visited Kendal Castle, and found out more about castles from other sources in order, first, to create a role play of what a medieval banquet in Kendal Castle may have been like and, second, to make a children's information board for the castle, since the children said that they found that the board on the site, written for adults, was difficult for them to understand. This project (Cooper 1998) preceded the *National Literacy Strategy*, so it is interesting, though not surprising, that each of the activities had both *National Curriculum for England and Wales* (DfEE/QCA 1999) learning objectives and *National Literacy Strategy* text level objectives.

First the children were asked to 'draw and label a picture of a castle: the ideas that come into your head when someone says "castle"' (Figure 10.1). Students scribed for younger children. This was in order to find out what children already knew (and possible misconceptions); what images they had of castles. Some children had a lot of factual knowledge, about moats, drawbridges, arrow-slits; others were dominated by fantasy – garlands of flowers around the turrets, Max from *Where the Wild Things Are* in a boat on a rescue mission across the moat (Sendak 1970).

Then the children were told that they were visiting Kendal Castle in the afternoon and asked what they would like to find out about it. Their questions were listed on a flip-chart and grouped into four focuses:

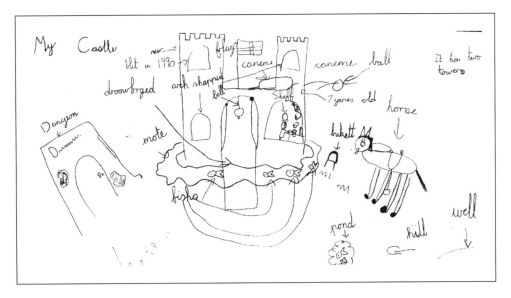

**FIGURE 10.1** Concept map of a castle, drawn before visiting Kendal Castle.

- **Now and then**: What can you see from the castle mound now and what would you have seen a long time ago – certainly; possibly?

- **Attacking the castle**: Why was it built here; how could you attack? where?

- **Daily life**: Where did they cook; wash; get water; have banquets?

- **Survey of the site**: Measure curtain wall, windows, doorways; note materials, where did they come from?

In the afternoon the children worked in groups on the site to record information in notes and lists. Some children organised their notes under headings, others recorded as small drawings, with labels scribed for them where necessary.

Next day preparations began to reconstruct a banquet at Kendal Castle in the time of Catherine Parr, who had lived there as a child. In order to find out how to dress, children made rubbings of replica medieval brasses, including one of Catherine Parr. This gave them lots of information about ladies' headdresses, 'belts with tassels', patterns on dresses; about knights' chain mail, armour, helmets, swords, coats of arms on shields. Then each child chose a small item of dress from their rubbing, a necklace or a shield, for example, and made a replica, from card, fabric or shiny paper, which they could wear to the banquet.

They found the rest of the information they needed to plan the banquet from books – usually from illustrations, either artists' reconstructions or contemporary pictures. *The Medieval Cookbook* (Black 1992), although an adult book, has splendidly vivid pictures of medieval feasts to accompany the recipes: killing the boar, baking the bread, roasting birds on spits, etc. Invitations were sent (modelled on familiar party invitations), menus were written and programmes for entertainment devised. These were divided into subheadings: during the meal – stories, jesting, lute – and after the meal – singing, jesters, dancing and tournaments. Samantha's drawing of the joust (Figure 10.2) and accompanying writing (Figure 10.3) show how the interpretation of medieval people on the brasses was brought to life by her further enquiry using information from book illustrations of knights, which informed the joust role play following the banquet. Stories were written, to be read during the meal, modelled on the familiar conventions of fairy stories about princes and princesses. Jokes were remodelled suitably for medieval jesters: why did the chicken cross the drawbridge? Replica food was prepared (finding from their researches that squirrels were eaten, as well as boars' heads, a lugubrious pig's head and some surprisingly perky-looking squirrels were carried to the table with great care on a large silver salver). Following the banquet, jugglers caught most of the balls, everyone laughed at the jesters' riddles, and Baron Dorset, looking remarkably like the head teacher, joined in the dancing to the viol, the harp and the crumhorn, using a tape of medieval music.

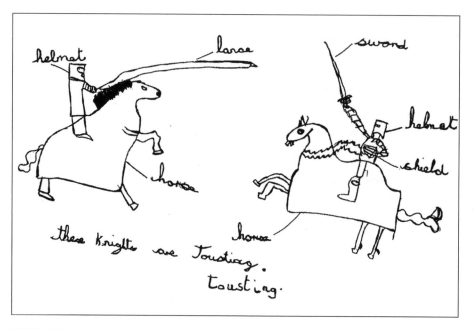

**FIGURE 10.2** Samantha found out about jousting from information books.

The various examples of non-chronological writing on the children's information board (Figure 10.4) were an excellent assessment of the enormous range of detailed information the children had acquired over the intensive three-day project and the site plan of Kendal Castle, with its topographically accurate key to the plan of the castle, showed a significant development from the fairy-tale fantasy castles of the initial concept maps to a factual labelled diagram.

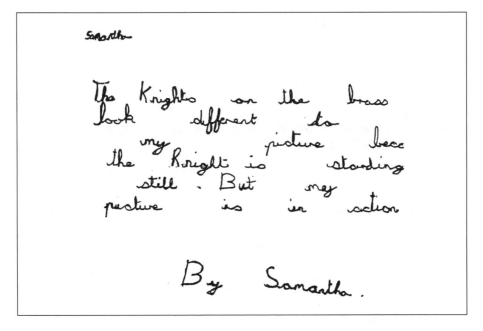

Samantha

The Knights on the brass look different to my picture becc the Knight is standing still. But my picture is in action

By Samantha.

**FIGURE 10.3** Knights on brasses look different from illustrations in books.

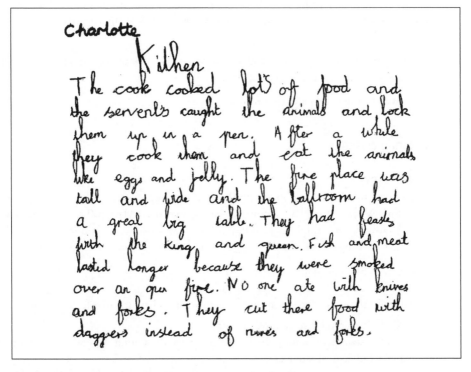

Charlotte

Kitchen

The cook cooked lot's of food and the servent's caught the animals and lock them up in a pen. After a while they cook them and eat the animals like eggs and jelly. The fire place was tall and wide and the baltroom had a great big table. They had feasts with the king and queen. Fish and meat lasted longer because they were smoked over an open fire. No one ate with knives and forks. They cut there food with daggers instead of nives and forks.

**FIGURE 10.4** Children made an information board for Kendal Castle.

## More history and literacy

The challenge for the students in this workshop was to explore ways in which history and literacy objectives might both be combined. The focus was on reading and writing non-fiction from Year 1 to Year 6.

## Year 1/2: Finding out about Victorian washday: reading and writing instructional text

This could be applied to explaining how any artefact was used.

### History objectives

Use common words or phrases related to passing of time. Identify differences between ways of life at different times. Find out about the past from a range of sources. Communicate awareness and knowledge of history.

### Literacy objectives

Read simple instructions. Note structured features: statement of purpose at start, sequential steps in list; direct language. Write simple instructions. Organise sequentially (lists, numbers) each point depending on the previous one. Use appropriate register (direct; impersonal).

Reread own writing for sense and punctuation. Use simple organisational devised to indicate sequence (arrows), boxes, keys.

New words linked to particular topics.

### Victorian washday

#### *Whole class*

Show wash tub, scrubbing board, postle, iron, line, pegs, soap. What were these things used for? When? Why? By whom? What do we use today? Who does the washing today? How do you think the scrubbing board was used? Can you follow Mrs Tiggy-Winkle's washing instructions?

To wash a shirt you will need:

- Child mimes as instructions are read from flip-chart (or overhead transparency).
- Were they good instructions? Why?
  Identify statement of purpose, sequential steps; each point depends on previous one, direct impersonal language.
- Do you know what the other things are called? (Label)

■ How do you think you use the postle?

■ Child mimes as class read scrubbing board instructions, changing as necessary for postle.

■ Explain class are going to make a book of Mrs Tiggy-Winkle's washing instructions.

You will need:

■ a scrubbing board
■ a wash tub
■ hot water
■ soap.

Half-fill wash tub with hot water. Put in dirty clothes. Stand scrubbing board in the wash tub. Stretch dirty shirt across scrubbing board. Rub the shirt with soap until it is clean. Wring out soapy water. Rinse the shirt in clean water. Hang on outdoor clothes line to dry with pegs, or on clothes horse by kitchen fire, it if is raining.

### Independent groups

You are going to write instructions for using the postle. Either write the instructions as for the scrubbing board, or draw pictures or a diagram with labels. Remember: purpose, sequence, register.

### Focus group

We are going to explain how to use a flat iron (key instructional features, but new information).

### Plenary

Read instructions for using postle and iron; child mimes. Evaluate for inclusion in Mrs Tiggy-Winkle's washday book.

## Year 3: Humorous verse. Cautionary tales. *Matilda, Who Told Lies and Was Burned to Death* (Hilaire Belloc)

### History objectives

Characteristic features of period and experiences of middle-class child. Find out about the past from a variety of sources. Discuss clues in illustrations about when poem (Belloc 1991) written:

■ tea in the drawing room – servants
■ fire engine
■ street scenes
■ clothes
■ carriages.

## Literacy objectives

Consider credibility of events. Discuss character behaviour.

Compare forms of humour, e.g. cautionary tales. Prepare, read aloud and recite by heart, poetry that plays with language or entertains; recognise rhyme and patterns of sound that create effects. Compare and contrast works by the same author.

Use speech marks and other dialogue punctuation.

## Matilda

### Whole class

Read poem: what is it about? Is it likely? True? Is Matilda reasonable? Brave? Foolish? Discuss clues in illustrations about Matilda and her life; similarities with and differences from children today. Introduce concept of 'cautionary tales'. What makes it fun? Identify rhythm. Mark a photocopied page (interactive whiteboard). Introduce other Belloc cautionary tales to read at another time.

Identify speech and punctuation marks: 'Matilda's house is burning down!' using photocopied page on whiteboard. They only answered 'little liar'.

Tap out syllables. Reread. List any new words (e.g. gallant, frenzied).

### Independent group work

Give children photocopied pages to read; to mark rhymes; syllables; prepare to recite.

### Guided group work

Give children sheets marked with lines of eight dashes (one per syllable). Help them make up their own, modern, cautionary verse.

### Plenary

Class recite their pages, to read complete poem in sequence. Guided group read their poem. Discuss what makes them effective. How is a Victorian poem the same/different from modern version?

# Year 4: What were Ancient Egyptian houses like?

This model could be used to find out about a key aspect of any area of study from a variety of reference books.

## History objectives

Ask and answer questions about the past, using variety of sources. Understanding why there are different interpretations of the past.

## Literacy objectives

Appraise a non-fiction book for its contents and usefulness by scanning (e.g. headings, contents list). To prepare for factual research by reviewing what is known, what is available and where one might search. To scan text in print or on screen to locate key words or phrases, useful headings and key questions and to use these as a tool for summarising text. Mark extracts by annotating and by selecting key headings, words, sentences. Identify key features of explanatory text (e.g. to answer a question, use of illustrations and diagrams).

Use cues (phonic, graphic, grammatical knowledge, context when reading unfamiliar texts). Understand that vocabulary changes over time (e.g. discuss why some words have become little used).

## Egyptian houses

### *Whole class*
On interactive whiteboard show of a page about an Ancient Egyptian house from a reference book. What do you already know about houses in Ancient Egypt? How can we find out more? (Archaeological remains, tomb, book.)

The information in books comes from making deductions and inferences about archaeological sources; different books may say different things. We are going to see what we can find out from these books: what is the same/ different; how useful the books are.

Where can we find out about Egyptian houses in this book? (Contents, index.)

Find text. Read page (on whiteboard). Mark key information. List it on flip-chart under headings. Discuss usefulness of text, illustrations, diagrams.

Discuss unfamiliar vocabulary: brewery, bakery, silo, granary. Do we still use these words today? When? How has their meaning remained the same/changed?

### *Independent group work*
Groups given other reference books at appropriately differentiated levels. Find reference to Egyptian houses. List key words/information.

### *Plenary*
Whole class list what they have found out on flip-chart, adding under original headings. Note differences between books; discuss reasons. Reorganise list under headings, sub-headings, numbered points.

# Year 5: Persuasive text: advertisements

Commercial advertisements can be read as a historical source. They both mirror and influence the ways of life, aspirations and social values of men, women, children and the ways in which these change from decade to decade. Children are familiar with the concepts of advertising and can understand them as persuasive interpretations. Text is minimal, supported by clear picture clues and illustrates a range of linguistic features. The History of Advertising Trust is an excellent resource (www.hatads.org.uk): posters for whole-class work; calendars that children can work on individually or in groups. Their collection on 'Women in Advertising – from Victorian Times to Today' was used to plan for the following learning objectives.

## History objectives

Ask and answer questions from sources about life in the 1890s; 1930 to the present. Characteristics of periods and societies, attitudes and experiences of men, women, children. Social diversity. Reasons for situations and changes. Make links between situations, changes, within and across periods. Reasons why the past is represented and interpreted in different ways.

## Literacy objectives

From examples of persuasive writing investigate how style and vocabulary can be used to convince the intended reader.

To evaluate advertisements for impact, appeal, honesty, focusing on how information about the product is presented: exaggerated claims, tactics for grabbing attention, linguistic devises; puns, jingles, alliteration, invented words.

To design an advertisement making use of linguistic and other features learned from examples. To understand how the grammar of a sentence is altered; statement to question; question to order; positive to negative. To use a range of presentational skills, e.g. print script for captions, headings for posters, range of computer-generated fonts. The opportunities to use these skills in order to discuss and evaluate messages of old advertisements, and compare them with those of today offer an exciting variety of possibilities.

# Year 6: Diary of Anne Frank (21 August 1942) (interactive whiteboard)

Diaries and journals recounting experiences and events.

## History objectives

Find out about the past from a variety of sources.

Characteristic features of periods and beliefs, attitudes and experiences of men, women and children; social, religious, cultural, ethnic diversity.

## Literacy objectives

Personal responses to literature, identifying why and how a text affects the reader. Prepare a short section of the story as a script.

Distinguish between biography and autobiography, fact and opinion, implicit and explicit point of view.

Develop skills of biographical and autobiographical writing in role of a historical character through describing a person from different perspectives, e.g. police.

Develop a journalistic style; consider balanced ethical reporting.

Identify connectives to convey sequence; causal connectives.

## Anne Frank

### Whole class

What do you know about Anne Frank? Put diary extract in context; use website, photo scrapbook of story of her life, brief history of the Holocaust, and tour of the rooms where she lived (www.annefrank.com).

Read diary entry. What more does this extract tell us (weather, hiding place, holiday . . .)? What is special about a diary (not written for others; personal views, feelings, perspective, language)? What does it tell us about Anne's feelings, relationships, what sort of person she is?

How does Anne explain the time sequence (first three days, now, at present, already)? Identify causal connectives (because a lot of houses had been searched; because we all locked ourselves in the doorway).

List on flip-chart what you would need to consider in writing:

- a newspaper article about the discovery of the diary;
- a police account of the search for the hiding place.

### Independent group work

Write a newspaper account of the discovery of the diary. Write a police report on searching for the hiding place. Read/write another entry from Anne's diary.

### Focus group

Prepare a diary extract as a film script.

### Plenary

Compare interpretations; discuss fact/opinion; point of view, validity.

After sharing these literacy hour plans, which used a variety of texts across a wide age range, and encompassed both literacy and history objectives, the students agreed that they would have a go at developing these models in other contexts during their coming block placements in schools.

## Analysis of links between the literacy and historical thinking

The UK School Museums Group Conference invited a short paper on links between history and literacy, which they could use to ensure that discussions of their artefact collections with primary school children and the information labels, brochures and follow-up activities that they provide (quizzes, trails, worksheets) reflect and develop literacy as well as history objectives. They felt that this would enable them to justify to schools the time spent on visits to museums; a parlous situation – but an interesting exercise. The resulting analysis of different types of text that can be used in history lessons, with suggested levels of difficulty, is shown below.

### Types of non-fiction text

#### *Information texts*

| | Y1 | Y2 | Y3 | Y4 | Y5 | Y6 |
|---|---|---|---|---|---|---|
| Signs, labels, captions, lists | Y1 | | | | | |
| Non-chronological reports | | Y2 | Y3 | Y4 | | Y6 |
| Observations | | | Y3 | Y4 | Y5 | |
| Reports, articles | Y1 | | Y3 | Y4 | | |
| Describe and classify | | | | Y4 | Y5 | |
| Formal writing: public information, documents etc. | | | | | | Y6 |

#### *Instructional texts*

| | Y1 | Y2 | Y3 | Y4 | Y5 | Y6 |
|---|---|---|---|---|---|---|
| Instructions | Y1 | Y2 | Y3 | | | |
| Rules, recipes, directions, instructions showing how things are done. | | | | | | |
| Explanations | | Y2 | | Y4 | | Y6 |
| Puzzles, riddles | | | Y3 | | | |
| Viewpoints, fact/opinion discussion, debate | | | | Y4 | Y5 | |

#### *Chronological texts*

| | Y1 | Y2 | Y3 | Y4 | Y5 | Y6 |
|---|---|---|---|---|---|---|
| Recount events, activities (visits) | | | | | Y5 | |
| Observations that recount experiences over time | | | | | | Y6 |

## Technical vocabulary

The technical terms that should form part of pupils' developing vocabulary for talking about language can be used in the discussion of and writing about artefacts or other historical sources. Again these develop from simple questions and instructions, an old recipe, how to play a simple Victorian game or use a butter pat at Key Stage 1, to the language of probability, opinion and argument in Year 4 and of hypothesis and perspective in Year 6.

Y1  Question, label, instruction, list, non-chronological writing.

Y2  Explanation, fact, notes, skim, scan.

Y3  Definition, bullet points, past tense, legend, myth.
    Conjunction: if, so, while, though, since, when; time – first, then, after, meanwhile.
    Argument
    Debate
    Discussion – argument for and against
    Opinion

Y5  Chronological sequence
    Point of view

Y6  Word derivation
    Hypothesis
    Viewpoint

## Scaffolding children's historical thinking

Bruner's notion (1966) of devising scaffolding frameworks for supporting and developing children's thinking processes has been applied to thinking in history through research and in published history resources (Counsell and Thomson 1997; Wray and Medwell 1998). Many of these writing frames can be used to enable children to develop the literacy skills defined in the technical vocabulary in historical contexts.

Children can use them to write structured reports about artefacts or sites; this report is about . . .; detail a, b, c, d; conclusion. They can write explanations of historical events, or of why people in the past may have behaved in a certain way: I want to explain why: reason i), ii), iii), iv); so now you see why . . . They can use a series of steps to sequence instructions ranging from how to make a peg doll to how to navigate a course to the East Indies in an Elizabethan ship. They can use a template to identify an issue, list arguments for/against, and write a conclusion. If the writing frames are linked to ICT this allows the flexibility to reorganise text, to work collaboratively, and it gives a structure for comparing responses.

## History, literacy and fiction

There has recently been a renewed exploration of ways in which story and, in particular, fiction set in the past can help children to develop historical understanding (Hoodless 1998; English Heritage 1998a; Bage 1999). When a group of Year 3 BA QTS students worked in pairs, brainstorming texts they had actually used, they found that between them they had already used a number of the genres in their history teaching. One interesting fact to emerge was that all kinds of historical texts and genres had been adapted for use at a range of levels: the Year 1 spidergraph, for example, recorded that five-year-old children taught by these students had worked on Egyptian and Greek myths and legends, Saxon and Viking sagas and Chaucer. Year 6 children had worked on extracts from Dickens, Leon Garfield and Rosemary Sutcliff and written their own scripts after hot-seating as factory owners and child workers.

One student, Hannah Dewfall, said that 'it was my own delight in historical fiction that fuelled my enjoyment of history'. But she was also aware of the dilemmas of teaching history through fiction:

> While English teachers often see historical fiction as a minor genre, history teachers often see it as an inaccurate view of historical events. If a historical novel is to be used to teach history, social conditions and public events must be thoroughly researched, free from anachronisms and an integral part of the text.

She went on to explore ways in which literacy objectives for fiction might deepen children's historical understanding. Her Year 5 class were reading *The Machine Gunners* (Westall 1975). She focused on two statements to discuss how the central character, a child, is presented through dialogue, action and description and how the reader responds to him through examining his relationship with the other characters.

> 'Chas watched them as if they were ants, without sympathy, because they were a slummy kind of family.'

and

> 'Besides the dead German would scare the silly little cow. She wouldn't interfere in men's business again.'

Hannah used these statements to help the children discuss reasons for attitudes to class, race and gender, now and in the past, and why these might change over time.

Another student read extracts from three stories about the Second World War. *Rose Blanche* (McEwan 1985) a fictional story about concentration camps, *After the War is Over* (Foreman 1995) a story about real children and events in the history of a village and the *Diary of Anne Frank* (Frank 1989), an eyewitness account.

Through focused discussions her Year 6 children considered how the authors handled time and conveyed the passing of time, and the influence of the viewpoint of narrators on the readers' view of events as well as differences between fact, opinion and fiction.

We need such creative teachers who are proactive in interpreting requirements in ways that give them ownership and reflect their professional judgements. We do not want passive, mechanistic teachers who are targets for political manipulation. We need literacy to be taught, not by teachers who enable children to read, write and cipher by rule and recipe, but in ways that provide children with new tools for thinking.

## History, literacy and non-fiction

Baldwin (2003) has identified literacy objectives in comprehension throughout Key Stage 2, which can be used in connection with interpretations in history. These range from distinguishing between fact and fiction and comparing the way information is presented in Year 3, to comparing how different texts treat the same information in Year 5. He also lists non-fiction writing composition objectives, which can be applied to interpretations in history, ranging from presenting a point of view in Year 4 to describing a person from different perspectives in Year 6. Taylor (2001) describes how her Year 6 class learned history through a topic on Charles Dickens. They researched his character in order to write a biography and a CV. They watched the beginning of the film *Oliver Twist* to compare their lives with his, then used dialogue from the text to write a play script. They read a description of Coketown from *Hard Times* (underlining and finding the meaning of unknown vocabulary), to find out about the impact of the Industrial Revolution. This led to paintings and poems describing a walk through Coketown and discussion of the benefits and disadvantages of industrialisation.

## Engaging in fictional and non-fictional writing

The children's author Stewart Ross worked with Year 6 at St Illytd's School in Swansea, using the internet, as part of the Adopt an Author Scheme funded by the National Endowment for Science, Technology and the Arts (Nesta) (Ross 2004). The aim of the project was to give children, and particularly boys, an insight into the way professional writers operate. He was working on *Tales of the Dead: Ancient Rome* (Ross 2005a) and began by asking the children to compose their own storyboards, twenty frames of words and pictures, that would be their smaller version of the book he was preparing for Dorling Kindersley. He sent them some of the roughs, which they used as a guide for spreads of their own, choosing subjects from the agreed book map. They were invited to write attention-grabbing openings and develop them to a cliffhanging end. At the end of the project the teacher said that the children had looked at fiction and non-fiction in depth, confronted issues such as slavery, seen that writers are normal human beings, and had their confidence considerably reinforced.

## Historical fiction

A sense of other times and experiences may be more successfully drawn from fiction, a more nourishing food for the imagination than many 'historic experiences' available. Some recent historical fiction is humorous and instantly readable. *The Silver Spoon of Solomon Snow* (Umansky 2004) is the story of a foundling's journey in search of his true identity, with terrific verbal and visual jokes on the way. *Jammy Dodgers on the Run* (Sivers 2004), set in the Victorian underworld of Seven Dials, is gruesome in places but also full of fun. *Joshua Cross and the Queen's Conjurer* (Redmond 2003) is a time-slip adventure set in Tudor times. *Tread Softly* (Pennington 2004) is historical fiction about Elizabethan plotting and intrigue on a more serious level and *Anne Boleyn and Me: the diary of Elinor Valjean* (Prince 2004) presents, in diary format, the reactions of a young Spanish woman to Henry VIII's rejection of Catherine of Aragon.

Older classics for children, such as *Tom's Midnight Garden* (Pearce 1976), may be read simply as stories that take you to other times, or they could be used to explore what they also tell us of the times in which they were written. Do they reflect a nostalgia to retrieve vanishing ideals or a community outliving the transience of individuals? Dan Dare, hero of the post-Second World War *Eagle* comic, can also be seen as representing the values of the Festival of Britain: liberal (slightly evangelical) nationalism. It is interesting to compare the predictions for space technology of the time with reality, which turned out to be far more advanced – although Dan was able to relieve the rationing crisis with food from Venus. Dan Dare can tell us a lot about the 1950s.

*Narrative Matters* (Bage 1999) looks in depth at the use of story in history. *History and English in the Primary School* (Hoodless 1998) is a theoretical examination of case studies that link the two subjects. The Literacy Through History Project (Nichol 1998, 2000; Lewis and Wray 1998) makes links between a discrete literacy hour and history.

## Speaking and listening

Speaking and listening are important aspects of assessment for learning. They are also crucial for extended thinking and clarifying and embedding new concepts. There are, of course, many contexts for speaking and listening in history: group discussion, discussing interpretations of sources, justifying statements, problem solving and evaluating learning.

## Drama

Drama, in its different forms, extends and clarifies thinking through speaking and listening in role. I watched a Year 1/2 class responding to a student in three separate roles. A Roman sandal had been lost and was now in a museum show case (under an upturned aquarium). The student used different signifiers for each role. She was in turn the Roman child who had lost the shoe, the archaeologist who discovered it and the museum curator. The children listened and questioned her in each role without difficulty and with great interest.

Steve Mynard decided to take a break from teaching and set out to explore some ideas of his own about rejuvenating the curriculum with the intention of putting 'some of the creativity and imagination back' into professional development. He runs a living history course, which is held all over England (steve.mynard@blueyonder.co.uk).

This year I was asked to run a session to 'tell a group of postgraduate distance learning students all they need to know about history'. Hmm. I used a session my colleague Mike Huggins (1997) had written about, which required me to give an arresting knock on the door with my stick and appear bent, wearing my second-best long black dress and wrapped in a piece of hand-dyed and woven cloth I had found in Ireland. I was in role as a Kendal woman in 1589. This caused a sensation. There is no space to recount this interpretation but it involved the students in each choosing a name, photocopied from the parish records of the time, and responding in role. They chose a house from a contemporary map and a lifestyle indicated by the places named on the map (e.g. tenters' field). From a series of contemporary woodcuts they each chose an occupation. I developed the scenario from key documents throughout the year that record how the plague arrived, its effect and the problems the inhabitants faced in knowing how to deal with it, what to do with those who were ill, whether to close the market . . . The role play started as great fun as people developed their roles and addressed each other by name. But what astonished me was how the atmosphere gradually changed, became muted, until some people were practically in tears. It ended with a reading from the vicar's sermon at the end of the year when the plague had subsided, attributing it to the misdeeds of the people. The people, living and dead, and looking forward to returning, chastened, to their previous, happy community.

The session involved making inferences from maps and a variety of primary written sources, considering problems from the points of view of those living at the time, beginning to understand how different people may have felt and filling in the gaps, by extrapolating from evidence of what was known and tracing the events chronologically through the year. Everyone felt relaxed about talking freely in role. The session was also very informative. There had been no reading or writing but a great deal of speaking and listening.

Charlotte Mason, an innovative nineteenth century educator, set great store by drama as a means of getting into touch with and interpreting or reconstructing the past.

> They play at history lessons, dress up, make tableaux, act scenes – or they have a stage, paint the scenery, make speeches. There is no end to the modes of expression they find when there is anything in them to express . . . Let a child have meat he requires in his history and imagination will bestir itself without any help of ours. The child will play out a thousand scenes of which he only gets the merest hint.

Penelope Lively, the novelist, who grew up in Cairo during the Second World War and whose books are all concerned with the concept of time, was educated through Parents' National Education Union, an international distance learning organisation created by Charlotte Mason. Lively describes, in *Oleander Jacaranda* (1994) how she could, 'slide off into another world at will [. . .] hidden in the garden. I became Helen lying in the arms of Paris Achilles nobly dying.'

## Oral history

Claire (2004) gives excellent guidance on how to plan for oral history. She also refers to Howarth (1998), a good book for teachers interested in developing their personal understanding of oral history, and to practical books on oral history in schools (Hewitt and Harris 1992; Redfern 1996). She suggests putting 'Oral History' into Google for a wealth of websites.

## History and mathematics

Mathematics contributes to many subjects that may form the starting point of a mathematics lesson or be applied in the context of other lessons. Examples of contexts in history using numeracy objectives from reception to Year 6 are given in Table 10.1.

While the key learning objectives of numeracy must clearly be to develop confidence and competence in mathematics it is often possible to do this in the context of a historical topic. The concepts of measurement, scale and the properties of 2D and 3D shapes could be taught by making and describing models through a sequence of structured lessons. Key Stage 1 work on counting, sets, number sequences in relation to money and real-life problems could be linked to role play on Victorian market sellers.

### A Victorian market

Mike and Edward, both aged six, devised their street cry (Figure 10.5) as part of a mathematics lesson:

> Oranges, oranges, roll up, oranges 5p for 1, 10p for 2, 15p for 3, 20p for 4, 5 for 25p! All your oranges!

**FIGURE 10.5** Mike's and Edward's street cries written in a literacy hour could easily have been part of a numeracy hour.

**TABLE 10.1** Examples of links between numeracy and history.

|  | Numeracy | History contexts |
| --- | --- | --- |
| Reception | Use number names in familiar contexts. | My sister is two, I am four |
|  | Use language such as more or less; heavier, lighter. | Old iron is heavier, new iron is lighter |
|  | Sort into sets | Old/new |
| Year 1 | Count on and back, in ones and in tens; addition and subtraction; mental calculations | Timeline calculations |
|  | Compare, measure in non standard units: two |  |
|  | lengths | Old/new building |
|  | masses | Old/new artefacts |
|  | capacities | Old recipes |
|  | Everyday language to describe 2D and 3D shapes | Doors, windows, tiles, brickwork |
| Year 2 | Count, read, order numbers to 100; count on or back | Timeline calculations |
|  | Estimate, measure, compare | Describe artefacts in class museum, |
|  | Sort shapes | costumes, gloves; buildings, recipes |
|  | Use mathematical vocabulary to describe position, direction, movement | Tiles, bricks, mosaics |
|  |  | Journeys, maps |
| Year 3 | Read, write and order numbers to 1000; count on and back | Timeline calculations |
|  | Use units of time and understand relationship between them: hour, day, week, month, year | Calculations: journeys, letters, newspapers, diaries, timetables |
|  | Solve given problem organising and interpreting numerical data | Census, street directories, graveyard studies, population statistics, trade figures, questionnaires and surveys |
| Year 4 | Know and use relationships between familiar units: length, mass, capacity | Recipes, diet, loads carried, weight of artefacts |
|  | Use appropriate number operations to solve problems | See Year 3 suggestions |
| Year 5 | Understand, calculate area e.g. of rectangle | Maps, changes in land use, sites and buildings |
|  | Use all four operations to solve simple word problems involving numbers and quantities, including time | How long? Longer, shorter, before, after, how many? |
| Year 6 | Measure acute and obtuse angles to nearest degree | Journeys, buildings |
|  | Use appropriate operations involving numbers and quantities | Trade, population |
|  | Extract and interpret information in tables, diagrams, charts | See data presentation Year 3 onwards |

At other times, as with some history-literacy links, the mathematics calculation may also be an integral part of a historical investigation. This is particularly relevant to making timeline calculations in order to consider sequence, duration and causes and effects. Numerical calculations are also fundamental in organising and making probabilistic inter-pretations of data: for example making inferences about reasons for changes in population size, occupations, movement, family size in your locality, and the extent to which they reflect national changes. Children could devise techniques to analyse the proportions of Palladian buildings in photographs to see how accurately they reflect the 1:1.6 proportions of the Golden Rectangle, in order to demonstrate the influence of Greek architecture on subsequent buildings. *A Teacher's Guide to Maths and the Historic Environment* (English Heritage 1998b) is packed with further ideas, and museums such as the Weald and Downland Open Air Museum, are developing structured numeracy programmes linked to museum visits.

Mathematics contributes to many subjects of the curriculum, often in practical ways. It identifies opportunities to collect data, by counting and measuring of all kinds, to relate ratio, scale, position, direction and coordinates to maps, to relate problems to the measurement of time, in days, weeks, years, decades, centuries. With imagination they can be developed both within the numeracy hour and extend beyond it. Historical questions can be identified and data collected from a site visit: measurements, gravestone information, shapes and patterns in buildings and fabrics. Key knowledge and skills in mathematics can be developed through teaching and activities during a mathematics lesson and linked to work in other subjects.

## History and numeracy: two examples

Besides applying mathematical calculations to historical enquiries children can gain historical insights by finding out how people in the past represented numbers and worked out arithmetic. The late Robin Foster, a colleague who lectured in primary mathematics education, made this point when I discussed this section of the book with him. 'The arithmetic we take for granted as simple or trivial taxed great minds in the past', he explained. 'Making children aware of how mathematics developed, and how others too found it difficult can be supportive and illuminating.' It was not long before he was persuaded to put his theory into practice. Here are his plans for two numeracy hours he taught to a Year 2 and a Year 6 class.

### Year 2: Tens and units in a Victorian classroom

#### *Resources*

- Picture of a Victorian school room.
- Picture of a Victorian abacus (Figure 10.6).
- A modern two-pronged abacus.
- Worksheets with empty two-pronged abacuses for children to complete.

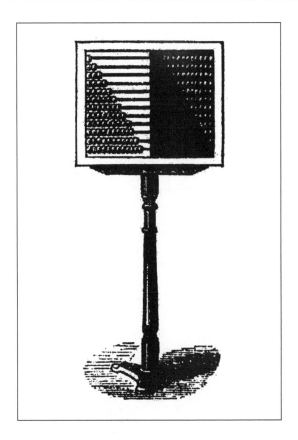

**FIGURE 10.6** A Victorian abacus.

### Intended learning outcomes

At the end of the session the children will have:

- used vocabulary relating to the passing of time; identified similarities and differences between their classroom and a Victorian classroom using visual sources;

- have seen ways of representing tens and units and relate this to particular numbers.

### Mental activity

- Have a piece of wire or string with six beads on it. Show the children the beads. *How many beads are there?*

- Separate and cover up some of the beads with your hand. *How many are hidden? How many can you see?*

- Repeat this for other values of beads. Talk about how in earlier days children did not have much equipment to help them with their mathematics.

## Main session

■  Show the children the picture of the Victorian classroom.

The picture is in black and white, is it a photograph? Imagine the scene in colour. How is it different from our classroom? How is it the same? What do you think the object in the picture is for? What is an abacus?

■  Show the children the close up picture of the Victorian abacus.

*How could you count using this? What happens if I wanted to show 23?*

Demonstrate how you could have 23 beads or use 20 (as two tens) and three as three ones. Show a simplified idea of using a two-pronged abacus to show numbers up to 99.

## Individual or group work

■  Supply the children with pictures of two-pronged abacuses and ask them to represent particular numbers (Figure 10.7). (Vary the numbers according to the individuals.)

■  Use the abacus to show 56. *If you had five beads, what number could you make? Which is the biggest/smallest?*

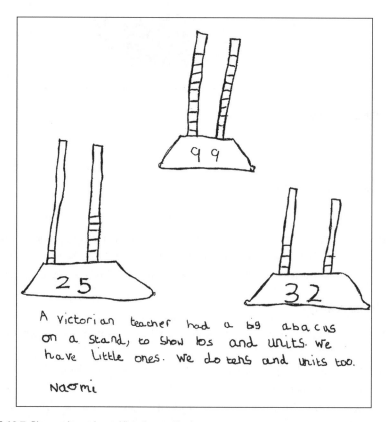

**FIGURE 10.7** Place value using a Victorian method.

## Plenary

- Relate their answers to the Victorian abacus. Allow them to compare their results.

- *What about numbers that are greater than 99?*

## Year 6 Elizabethan multiplication

### Gelosia algorithm – background information

This method, which was used in the reign of Queen Elizabeth I to multiply two-digit numbers, was probably introduced from India. The example shows how it is used to multiply 13 by 49 (see Figure 10.8).

- Draw a lattice grid of 2 × 2 cells; divide each cell with a diagonal line as shown.

- Put the numbers to be multiplied above and to the right.

- Multiply each digit on the top by each digit on the right; record the tens part of the number at the top left of the cell and the units in the bottom right of the cell.

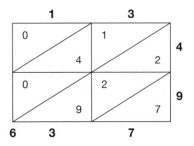

**FIGURE 10.8** Example showing the working of Gelosia algorithm.

$1 \times 4 = 04$
$3 \times 4 = 12$
$3 \times 9 = 27$
$1 \times 9 = 09$

- Add the digits diagonally starting from the bottom right to obtain the final multiplication result of 13 × 49 = 637.

Careful consideration of the place value will reveal that the only units in the result are in the bottom right-hand part of the grid. The next three digits above and to the left are the tens digits, the next diagonal represents the hundred digits and so on. This is an indication of how the algorithm works, but is not really a requirement of anyone successfully employing it.

### Year 6 numeracy hour: designing and working some 'Tudor' calculations

#### Resources

Worksheets with empty Gelosia grids.

#### Desired learning outcomes

Children will:

■ have considered possible multiplication problems people in Elizabethan times may have needed to solve; that they used a calculation method different from those taught today, which was probably introduced from India;

■ be able to compute these problems using an Elizabethan method (Gelosia).

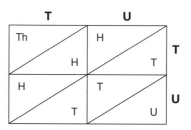

**FIGURE 10.9** Place value demonstrated in Gelosia algorithm.

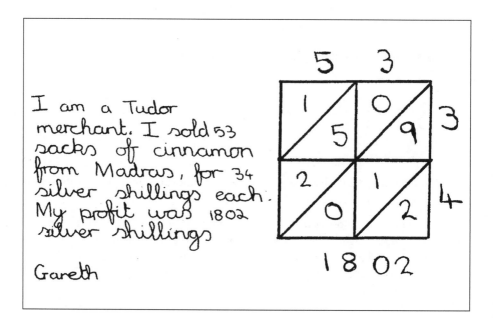

**FIGURE 10.10** 'Elizabethan problem' calculated by Gelosia algorithm.

## Mental activity

Oral multiplication questions (e.g. 7 × 3). Teacher records answers on board using lattice-type grid.

## Main session

Brainstorm possible two-digit multiplication problems people in Elizabethan times might have needed to calculate (e.g. English pirates capture Spanish mule train of 52 donkeys in Central America, each carrying 25 bags of silver coins; profit from 30 sacks of peppercorns from Madagascar sold at 63 shillings a sack; 1 quart of beer per day for a ship's crew of 45 on a 30-day voyage; distance of a 25-day voyage, average speed 25 knots each day).

## List problems on flip-chart

Demonstrate how to use the Gelosia method to calculate answers to some of the problems. Supply children with blank grids. Ask individuals or groups to work out remaining problems (or design others) using Gelosia algorithm.

## Plenary

Individuals demonstrate particular examples.

Compare results and lattices for 37 × 25 and 25 × 37. *Are the results the same? Look carefully at the tens place of the answer. How was it worked out?*

Discuss the place value aspects of this method of recording.

# Developing investigations

Clearly the teacher also has a management role in supporting and extending an investigation through a sequence of activities identified in the medium-term plan and in preparing classroom organisation to maximise existing resources, by allowing children to plan and develop computer work while away from the computer. Working together to construct and interrogate a database and discuss and interpret findings is one example of planning over time and organising limited resources.

## Databases

A database involves collecting information (records), with shared characteristics (fields), in order to look for patterns and trends. These can be recorded graphically as pie or bar charts, graphs or Venn diagrams. In the context of a historical investigation, such sources may be:

- street directories, census and parish records of births, deaths, age, sex, occupation, address;

- other statistics relating to population (illness, height, diet);

■ trade figures (cattle sold at Smithfield, price, weight, numbers);

■ information about buildings or archaeological sites with some shared characteristics (e.g. plans of Roman villas, recording shape, size, hypocausts, mosaic pavements);

■ place-name endings in an area indicating time and date of settlement (Roman, Viking, Saxon).

Such sources could be investigated through asking questions about change and about the causes and effects of change and interpreting the findings in the light of incomplete evidence, uncertainty, probability and what is known of the period. Each child can collect information for at least one record – a gravestone, for example – as part of a churchyard study, complete a 'record sheet' on paper, categorising the information in fields to ensure that s/he can structure the information in this way, then type the record onto the database. Next, when all the information has been collected, each child can fill in a second sheet setting out a question and the correct format for asking this question of the database. When children have the responses to their questions they can fill in the last part of the sheet, saying what inferences they can make from them. This tried-and-tested method ensures that everyone understands how to use the database, and has equal access to creating and interrogating it in a short time, although the complexity of the questions and sophistication of the deductions can vary considerably. Alternatively children could interrogate an existing database, each constructing a question, finding the information, then trying to interpret it. One interesting finding from a local workhouse database was that most of the inmates were described as paupers; one of the few other groups was 'female school teachers'. Deductions? Another finding was that there were few girls in the workhouse but a lot of young boys. Reasons?

## History and ICT

Children are required to use information technology sources to support and develop their enquiries in history, to select and analyse information, to share ideas as part of this process, and to organise and communicate their findings. At Key Stage 1 they might gather information (text, images, sound) from a range of sources (CD-Roms, videos, television), and use them to create databases; at Key Stage 2 these sources might be extended to include the internet, with more emphasis on selecting suitable sources, and working with others to interpret, analyse and check relevance.

This investigative process may be developed at Key Stage 1 by planning and writing instructions, exploring real or imaginary situations through simulations; at Key Stage 2 there may be more emphasis on bringing together and cross-referencing text, images, sound or tables and on reviewing ideas in the light of what others have done.

The findings of the investigation might be presented as a display at Key Stage 1; and at Key Stage 2, through writing brochures, posters, animations or internet publication on the school website, with a sense of appropriate audiences – other pupils, parents, a wider and impersonal audience.

## ICT and history: decisions

Perhaps the most appropriate ways to use ICT are as sources of information and to make it easier to organise and communicate findings, but clearly this can involve all the other key elements of historical thinking: knowledge and understanding, chronology and interpretations of the past. The wealth of opportunities to use ICT to develop children's historical understanding is daunting and clear decisions need to be made about how this is planned and organised.

## Imaginative examples of using ICT in history

Interactive whiteboards make possible the interaction between resources such as CD-Roms, website pages, Word documents and PowerPoint® slides. They can be used to model how to complete tasks, to gather the views of a class, and to shuffle up and move around text and pictures by dragging and dropping. Pupils can play with ideas using frameworks such as circles or rectangles to create interactive exercises, hierarchical ordering schemes and thinking organisers; this helps them to memorise concepts and ideas, which might not otherwise stick in their minds.

## Modelling how to analyse characteristics of a period

The teacher could model for the whole class how to sort a variety of images of a given period using one set of criteria, for example, 'rich' and 'poor'. The children could then work in groups on their laptops or desktop computers sorting the images according to other criteria: men/women, adults/children, town/country or whatever criteria they may devise. The whole class could share the work of all the groups and work out what they could deduce and infer about the period.

## Modelling concept development

A variety of images of, for example, Victorian houses, could be collected then sorted into categories: semi-detached, detached, terraced. Groups could sort according to other criteria: part of the country, materials made from, size, town or country. This would involve further research and inferences. Sharing their findings children could discuss: Why were they built? Where did the money come from? Similarities and differences in 'Victorian houses'. This would stimulate far more complex thinking than 'a model of a Victorian house'. They might then look at Victorian houses in their locality.

## Modelling sequencing activities

The teacher could model with the class the kinds of discussion and reasoning involved in deciding how to sequence, for example, types of transport since 1930. How do we decide which came next? What changes are illustrated? What caused these changes? What were the effects on people's lives? Do changes occur at equal intervals? Can we find by dating them and linking the images to a timeline?

In groups children could repeat the activity with other key features: clothes, houses, leisure activities, jobs. Then the whole class could consider interactions between changes and reasons for them. This would work well for the nineteenth century too: inventions, factories, transport, trade, town sizes.

## Modelling place-name analysis

The teacher, with the whole class, might identify place names with a particular Viking (or Saxon) ending on a map (e.g. beck – a stream). In groups the children could identify other Viking endings (e.g. thwaite, how, rigg), possibly using maps of differentiated scales. The information could be combined to find out where the Vikings settled and discuss why they chose those places.

## Using a data projector to discuss artefacts, paintings, photographs

This is particularly useful for discussing small artefacts as a class. A small coin, for example, could be put on a table and projected onto the screen. Or the detail on a larger artefact could be zoomed in on, in order to discuss: what we know, what we can guess, what we should like to know.

The teacher could show the class how to explore a painting or photograph by moving around the image with a mouse or graphic pen pointer and magnifying small details. This could be radio connected and passed around the class. Crowd scenes, such as Frith's *Railway Station*, come to mind. Or two different interpretations could be compared, contrasted, explained, or two images that illustrate changes over time. A whiteboard with a graphics tablet could be used in the same way and would be a cheaper option.

## Virtual tours using PowerPoint®

Stuart Roper's class used an interactive whiteboard to look at the Victorians through the eyes of the eyes 1851 Great Exhibition (Roper 2006). On a PowerPoint® file he placed a plan of the Crystal Palace, and a picture of the inside of the building. Pupils were asked, for example, to find something few people had used before. In turn, using their floor plans, they looked for the place on the whiteboard. Each correct spot had been given a hyperlink. Pressing on the link took pupils to a picture that they could discuss: how was it made, who used it, how did it impact on their lives? The people in the picture were made to ask questions by pressing a sound recording inside a speech bubble. The pupils were individually asked to pretend they were standing next to the person and record an answer. This model could be used imaginatively in any setting or period.

## Labelling, clueing and information gathering using PowerPoint®

This activity could be used in preparation for or as follow-up to a visit. If it follows a visit the children could take it in turns to collect their own images using a digital camera. This would teach them that there are decisions to be made about what to include and what to leave out in creating accounts and documentaries.

A hyperlink in PowerPoint® can be created by clicking and dragging a shape over the portion of the picture you want to be linked to another file. Click on the 'slide show' and on the menu click on 'action settings'. In the dialogue box that appears, highlight the 'hyperlink' option. By pressing on the scroll down arrow you are presented with the option of linking to another PowerPoint® slide or any file, page or sound. Choose where you want the link to take you to review the slide show. Once thoroughly tested, use 'line' and 'fill' colour option from the drawing tool bar to hide the link; select 'no fill' and 'no line' to make the shape completely transparent. (Hint: use very specific windows.) The shape needs to have no fill-in colour and no line. This means it is a hidden link.

This could be used for labelling, and adding information. For example, make a square over the portcullis so that when a child clicks on it a label saying 'portcullis' appears. Or it could reveal a clue, pose a question, or link to another page of information. By moving the mouse over the image at random the child may accidentally find other information.

You could create a virtual tour of the building in this way, prior to a visit, opening different doors inside a building, to familiarise children with the place or to help them to plan an investigation in advance of a visit.

## Creating a sound recording in a PowerPoint® document

Another possibility would be to insert sound into an image. Sailors on a picture of a Tudor ship might explain their diet, their role on board ship, the purpose of their voyage. An image of a job or craft that no longer exists could be explained by a former practitioner. Clips from an archive of speeches could be linked to images of the speakers.

Plug a microphone into the computer. From the menu select 'movies and sounds'. Click on 'record sound'. A dialogue box appears that allows you to record your own voice. When finished click on 'OK' and the speaker icon will appear in your file. To run as a slide show, click on the icon for playback.

## Interpretations and technology

### Using a desktop to compare interpretations

You could put visual information into a photo-editing program (Windows/digital/photo-edit/paint), in order to show why there are different interpretations of what a derelict place or ruined building may have been like in the past; for example a Roman villa, a ruined castle, a disused Second World War airfield. Children could look at a picture of the ruin, draw their own interpretations of what different parts may have been like, print these out and compare and evaluate them. (Why did you think it was like this? Which seems most likely? Why?) Then they could see artists' interpretations and compare them with their own. This is a way of scaffolding children's historical imagination.

### Making reconstructions using technology

### Key Stage 1

Hugh Moore helped Key Stage 1 children to manipulate digital photographic images to convey what they thought their own area looked like in the distant past (Moore 2004). They took a digital photograph of an area where they could see houses and a road but also plenty of trees and green. Then he used a photo-editing program (Photoshop) to cut and paste trees, green, marsh and so on all over the houses and roads. (Do not resize or crop.) The children then used PowerPoint® to 'dissolve' or 'fade' transitions to make all the buildings and roads seem to disappear from the original photograph. This was done by matching up the before and after images on consecutive slides in PowerPoint®, the modern photograph first. When children viewed the show and clicked on the mouse button to bring on the next slide, the houses and roads seemed to disappear but the areas of the photograph not worked on remained.

### Key Stage 2

Russel Tarr (2006) suggests many advantages in encouraging children to make their own digital videos. Windows PCs now come with Microsoft Moviemaker as standard and it is possible to get a digital camcorder for little over £100. Tarr suggests video-recorded role play can be used for assessment, self-assessment and peer assessment.

At Key Stage 2 children may, for example, make a video that is the culmination of a long-term role-play project, with settings, characters and events gradually built up through research. Pupils may take on roles as directors, editors, artists, musicians, camerapersons, researchers and scriptwriters as well as actors. Tarr suggests that, on a site visit, which pupils record, they will use their cameras to record key aspects of the day and furiously scribble down accompanying notes. On their return they can edit their film and so reflect upon the day more than they would otherwise.

## Then and now

Elaine Dawe, a primary school teacher, has described how she uses word-processing or desktop publishing software across the primary age range to help children compare 'old' and 'new' in their locality (Dawe 2003). Children can, for example, identify images that are old or new in a photograph and add a text box to explain why as a basis for discussion, and also for assessing progression in chronological understanding.

## 'Ready-made' resources for teachers

There are, of course, many complete kits available for the less confident, which can be modified. A resource pack from the Museum of Antiquities in Newcastle upon Tyne on Romans and Celts on the northern frontier contains lesson plans and additional resources (www.museums.ncl.ac.uk/reticulum).

## Creating a website

Coventry's Herbert Art Gallery invited Year 3 pupils to create a website about significant periods of Coventry's history (Ross 2005b). The children became 'experts', looking at notable websites and explaining the use of objects. They dressed in costume for the launch. They were consulted about their own knowledge and opinions (www.the herbert.org/learning).

## Examining artefacts on line

David Mason says that artefact databases give us access to information and stimulate children to ask genuine questions, like historians, and to discuss interpretation through whole-class investigations using a data processor or group enquiries using a computer, or by annotating the images on an interactive whiteboard (Mason 2002). He describes using www.britishmuseum.co.uk. This contains 3,000 artefacts. Children click on 'explore', then on 'compass', then type a keyword into the 'quick search' box. 'Sutton Hoo' will bring up all the artefacts associated with Sutton Hoo; a click on 'thumbnails' will tell you more about each artefact. But there is still much to conjecture about. Children's inferences about the Sutton Hoo purse can be collated under headings, for example evidence of wealth, imagination and technical skill, extensive trade links, use of a range of materials; they could speculate about the possible symbolism of the decorations. Such activity models the process of asking questions and making inferences about sources which, with time, children become able to do independently. The ability to download the British Museum into your classroom stimulates both teachers and children.

## Virtual interactive tours

These may be DVDs, for example, 'Pyramid: beyond imagination' (BBC Interactive Factual and Learning) or virtual tours on the BBC interactive website (www.bbc.co.uk/ history/multimedia_zone).

# Online resources

In the resources archive on the Historical Association website (www.history.org.uk) Terry Haydn gives excellent suggestions in using ICT in the teaching of history. By using the internet to investigate connections between past and present he says that pupils can see the relevance of history to their lives. For example if we are analysing Tudor portraits should pupils not have some contemporary portraits with which to compare them. He also says that finding ways of using the internet, television and the scanner, film, newspaper archives, the census and television in ways that will help pupils to engage with the past will also develop teachers' pedagogical knowledge in history. Newspaper archives (e.g. www.thepaperboy.com) link the many contemporary issues, such as economic change, religion and emigration to the past . Information on the internet provides original sources of all kinds and also causes pupils to challenge interpretations.

Paintings can be scanned and shown on a PowerPoint® presentation, zooming in on details. This has worked successfully, for example using Frith's *Derby Day*, or *Railway Station* to consider the different social groups, how they differ and why they may be there. Postcards, for example of artefacts in museums, can be interpreted, their materials, how they may have been made and used – or postcards showing different interpretations of seaside holidays in the past – the saucy and the serious! Some even have contemporary messages on the back: 'Top hole. Everything here just tickety boo'.

## Really simple syndication (RSS)

This is useful to capture those moments when you are watching something just perfect for your next project. If you have broadband you click on the RSS button and save the clips on your desktop.

## Podcasting and parents

Of course, parents can be involved in all of the above activities but with podcasting they can also go on visits, share parts of lessons and become involved in work at home. For example, you could make a movie of the local area that you are studying, or of a lesson or visit, with suggestions for how to follow it up, and pod cast it. It will then be permanently available on your server for anyone given access to it to download when they are able to.

## The golden rule for using ICT

The golden rule is only to use ICT if this is the best way to achieve your learning objectives. Is it allowing you to access sources that are better than is otherwise possible? Looking at a real object or painting in a museum conveys the feel, the texture, the size and weight of an artefact better than an image on screen. Is this the best way to develop children's historical thinking in a particular context? Sometimes scribbled diagrams on a whiteboard are a more immediate response to a question than a beautifully crafted PowerPoint® presentation. Sometimes drawing on a site or in a museum forces you to observe and reflect much more carefully and to remember better than a more wide-ranging video recording. Does the interactive whiteboard or a video recording stimulate more discussion than would otherwise occur or does it encourage passive viewing? On the other hand, technology is seen as 'cool'!

# Useful resources

## The Public Record Office website, the Learning Curve (www.learningcurve.gov.uk)

The Snapshots section is particularly good for Victorian homes, prisons, schools. The Learning Curve, launched in 1999, has become highly valued by teachers. Only digital cameras were ranked equally as useful as the Learning Curve, among the best ICT resources for history teachers. As well as the source material there are interactive quizzes. Pupils can, for example, joust with each other or take a tour around an Elizabethan garden.

## The British Museum Collections database (www.thebritishmuseum.org→collections database)

This can be used very effectively by pupils planning a museum exhibition on any period. They can select a range of objects to go into the museum and write explanatory notes based on the curator's notes given, or use the notes to devise a quiz or for further research.

## The Smithsonian Institution (www.si.edu)

This site has specialist exhibitions in under-resourced areas such as the African Voices Exhibition and good archaeological resources.

## The British Film Institute and the Public Record Office (www.bfi.org.uk) (www.learningcurve.gov.uk/onfilm/default.htm)

These are moving image sources. These resources are trailblazers and promise to be an exciting development. Newsreels can be found on www.britishpathe.com.

## Census material

This can be used in all sorts of ways to research and present information about, for example, occupations in a locality, life expectancy, family size, movement into the area, employment.

## Anglo Saxon burials (www.ucl.ac.uk/archaeology/research/projects/ tribalhidage)

This is the site of a project in progress that will provide, among other things, a data base of Saxon grave goods. Pupils could make graphs of numbers of different types of grave goods, brooches, rings, javelins and so on, and make inferences about the beliefs of the people buried with them. This would link well to mathematics (see p. 48).

## Manuscripts

The virtual classrooms on this site enable schools to book sessions at Key Stages 1 and 2 that allow pupils to engage with documents in the National Archives with interactive online support.

## Other websites

Steve Mynard, runs living history sessions and workshops for teachers. He recommends the following websites:

- www.britarch.ac.uk/yac the home page of the Young Archaeologists Club;

- www.bbc.co.uk/history/forkids/ for its loads of interactive material;

- www.spartacus.schoolnet.co.uk for your own research purposes;

- www.seasidehistory.co.uk for its photographs and archive material;

- www.local-history.co.uk.

# Support for teachers

The Historical Association (www.history.org.uk) offers excellent support for the teaching of history 5–11, including the opportunity for teachers to share good ideas and experiences and ask questions.

English Heritage (www.english-heritage.org.uk/education) helps teachers to use the environment as a resource, supported by a huge resource catalogue of books, videos and photopacks.

# Museums and galleries online

### Virtual Library Museums Page (http://icom.museum/vlmp/)

Suggested for regional studies.

### Museum of London (www.museumoflondon.org)

This site has a rich variety of sources, videos and pocket histories online.
Peat warns about the downloading time, inactive links, and the importance of teachers allowing themselves plenty of time before deciding what to use with pupils.

## Theory linking history and art

One of the reviewers asked to comment on the proposal for this second edition said that s/he 'would like to see more about links with art'. Although it is beyond the scope of this book to examine all cross-curricular links with history in depth, I have always enjoyed using art in different ways as part of a history topic and so have succumbed to this suggestion.

First in art and design children should learn about the similarities and differences between the work of artists, crafts people and designers in different times and cultures, for example photographers, sculptors, architects and textile designers.

# Visual images as sources

Visual images, paintings, sculpture, photographs, cartoons from past times are important historical sources. They are embedded in the narrative of history. Simon Schama's television series, *Power of Art*, demonstrates the combined educational power of art and history.

Arnheim (1970) says that every visual pattern, whether a painting, building, ornament or chair, makes some statement about the nature of human existence. This may be a brief statement but it is worth reflecting on what he means by this.

# Interpreting images as sources

## Power relationships

Gombrich (1982) discusses how strong feelings can be displayed by images. For example, *The Kneeling Captive* (Biblioteque Nationale Paris) demonstrates through posture the stark contrast in statues of imperial Rome between figures of authority and submission. Can you think of other power relationships shown visually?

## Questioning images

Innumerable images of thirteenth-century saints, donors and worthies in churches, with their folded hands, evoke piety. Remember Samantha's comments on the image of a praying knight in a brass-rubbing and her vivid drawing of him on the battlefield (pp. 152–3)?

## Well-known stories – personal emotions or symbols?

Greek vases illustrate familiar narratives while nineteenth-century domestic paintings tell stories about strong feelings, jealousy, fear, love, loss. Images of Christ, saints or parables in stained glass windows in churches turn metaphor into symbolism.

## Connecting with thoughts and feelings in the past

Philosophers in ancient Greece highlighted the importance of the visual image. Plato expressed this poetically, saying that the gentle fire that warms the human soul flows out through the eyes in a stream of light and establishes a bridge between the observer and the observed object over which light rays travel through the eyes to the soul.

Collingwood (1925, 1938) was a philosopher who wrote extensively about both art and history; he was an archaeologist and a historian. The connection between art and history was clear to him. Art is a personally constructed interpretation and so reflects the culture that led to its creation. It is not possible to understand the thoughts of people in the past by describing their actions. But, Collingwood claims, through looking at a piece of art the artist and the spectator come to share certain mental states with the artist.

Dewey (1932) similarly said that through an expressive object the artist and the active observer encounter each other, their material and mental environments and their culture at large. This demonstrates the connection between art and everyday experience. Dewey says that to emphasise what is aesthetic is to emphasise a manifestation of a record, a manifestation of a civilisation and of the quality of that civilisation.

## Face value or values?

Interpreting a visual source can help us to move from the concrete to the abstract. Arnheim (1970) points out that a picture combines sensory appearance and reasoning. A portrait may be of a particular individual, portrayed as having particular physical characteristics and personality but is also a symbol displaying more. He explains how paintings and sculptures that portray figures, objects, actions in a more or less realistic style make no sense of what life was like in the past until the viewer can read what each symbolises. This requires thought, language and discussion. Which of two images of nineteenth-century harvest tells us more about what life was like for those portrayed: a ragged and hungry labourer taking a break and munching bread or a painting of a rejoicing, rosy-cheeked group sitting among the harvested corn? This is not is a simple question.

A realistic portrait of Winston Churchill, for example, may portray him as a stout, thoughtful, elderly statesman but it may also be a symbol of more abstract qualities of the period: of oppression and resistance, determination and inner containment. Frith's *Railway Station* describes the departure platform at Paddington Station but it also a symbol from which to deduce abstract concepts: causes of the Industrial Revolution – coal and iron mining, steam power, speed, social mobility; and its effects – railways, communication, travel, trade. A photograph of a Victorian lady on a bicycle, taken in a studio, tells something about the importance of the invention to her, the freedom and mobility and independence it gave her, and about the changing lives of women.

## Visual images promote learning in history

Bruner (1963) stressed the importance of using imagery (iconic representation) in such a way that the pervading powerful ideas and attitudes in a discipline are given a central role. In 1966 he emphasised the need to understand the questions to ask about an image in order to do this and said that this enabled children to transfer their thinking independently to new similar material and so avoid dependence on facts and memory. Once you know how to read a portrait or landscape you can both remember the painting and transfer the skill to understanding other paintings.

Charlotte Mason (1842–1923) had a great interest in history, art and literature and suggested that children should be shown typical examples of, for example, medieval windows: one an early Gothic lancet window (c. twelfth century) and one a perpendicular Gothic window (c. fifteenth century). By storing these images children can could build their own image banks and work out the ages of other buildings they see with similar style windows. In *The Original Home Schooling Series* (Mason 1993, vol. 4: 38) she explains that, 'Great artists, builders and musicians have the power of showing us their visions and we, by a similar power of imagination, may share their visions.'

Klausmeier (1979) discusses the role of images in concept formation. He says that images are stored. Shared characteristics can be abstracted, new information added and generalisations made. The more Georgian buildings we see the more we understand about the characteristics of Georgian architecture.

Arnheim (1970) similarly links visual perception and thought. He says that by collecting images of kinds of qualities, kinds of objects and kinds of events the mind grasps what they have in common and so organises concepts. What are the common factors in images of 'a mob' or 'a riot'? How many images of pride or of grief can you recollect? By reflecting on our 'image banks' we are able to make connections between people and events across generations and cultures.

## Art, history and personal development

Learning through visual images prompts individual responses, which enrich and enhance a pupil's development. Egan (1992) emphasised the importance of forming and articulating vivid images in teaching and learning. Bruner (1963), Arnheim (1970), Dewey (1932) and Collingwood (1938) provide a firm foundation for bridging art and history, since they understand the centrality of history in the curriculum which aims to educate the whole child.

Gardner (1990: 31), having introduced his theory of multiple intelligences, concluded that the most promising way of integrating the various forms of learning is to 'situate them'. When pupils see adults moving between various forms of knowing, combined in natural situations they too are participating in a rich, engaging project. Here are some examples of adults working with children and moving between art and history.

## Understanding history through making art

### Developing understanding and skills in art and design

Children develop skills and understanding in art and design through first-hand observation, experiences, imagination and exploring ideas. They investigate a range of materials and processes used in art, craft and design, for example print making, drawing, painting, textiles, sculpture. They should try out different tools and techniques, in order to represent observations, ideas and feelings, through designing and making images and artefacts. They should learn about colour, pattern and texture, line and tone, shape form and space. They should learn through investigating different aspects of art craft and design during visits to museums galleries and sites and the locality.

## Examples of children recording and making deductions and inferences about sources through art

This section allows me to take a trip down memory lane and remember some of the art and history combinations I have worked on with children over the years. By engaging in the processes of art and design children can also develop their historical thinking.

Interpreting sources requires close and detailed observation. Drawing artefacts and buildings and especially drawing details and decoration engages children. It helps them to focus and concentrate on an object for a long period. This both raises questions and generates ideas and also records the object for discussion and further research at a later time.

## Drawing

I have many photographs of children with clipboards sitting on museum floors in front of showcases, drawing with immense concentration. Sadly the only remaining example of such work is an Iron Age pot (Figure 10.11) drawn in the British Museum by N.B. (I remember who you are N.B.!).

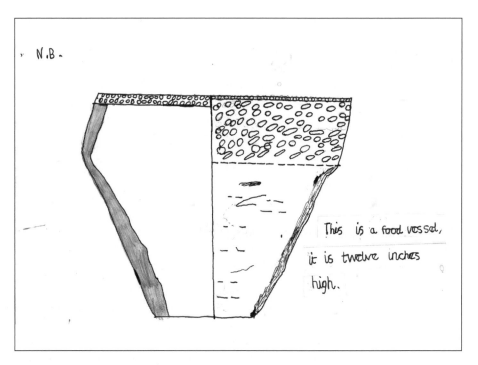

**FIGURE 10.11** Drawing of an Iron Age Pot in the British Museum.

## Silk screen printing

I was responsible for art in one of my schools, so had fun buying new equipment and experimenting with different techniques. One of these was screen printing. This technique involves a wooden frame with fine gauze stretched and pinned across it. The gauze is blocked out by painting a glue onto it or sticking brown paper onto it. Then a squeegee (I love the name!) is used to spread the dye, which penetrates the unblocked areas.

Our first endeavour was to screen print lengths of material with a repeating eighteenth-century design based on a Georgian church and houses in a Georgian square. We had seen the church and the square on a class visit to Georgian London and taken photographs of them. We based the silhouettes on the photographs. We had also read the parish records, showing who had lived in the square in Georgian times. Because of the visit, the photographs and the records the screen print was based soundly on evidence. (We also found some broken eighteenth-century clay pipes in the square, which was an added bonus!) The silk screen printed fabric was finally made into curtains for the classroom.

I still possess one example of screen printing, as it was used as a textile drape for displays. It is based on the border of a Roman mosaic floor we had seen on a site visit and photographed. The screen print was remarkably easy to make as the lines were straight so that brown sticky tape could be used to block out the screen.

## Spinning, weaving, dyeing

Having found out, from a visit to Butser Iron Age village reconstruction, that the Iron Age people spun wool from their Soay sheep and wove it into checked patterns, we had a go at spinning with spindles. The wool was provided by a local farmer. First it had to be carded so that the threads all lay in the same direction. Then a thread was twisted and attached to the spindle. This was drawn out as the spindle spun like a top on the floor and the hooks on each thread joined together. That's the theory anyhow. We did not produce a large quantity of wool. But we had enough to weave on two small hand-made looms (based on the design seen at Butser) and to dye one piece of cloth with onions and one with blackberries. The plaid pattern was beyond us.

## Pottery

We had a kiln so had lots of opportunities to make replica Iron Age food vessels, with designs as recorded in the British Museum. The class who studied the Georgians also made a model of St Martin in the Fields church, glazed in white. Another pottery success was a replica Roman board game, which involved clay balls, glazed in different colours.

## Embroidery

While working on the Elizabethan project some of the girls found designs for Elizabethan embroideries. They enlarged parts of the design and drew them on white cotton. It was interesting to overhear them one day discussing exactly which of the many shades of green thread was the best match for a particular leaf.

## Lino cuts and scraper board

This technique lent itself particularly well to copying or imitating Tudor woodcuts and made very effective designs for the broad sheets describing the approach of the

Armada. Some were cartoons (Figures 8.4 and 8.5). Others included gruesome warnings of what would happen to Catholics who were caught.

Other printing ventures included marbled paper to make frames for children's sepia printed 'Victorian' photographs (with the addition of some seashells for good measure) and printing 'Victorian wallpaper'. Some Year 6 children used scraps of velvet, silk, lace or beads, as found in a Victorian pattern book. Others made prints with cardboard cut in the shapes of leaves, birds, fruits and vines inspired by William Morris designs. This was an interesting way of illustrating how patterns, colours and textures reflected changes in nineteenth-century design.

### Leather artefacts

I particularly remember, having been given a bag of soft leather off-cuts, the 'Iron Age shoes' and 'Iron Age bags', which were part of the Iron Age display.

### Combining sources

The artwork based on studying sources can contribute to a summative display of work related to a topic, beside the source, with deductions and inferences about the source and how the art was made.

## Examples of children creating interpretations through art

Historical interpretations, constructed through art, may be paintings or drawings of an event based on evidence. Or they may be models, possibly based on incomplete evidence, part of the floor of a Roman villa, post holes of an Iron Age hut, or a reconstruction of a room. One class collected Victorian artefacts to recreate a Victorian room in the corner of the school foyer, which included a Victorian armchair, and birds in a glass dome, donated by the head teacher.

### Reconstructions illustrating events

Charlotte Mason described how she encouraged her pupils to listen to a contemporary description of a historical event then asked each child to illustrate the story based on evidence (1993, vol. 1: 292–4). Their drawings not only showed extraordinary power of visualising:

> What they visualise they know. It is their life's possession. The children's drawings are psychologically interesting, showing what various and sometimes obscure points appeal to the mind of a child and also that children have the same intellectual pleasure as persons of cultivated mind in working out new hints and suggestions.

Mason describes how children who had been reading *Julius Caesar* were asked to make a drawing of their favourite scene. The resulting interpretations are fascinating. One girl focuses on architecture.

You look through an arch, which leads into a side street, and, in the foreground, Antony stands on a platform at the head of a flight of marble steps. Antony's attitude expresses indignation and scorn. Below, is a crowd of Romans wearing the toga, whose attitudes show various shades of consternation and dismay. Behind, is Antony's servant in uniform, holding his master's horse; and on the platform, in the rear of Antony, lies Caesar, with the royal purple thrown over him. The chief value of the drawing, as a drawing, is that it tells the tale.

Another girl, for example, draws Calpurnia begging Caesar not to go to the Senate. Caesar stands armed and perturbed, while Calpurnia holds his outstretched hand with both of hers as she kneels before him, her face raised in entreaty; her loose blue night-robe and long golden hair give colour to the picture. Mason concludes that in these original illustrations we get an example of the various images that present themselves to the minds of children during the reading of a great work.

More recently Yapici Dilek (2010) has investigated students' ability to combine visual and historical thinking skills. She found that drawings were an effective way to access pupils' historical thinking and that artwork which visualises the past supports historical problem-solving. For example, having studied written and visual sources, pupils were able to convey their understanding of chronological changes in the position of women in Turkey, and their feelings during different periods, through succinct drawings with captions showing changes in body language, facial expressions and dress. In a series of drawings a boy drew a couple under the Ottoman monarchy, in which the man is showing the woman the door. She wears the veil and chador. This illustrates that women were second-class citizens with no divorce rights. A drawing of the early twentieth century shows a woman campaigning for women's rights, wearing a chador but no veil. In a third drawing of the Republican era the boy illustrates women's acquisition of political rights showing a picture of a woman deciding who to vote for and of another woman electioneering.

Or an interpretation of events may be recorded as a picture story; for example, Figure 10.12 retells the first part of the story of the siege of Troy, enthusiastically drawn by an eight-year-old who found writing difficult.

## Model making

I recall two doll's houses made by Key Stage 1 children in cardboard boxes. One was 'an old doll's house' based on a picture of a Victorian doll's house seen in the Museum of Childhood. The other was 'my house', which featured electric lights run from a battery. These models were made to demonstrate time and change, similarities and differences, now and then. Another model that springs to mind is the timber frame house described on page 88, which was made in balsa wood to explore the strength of different roof truss designs in a Tudor house the class had visited. By contrast the Tudor model house (p. 129) was made to explore the history and mathematics, rather than science, technology and historical understanding.

# The Trojan Horse

Long ago in ancient Greece there lived a man called Ulysses and his wife Penelope and his son Telemachus

One day a princess called Helen was captured by a foreign prince and taken to Troy

Ulysses and the other Greek Kings gathered their armies. Together they sailed to Troy to rescue Helen

The Greeks fought many battles with the Trojans but they could not capture Troy. They camped on the beach outside the city and tried to break down the huge walls

**FIGURE 10.12** Beginning of a picture story of the siege of Troy.

## 'Set design'

In this category I remember the imaginative sets designed and made by Year 6 children who were working on a Victorian topic that included a performance of *Mary Poppins*. On another occasion it was *Oliver*. A similar reconstruction was of a Stuart room, after visiting the Geffrye Museum, which has a series of rooms from particular periods. One Year 5 group decided that they would recreate the Stuart room using two screens and a corner of the classroom. They did this very effectively by projecting slides from the museum onto the four walls drawing them in detail then painting them. Then they borrowed some Stuart costumes from a local dramatic society and put these on stands in the room. They had created their own 'museum', which led to informative talks, to story writing and drama.

A similar reconstruction was of a Greek temple in the corner of the room using drama blocks as steps and huge corrugated card tubes painted white, wound around with ivy for the pillars. The portico was decorated with a genuine design enlarged on the photocopier then printed in sequence. This temple housed research on Greek gods and myths.

A third reconstruction was a Stone Age cave. A slide of a cave painting was magnified onto a large wall using a projector. Then the animals were painted using oxides from the pottery area. The cave entrance was decorated with branches and leaf rubbings. This prompted various dramas and story scripts over a long period.

## Practical details

You may be wondering how so much time could be justified on such work. It was interesting that most of the ideas came from groups of children themselves. Since it was their initiative most of the construction was done at playtimes and lunch times or done at home. Not all the children would be involved and participants drifted in and out of the project. But such pupil-initiated ideas both stemmed from and generated an enormous amount of dialogue, presentations, explanations, questions, planned research and story writing.

## Book making

Finally it was the tradition of the school for each child to collate all their work on a project in a handmade book (excellent for assessment). The cover design, as in any expensive cloth-covered book, would reflect the contents; for example a black paper silhouette design might reflect the Georgian project, or a scraperboard diagram of a spinning jenny might decorate a project on the Industrial Revolution. (Parents were delighted with these. One parent told me recently that she still had them, stored them all in her attic.)

# Conclusion

This chapter has considered what the *Cambridge Review* described as dimensions of the curriculum, which require time: time for reflection, discussion and problem solving. And it suggested links between history and other subjects, in particular literacy, mathematics, ICT and art, based on case studies, which demonstrate how working across curriculum areas made for effective time management.

# References

Arnheim, R. (1970) *Visual Thinking.* London: Faber & Faber.

Bage, G. (1999) *Narrative Matters, Teaching and Learning History Through Story.* Lewes, UK: Falmer Press.

Baldwin, G. (2003) 'Questions you have always wanted to ask about . . . historical interpretations', *Primary History*, 33, 20–2.

Belloc, H. (1991) *Matilda, Who Told Lies and was Burned to Death.* London: Red Fox.

Black, M. (1992) *The Medieval Cookbook.* London: British Museum Press.

Bruner, J.S. (1963) *The Process of Education.* New York: Vintage Books.

Bruner, J.S. (1966) *Towards a Theory of Instruction.* Cambridge, MA: Harvard University Press.

Claire, H. (2004) 'Oral history: a powerful tool or a double edged sword?' *Primary History*, 38, 20–3.

Collingwood, R.G. (1925) *Outlines of a Philosophy of Art.* Oxford: Oxford University Press.

Collingwood, R.G. (1938) *The Principles of Art.* Oxford: Oxford University Press.

Cooper, H. (1996) 'Threat of the basics instinct', *Times Educational Supplement*, History Extra, 6.

Cooper, H. (1998) 'Writing about history in the Early Years', in P. Hoodless (ed.) *History and English in the Primary School.* London: Routledge, 157–78.

Cooper, H. and Twiselton, S. (2000) *Art and Artists: Impressionism: reading for information.* Leamington Spa: Scholastic.

Counsell, C. and Thomson, K. (1997) *Life in Tudor Times.* Cambridge: Cambridge University Press.

Dawe, E. (2003) 'From past to present', *Times Educational Supplement*, 4 July.

Deary, T. (2004) *Horrible Histories: Villainous Victorians.* London: Scholastic.

Dewey, J. (1932) *Art as Experience.* New York: Berkley Publishing Group.

DfEE/QCA (1999) *National Curriculum for England and Wales: handbook for primary teachers in England.* London: DfEE/QCA.

Egan, K. (1992) *Imagination in Teaching and Learning.* London: Routledge.

English Heritage (1998a) *Story Telling at Historic Sites.* Northampton: English Heritage.

English Heritage (1998b) *A Teacher's Guide to Maths and the Historic Environment.* London: English Heritage.

Foreman, M. (1995) *After the War is Over.* London: Pallion.

Frank, A. (1989) *The Diary of Anne Frank.* London: Pan Books.

Gardner, H. (1990) *Art Education and Human Development.* Santa Monica, CA: The Getty Centre for Education in the Arts.

Gombrich, E.H. (1982) *The Image and the Eye: studies in the psychology of pictorial representation.* Oxford: Phaidon.

Hewitt, M. and Harris, A. (1992) *Talking Time: a guide to oral history for schools.* London: Learning by Design, Tower Hamlets Education.

Hoodless, P. (ed.) (1998) *History and English in the Primary School.* London: Routledge.

Howarth, K. (1998) *Oral History: a handbook*. Stroud: Sutton Publishing.

Huggins, M. (1997) 'Helping primary pupils access archive material in the context of Tudor local history', *Teaching History*, 87, 31–6.

Klausemeier , H.J. (1979) *Cognitive learning and Development*. Cambridge, MA: Ballinger.

Lewis, M. and Wray, D. (1998) 'Bringing literacy and history closer together', *Primary History*, 20, 11–13.

Lively, P. (1994) *Oleander, Jacaranda: a childhood perceived*. London: Penguin Modern Classics.

Mason, C. (1993) *Charlotte Mason's Original Home Schooling Series, Vols 1–6* (www.ambleside online.org).

Mason, D. (2002) 'Hoodunnit', *Times Educational Supplement*, 15 November.

McEwan, I. (1985) *Rose Blanche*. London: Jonathan Cape.

Moore, H. (2004) 'Ancient history: things to do and questions to ask', in H. Cooper (ed.) *Exploring Time and Place Through Play: Foundation Stage to Key Stage 1*. London: David Fulton Publishers.

Nichol, J. (1998) 'Literacy through history project', *Primary History*, 20, 14–17.

Nichol, J. (2000) 'Literacy, text-genres and history: reading and learning from difficult and challenging texts', *Primary History*, 24, 13–18.

Pearce, P. (1976) *Tom's Midnight Garden*. London: Puffin.

Pennington, K. (2004) *Tread Softly*. London: Hodder Children's Books.

Prince, A. (2004) *Anne Boleyn and Me: the diary of Elinor Valjean*. Leamington Spa: Scholastic.

Redfern, A. (1996) *Talking in Class: oral history and the National Curriculum*. Colchester: Oral History Society.

Redmond, D. (2003) *Joshua Cross and the Queen's Conjuror*. Cambridge: Wizard Books.

Roper, S. (2006) 'Crystal clear', *Times Educational Supplement*, 13 January.

Ross, S. (2004) 'Watch me write', *Times Educational Supplement*, 17 August.

Ross, S. (2005a) *Tales of the Dead: Ancient Rome*. London: Dorling Kindersley.

Ross, S. (2005b) 'Paperback writers', *Times Educational Supplement*, 25 February.

Sendak, M. (1970) *Where the Wild Things Are*. Harmondsworth: Penguin.

Sivers, B. (2004) *Jammy Dodgers on the Run*. Basingstoke: Macmillan Children's Books.

Tarr, R. (2006) 'Film focus', *Times Educational Supplement*, 17 March.

Taylor, J. (2001) 'History with a twist', *Times Educational Supplement*, 30 November.

Umansky, K. (2004) *The Silver Spoon of Solomon Snow*. Harmondsworth: Puffin.

Walsh, B. (2003) 'A complex empire: National Archives Learning Curve takes on the British Empire', *Teaching History*, 112, 22–7.

Westall, R. (1975) *The Machine Gunners*. London: Macmillan.

Wray, D. and Medwell, J. (1998) *Teaching English in Primary Schools: a handbook of teaching strategies and key ideas in literacy*. London: Letts Educational.

Yapici Dilek, G. (2010) 'Visual thinking in teaching history: reading the visual thinking skills of twelve year-old pupils in Istanbul', *Education*, 38(3), 257–74.

# Principles, theory and practice

# 11

# Creativity, innovation and research-based practice

Part 1 of this book began with small-scale research studies exploring ways of teaching the three strands of historical enquiry. Interestingly they were not all undertaken by English history educators. They included studies from Portugal, Turkey, Malta and Brazil, influenced by previous English research. Meanwhile history in English primary schools became marginalised. Yet many teachers have continued to develop innovative practice, as is evident from the articles quoted in this book that they have contributed to *Primary History*. Classroom-based research, which explores new approaches, analyses, evaluates and reflects on them, comes from freedom for teachers to take professional responsibility for the timetable and curriculum and freedom from fear of taking risks.

## Doing classroom-based research

### Deciding on a question

This need not take extra time. The 'data' is collected as part of normal teaching and its analysis will inform future practice (both yours and, if you publish it, that of others) in a more precise and useful way than unfocused reflection. Identify a small aspect of your teaching or children's learning that you want to explore. This will probably have arisen from something that puzzled you. It may be just one child's misconception. Why did they think that? How did you or could you intervene to take their thinking further? It could be a careful consideration of the evidence you collect from different children for summative level assessments; does this raise any questions? It could be keeping notes on how you make your own subject knowledge more secure; what is least time-consuming and most effective: internet information about content, reference books, doing research at your own level by, as a starting point perhaps, visiting a site before you take your class there, or watching a film on a historical subject made for adults and deciding you would like to find out more? It could be working with a practitioner to inform your subject knowledge as a leisure activity! One of my colleagues decided to join an archaeological dig at Hadrian's Wall, before teaching a unit on the Romans in Britain. It may be tracking the process of finding out how children and their parents work together: who finds out what? from where? (The dialogue between a child and a parent can be fascinating.) Or what did children learn from a living history reconstruction? All these opportunities arise through normal practice. Jotting down ongoing notes can turn into a fascinating process of discovery.

### Keep it small scale

Your 'data' may simply be a discussion with or observation of one child, or even with one parent. You are more likely to get interesting and manageable data from this than from talking to a class or even a group. Often this gives you insights far beyond the focus child and raises further questions. It is not necessary to involve everybody.

## Collecting the 'data'

'Data' can be collected by note taking, tick lists, using writing frames, tape recording or video recording. You may choose to ask 'semi-structured' questions – an open question followed by two or three key questions, but which allow open responses. You may observe children, identifying specific things to focus on: how they work together on a particular task, their roles, how they support, extend, correct each other. Video recordings take time to watch later but often reveal things that you did not notice at the time – and children and parents enjoy both making and watching them.

## Analysing the 'findings'

Remember what the question was that you were investigating. Perhaps it was the focuses of an observation, the sections on a writing frame. The question, and how you went about collecting the data, will have provided categories of information. Take each category in turn. There are almost certainly significant similarities, differences, or points that spring out. So now you can jot the information for each category under new subheadings. Gradually a picture begins to emerge that is multi-layered, meaningful, useful and interesting.

## Don't keep it to yourself!

Send your 'study' to *Primary History*, or the *Times Educational Supplement*. I speak from experience. Light years ago I was 'sent' on an afternoon computing course to learn how to make a database, using the cumbersome technology of the time. I felt my performance was so feeble that I decided to 'show them'. My class and I made databases of stone circles, Iron Age huts and Roman villas, using plans in an archaeology book, and decided on common fields to record and investigate. Next week I amazed everyone! I wrote about this and sent the article to *Junior Education* – who published it. I also sent a synopsis of my dissertation, written on a diploma course, to *Teaching History*. 'It may not be wise to leap into print so soon,' my tutor warned. But it was!

This chapter gives the flavour of research that I undertook as a Year 4 class teacher. It was an attempt to apply constructivist learning theories to thinking skills in history, through cross-curricular activities, site visits and class lessons teaching children to ask questions about sources, in order to build up the 'big picture'. This turned out to be quite a large study (Cooper 1991). Since 'invaders and settlers' is a popular history topic I shall begin with some Year 4 children's deductions, inferences and questions about Saxon sources they had not previously seen, then in Chapter 12 go on to describe other aspects of the study that could stimulate ideas for further classroom research.

## Discussion of Saxon sources

### Visual source: illuminated manuscript of harvest

This was a British Museum manuscript, F 21985, made into a slide. It shows one man apparently in charge of three bowed peasants, two carrying grain and one a sickle, and three others loading a two-wheeled cart. Children related details in it to abstract concepts learned in previous units: agriculture, community, communication, trade, crops, transport.

### Agriculture

In their 'archaeological reports', children talked about crops, farming methods and the cycle of the farming year.

> The people seem to be cutting logs and transporting them – maybe to trade them – if they live near a forest.
>
> They had flour, so they had bread.
>
> They could be putting animals and crops in barns. It's cold. It's wintertime.
>
> They had carts and sickles; they could shape wood and metal. They could move things around.
>
> There is only a small hole in the cart to pull with. It might have been pulled by a person not a horse.
>
> They carry loads on their back – which must be sore.
>
> Where did they store things?
>
> The cart could also be used to take a body and grave goods to the burial ground.

## Social organisation

Children referred to the jobs people are doing and the relationship between them. They recognised that the man on the left appears to be in charge and discuss what he is doing.

> We can guess the man on the rock is the leader. He looks as if he's telling them what to do. Therefore they had important people. The men carrying things are slaves – or they might be the king's servants.
>
> I think they had money, but not like ours. They learned to trade money for something like food.
>
> They are working in groups; they have got the jobs sorted out.
>
> There are two men on the cart. One is higher up and one is carrying a weight – perhaps a sheep. They are working together.
>
> Only men are working. Is the work too hard for the women?

## Communication

There are various suggestions about the meaning of the writing.

> Is it Latin? If so was it learned from the Romans?
>
> I guess it was learned through monks. I guess the monks wrote it. Therefore it would be Latin. Monks were taught to read and write in neat writing.
>
> Therefore they could write calendars and they could tell the months of the year and they kept in touch with the date.
>
> I think the picture goes with the writing to give the reader a clearer picture in his mind. It shows they had imagination.
>
> Yes but since it was done in Saxon times it is probably true.
>
> They could draw and write. Therefore they had literature.

# Plan: The Saxon church at Cirencester

## The building

The children had previously learned that St Augustine brought Roman-style Christianity from Rome to Canterbury (Wilson 1976).

The church apse design is Roman. Therefore St Augustine had preached and made that part Christian.

They could build proper buildings. Therefore they probably picked up ideas from the Romans.

The apse shows they could curve the end of a church.

Did the Romans live here before because I think I have heard of a Roman villa in Cirencester?

If St Augustine came here – because of the Roman bit – have all the churches round here got a semi-circle bit?

## The people

It's big. It could hold a lot of people. Therefore the population must have been high.

I guess it had more adjuncts that haven't been excavated.

It might have had more adjuncts because more and more Christians came to Cirencester. Maybe more Saxons were becoming Christians.

In some churches there is an echo. If it was crowded it might be very noisy.

Who paid for it?

We can guess a lord built it. Therefore he must be powerful. So they had powerful lords.

It must have taken time to build. I wonder what they used in the meantime?

They needed a church and they worked hard for something they really wanted.

Did it have more to it because I would like to see it being excavated. Did it have a graveyard?

Was it used for more than one purpose? The little rooms might be for discussing things.

They could share things and be part of a group.

Some of the rooms might be for storing bread and fuel.

I wonder if they had bells.

And finally:

I wonder if the monks enjoyed their life reading and writing because I get tired of it.

## Map: Croydon in Saxon times

The children were given a simple map that showed the meanings of Saxon place name endings (e.g. don/den, valley; stead, farmstead; ing, the people of). It shows chalk downs, the rivers and modern settlements along the spring-line a little way up the sides of the downs where the clay in the valley meets the chalk downs or on the top of the downs. The children had discussed the significance of the geology on settlements during, a visit to the downs with the field studies advisor. They learned that the settlements were along the spring-line between the clay and the chalk, and dated some of the hedges to 800 years. (Pace 100 yards; every new species represents 100 years.)

In discussing the map, children used their knowledge from maps discussed in a lesson, that the Saxons sailed down the tributaries of the Thames, and that settlement depends on suitable soil for crops and on a water supply.

> We know where they settled from the place names . . .
>
> Croydon is on a river and a spring. Therefore they might have a bigger community.
>
> How many springs do you get to one settlement?
>
> Are there any deserted settlements?
>
> They needed plenty of water because in them days they had to plough the fields and it was hard.
>
> I wonder why they moved to another place and if they sent someone on ahead to find a good place.
>
> We know that, unlike the Stone Age and the Iron Age they farmed on clay. Therefore they had more sophisticated ploughs.
>
> I guess there would be a track running between the settlements. Maybe they sort of banded together to protect each other.

## Written source: *Beowulf* (lines 824–38)

The children had read other extracts from *Beowulf* previously and discussed the idea that it is a folk tale idealising courage of earlier warrior bands in which Grendel personifies danger.

### Attempts to understand individual words

> 'Made good his boast' means he boasts for a reason – to be popular and get support for his next encounter.

'He had come from afar' means it took a long time to get there.

Why did they call it a 'gable roof'?

## Applying learned concepts

The children did not necessarily use the abstract concepts they had learned but used a range of subordinate concepts from their own vocabulary. Many of them described Beowulf as 'a hero', or as 'good, strong, clever, famous'.

## Significance of writing in Saxon times

It is a Saxon poem. Therefore they had different forms of writing. Beowulf was made up. Therefore it would have been a folk tale or a legend. There may have been this famous warrior.

Was it a lesson to people?

We know the Saxons could write. They probably had people who could write for the rich people. Stories meant a lot to them.

They may have made things up to make the story good to hear. They put the monster in the story. Therefore it is made up.

## Attempt to make a distinction between truth and fiction

It was probably a famous warrior. Therefore it would be partly true. It could have been set in a real place. Therefore they would know about it.

Where is Heorot, because I'd like to know if it was a real place.

It came from Denmark. Therefore a Saxon who knew it off by heart introduced it to the Saxons in England. Therefore it was passed around countries and settlements. Tales like Beowulf passed around countries.

The bit about the monster is not true because no monster ever lived. Anyone who saw him whole was eaten!

I would like to know how many times it had been changed because it would be interesting to know how it started off.

Why make it up? Because it sounds good!

### Understanding feelings, attitudes and values of another society

Grendel can't be true. Therefore it's a folk tale. Therefore in some ways we know the Saxons' beliefs.

Some people might have thought Grendel was going to come at night ... Therefore they might have been scared.

Beowulf was very brave. I guess they liked brave, strong people.

I know for certain it is a symbol of fighting. It must have been through lots of places. Therefore they wanted us to know they had courage.

I guess it was a symbol for fighting and braveness.

I guess they wanted more land for their crops so they had to fight before they settled. Was Grendel a monster or just an enemy?

I guess Beowulf was under God's power and he might have God's power and feelings in him.

Why did Beowulf like vengeance? Because he liked fighting?

This is a story of vengeance. Therefore Beowulf was a hero. They must have been glad they'd got Beowulf.

The concepts emphasised certainly identify characteristics of people arriving and settling in a new land.

## History/literacy links

A curriculum for English may include reading myths and legends, poetry from oral and literary traditions and texts from other cultures and traditions that represent different voices and forms. *Beowulf* satisfies these conditions and is a springboard for a wider understanding of heroes and heroines: the crucial journey, task or sacrifice. This can lead on to current heroes. Who are they? As part of a Key Stage 2 study of unit Invaders and Settlers, *Beowulf* identifies the values central to Anglo Saxon culture in the same way as the Norse myths do for the Vikings: family kinship, friendship, moral and physical courage, ritual, material pleasures and love of life. Alexander (1973) provides a version of *Beowulf* suitable for children.

## Construct your own Saxon village

Sue Bingham (2004) describes a project in which her school built an Anglo Saxon house in the school grounds. They contacted 'real archaeologists' through the East Sussex Museum. They helped them to make shingles and wattle walls, to dye, spin and weave wool, to make pots, to use a pole lathe to make furniture, to create a fire and make Anglo Saxon meals, even cooking bread in a clay oven. She says that she felt the project improved the children's questioning and problem-solving skills, their communication and mathematical skills, developed their imagination, their team-making skills and their ICT, through recording, researching and communicating with the experts by email. Children were able to follow the learning paths that interested them.

## A re-enactment

If you are in Viking territory, Kim Seddorn may be the man you should contact (Starkey 2004). As he and his companion-in-arms, equipped with specially made and authentic mail shirt, sword and helmet, shields and spears, advance towards them, children have been known to flee in terror! Kim Seddorn works in the Bristol area (kimseddorn @blueyonder.co.uk). Regia Anglorum is a nationwide company and will despatch the nearest Viking (or Saxon) to your school (www.regia.org). An alternative perspective is provided by Louisa Gidney (aka Sister Wisberger) (www.rentapeasant.co.uk). Her 'Rent a Peasant' workshop aims to put across the two fundamental aspects of life in the past: finding food and clothing. Children grind pulses and grain, are yoked as oxen, handle fleeces. Or children could create the role play themselves. They may wish to join the Young Archaeologists' Club (www.britarch.ac.uk). Chapter 12 describes the investigation, 'Young Children's Thinking in History', of which the Anglo Saxon data is a part.

## References

Alexander, M. (1973) *Beowulf*. London: Penguin Classics.
Bingham, S. (2004) 'Exploring Anglo-Saxon times', *Times Educational Supplement*, 19 November.
Cooper, H. (1991) 'Young Children's Thinking in History', unpub. Ph.D. London University Institute of Education.
Starkey, D. (2004) 'Back to the Viking invasion', *Times Educational Supplement*, 23 April.
Wilson, D. (1976) *The Anglo-Saxons*. London: Pelican Penguin.

# 12

# Young children's thinking in history

## The research design

Two 'experimental classes' of Year 4 children were taught during consecutive years using carefully defined and documented teaching strategies and compared with a control group in another school taught by an experienced teacher using his own methods. The three groups were initially compared for ability by analyses of variance and covariance using NFER Non-Verbal Reasoning Test BD as covariate. All three groups were taught the same four units of history – the Stone Age, the Iron Age, the Romans and the Saxons – each unit lasting half a term. Each unit was taught within an integrated curriculum with a historical focus. About two hours each week were spent specifically on history.

The teaching strategies for the experimental groups involved discussion of key evidence, differentiating between what you could know 'for certain', what reasonable 'guesses' you could make, and what you 'would like to know' about the evidence. The discussion involved selected key concepts of different levels of abstraction (e.g. arrow, weapon, defence). Each unit of study involved one visit to a local area where there was evidence of settlement at each period and one 'further afield' visit to extend beyond the locality. For example, the Stone Age 'further afield' visit was to Grimes Graves, and the Roman one was to Lullingstone Roman Villa.

At the end of each unit, all three groups took five written 'evidence tests', which each lasted about half-an-hour on consecutive days. In each unit these consisted of five different types of evidence about which children had to make inferences: an artefact (or slide of one), a picture, a diagram, a map and written evidence. The aim was to investigate whether they found 'concrete' evidence more difficult to interpret than more abstract maps and written evidence. A list of evidence used is given in Table 12.1.

The experimental groups were also given an oral 'evidence test'. The children made a tape recording of a discussion of each piece of evidence in small groups. During the first year the discussions were led by the teacher, and during the following year, no adult was present.

**TABLE 12.1** Evidence used in written and oral evidence tests.

| Unit | Test 1 Artefact | Test 2 Picture | Test 3 Diagram | Test 4 Map | Test 5 Writing |
|---|---|---|---|---|---|
| 1 | Slide. Palaeolithic flint hand axes c. 200,000 BC Museum of London. Slide OL91 | Slide. Font de Gaume Lascaux. Ray Delvert S. Lot. | Stone circle. The Druids Circle. Caernarvon. Stone circles of the British Isles. A. Burle | Map showing site of neolithic artefacts on North Downs | Petroglyphics from 'How Writing Began', Macdonald |
| 2 | Bronze helmet (1 BC) Slide BM | Uffington Horse photos | Little Woodbury. Iron Age house plan Wilts. In Cunliffe, R.K. 1974 | Lynchets of Iron Age Fields Butser Hill, Hants. | Strabo 1.4.2. Description of British exports |
| 3 | Shield boss found in River Tyne. Slide BM. | Detail from frieze of great dish, Mildenhall Slide BM PRB 47 | Villa plan Chedworth, Gloucs. | Roman roads across South Downs | Tacitus Annales XII 31–40 Boudicca Revolt |
| 4 | Replica of Sceptre. Sutton Hoo ship burial. BM Slide MZ 18 | Illuminated manuscript of Harvest made by BM F21985 | Plan Saxon church Cirencester | Saxon settlements in Surrey | Beowulf slays Grendel Penguin 1973 trans 824–38 |

Unit 2 Test 5 led discussion experimental group 1: JW, JB, GP, MS, BK, CB. T=Teacher

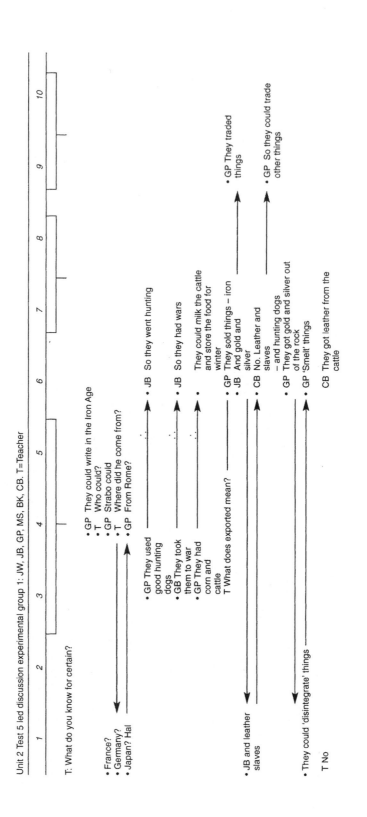

**FIGURE 12.1** Synopsis of led and unled discussion represented as a diagram.

Unit 2 Test 5 led discussion

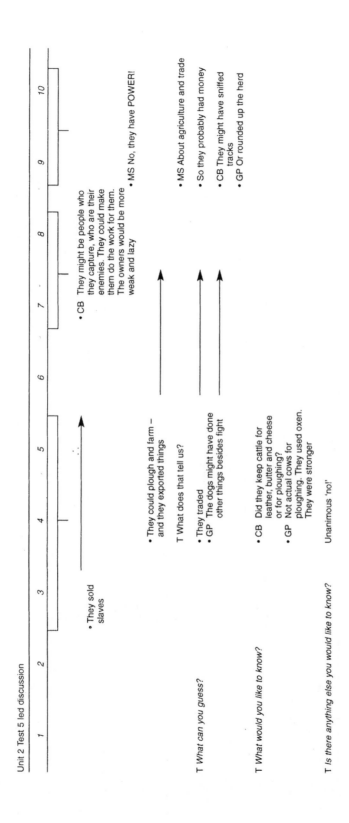

**FIGURE 12.1** *continued.*

Unit 2 Test 5 writing (Strabo 1.4.2.) Exp. Group 2. Unled discussion LW, JF, KB, FB, MS

|   | 1 | 2 | 3 | 4 | 5 | 6 | 7 | 8 | 9 | 10 |
|---|---|---|---|---|---|---|---|---|---|---|

• Most of the island was wooded

• They produced corn and cattle

• They could farm
• They probably kept the corn in good condition
• They probably had guards to stop people stealing the crops
• They probably traded corn to other countries

• The slaves probably worked all day

• There were many level districts

• They could build houses there

• They had gold, silver and iron

• and hunting dogs
• The Gauls used them for war

• They probably used the dogs to keep any eye on the crops
• And the cattle for meat
• The corn was to make flour to make into food build houses
• And to make their fires
• They must have fed the dogs well, and kept them in good condition
• They probably sent the slaves out to do the hunting.

FIGURE 12.1 *continued*.

In addition, the second experimental group was given a story-writing test. They were given a piece of evidence related to the topic, which was concerned with religion, beliefs, myth and ritual, so that it invited the children to piece together their knowledge into a coherent picture of the past and to attempt to consider and explain the beliefs and ideas of the period.

An assessment scheme on a ten-point scale was devised for the evidence tests. This was constructed from patterns in the development of deductive reasoning defined in cognitive psychology and in previous research relating this to history. It is not possible to quote it in detail, but it ranges from: *level 1* – illogical; *level 2* – incipient logic not clearly expressed; *level 3* – restatement of information given; *levels 4 and 5* – one or two statements going beyond the information given; *level 6* – an attempted sequential statement inadequately expressed; *levels 7 and 8* – one or two logical sequential statements, where the second statement is based on the first, connected by 'therefore' or 'because'; *levels 9 and 10* – a synopsis of previous points, using an abstract concept.

For example, given a map of an area of the North Downs where Stone Age implements have been found, a typical level 3 answer is 'There are clay areas, and chalk areas and steep slopes' (which are given on the map). A level 4 statement is 'They had rivers to get water from.' An example of a level 8 statement is 'Chalky ground is not wet, therefore the tools are found there because Stone Age people could live there. And they were near a river, so they could get water to drink.' An example of a level 10 statement refers to a diagram of an Iron Age hut: 'They had huts. Therefore they could build huts. They had vegetation. Therefore they had materials to make huts. They had houses, shelter and stores.'

A system was devised for analysing group discussions and recording points made using this scale by dividing a page horizontally into ten sections, recording synopses of points under levels and mapping the children's development of each other's arguments (Figure 12.1). This analysis could then be transferred to a variety of other diagrammatic forms (Figures 12.2 and 12.3).

The story-writing test was assessed using a scale based on Ashby and Lee (1987) and Piaget (1932). This ranged from no awareness of ideas, beliefs and values and so no attempt to explain them, through intermediate levels when children mention symbolic artefacts in passing, but do not reflect on the ideas they may represent, and finally to an attempt to suggest the significance of symbols.

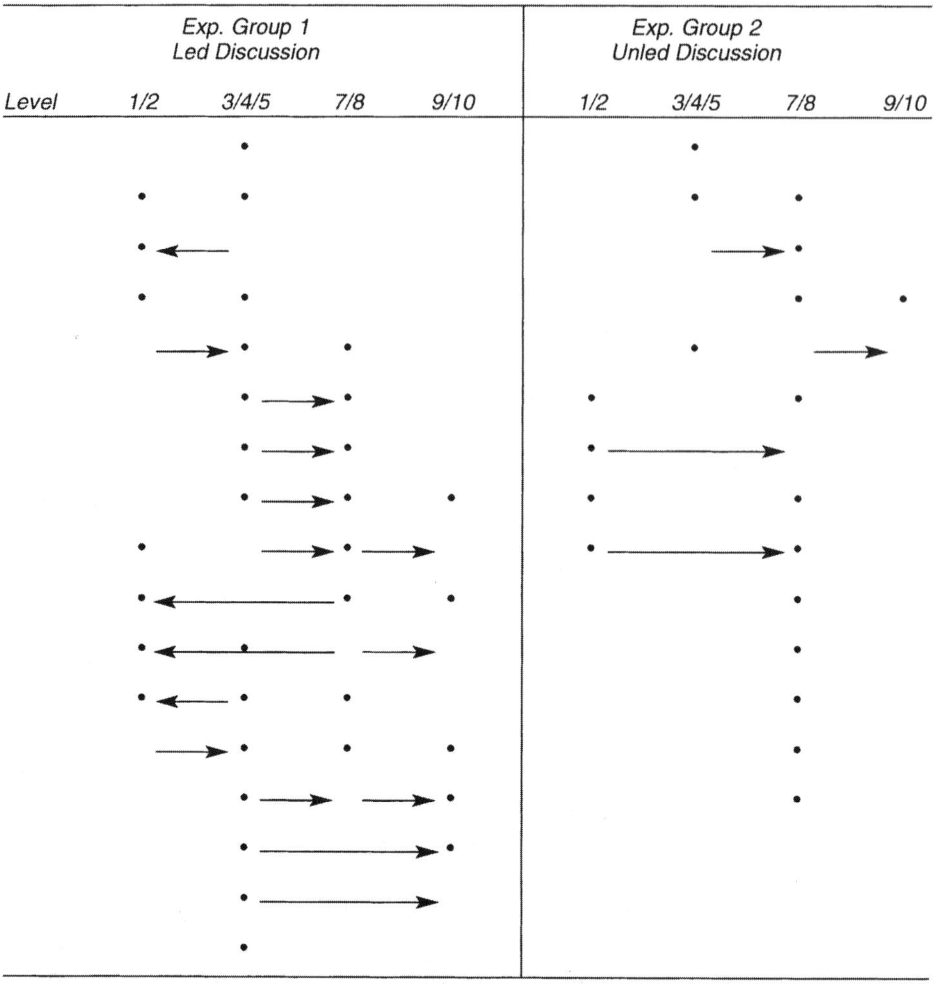

| | Exp. Group 1 Led Discussion | | | | Exp. Group 2 Unled Discussion | | | |
|---|---|---|---|---|---|---|---|---|
| Level | 1/2 | 3/4/5 | 7/8 | 9/10 | 1/2 | 3/4/5 | 7/8 | 9/10 |

*Points made at each level in led and unled discussions*

| Led Discussion | | Unled Discussion | |
|---|---|---|---|
| level 1/2 | 5 points | level 1/2 | 4 points |
| level 3/4/5 | 13 points | level 3/4/5 | 3 points |
| level 7/8 | 8 points | level 7/8 | 11 points |
| level 9/10 | 5 points | level 9/10 | 1 point |
| Total: | 31 points | Total: | 19 points |

**FIGURE 12.2** Led and unled discussions, unit 2, test 5, writing. Strabo 1.4.2.

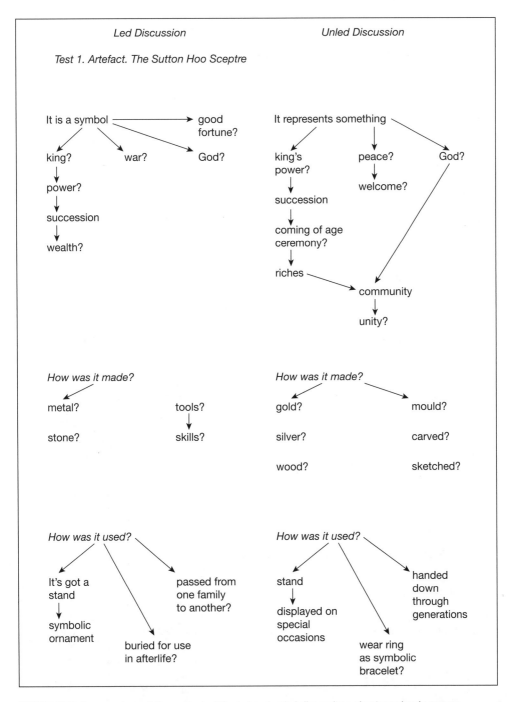

**FIGURE 12.3** A comparison of the content of the led and unled discussions about previously unseen evidence. Unit 4: The Saxons.

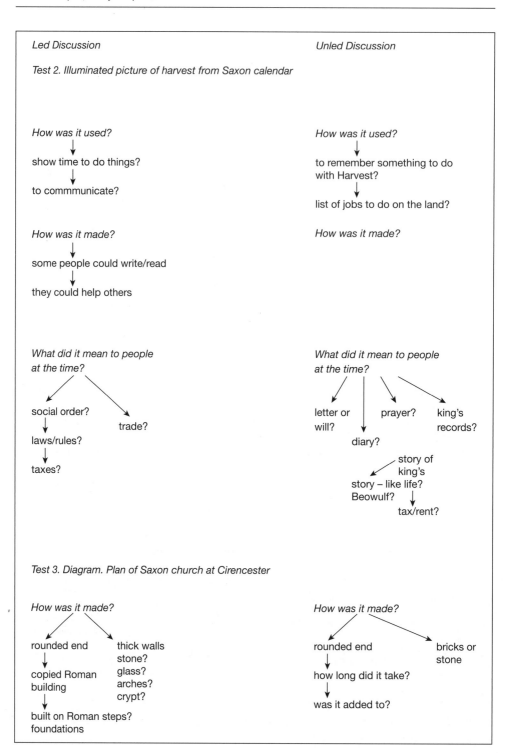

Led Discussion                              Unled Discussion

Test 2. Illuminated picture of harvest from Saxon calendar

*How was it used?*
↓
show time to do things?
↓
to commmunicate?

*How was it made?*
↓
some people could write/read
↓
they could help others

*What did it mean to people at the time?*
social order?         trade?
↓
laws/rules?
↓
taxes?

*How was it used?*
↓
to remember something to do with Harvest?

list of jobs to do on the land?

*How was it made?*

*What did it mean to people at the time?*
letter or will?   prayer?   king's records?
diary?
story – like life? Beowulf?  story of king's
tax/rent?

Test 3. Diagram. Plan of Saxon church at Cirencester

*How was it made?*
rounded end    thick walls
↓            stone?
copied Roman building   glass?
↓           arches?
built on Roman steps? foundations  crypt?

*How was it made?*
rounded end    bricks or stone
↓
how long did it take?
↓
was it added to?

**FIGURE 12.3** *continued.*

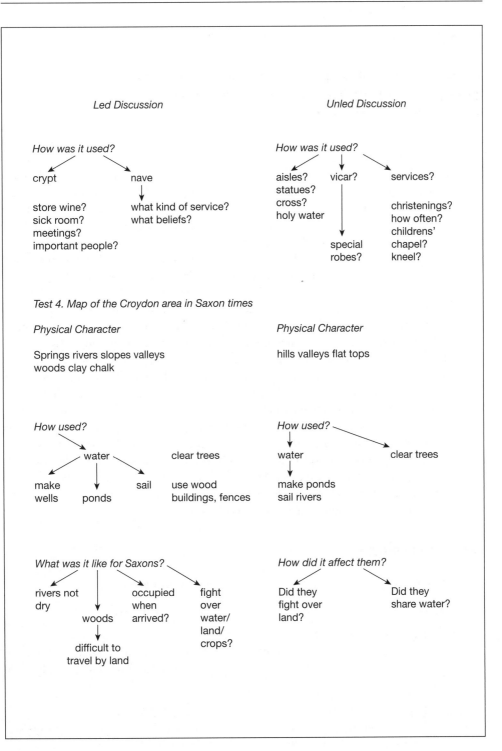

*Test 4. Map of the Croydon area in Saxon times*

**FIGURE 12.3** *continued.*

## The findings

### The relationship between interpreting evidence and the development of historical imagination and empathy – implications for story-writing

In analysing the written 'evidence tests' unit 1, The Stone Age, it became apparent that the deductive reasoning scale reflected levels of reasoning, but did not reflect a difference in the quality of the inferences of the control and experimental groups. The experimental groups' answers were more varied and more closely derived from the evidence, while the control group often simply repeated given information that was not rooted in the evidence. The control group displayed more anachronisms and stereotypes, and the assumption that people in the past were simple. Given a plan of a stone circle, for example, the experimental children suggested a variety of possible purposes (KM 'reckoned it was for war dances, trading flint, praying'), and they suggested how it may have been made. The control group's answers were dominated by repeating received information about 'magic oak trees', 'druids in white cloaks', and 'scary magic'.

This difference in quality was examined further in unit 2. Answers were grouped under Collingwood's (1939) three categories of historical enquiry: How was it made? How was it used? What did it mean to people at the time? The following analysis of the experimental groups' responses to the 'Waterloo Helmet' evidence (British Museum slide) shows how they considered each of these questions (although they had not been explicitly asked to do so). They had been asked 'What do you know for certain?' 'what reasonable guesses can you make?' and 'What would you like to know?'. Their answers suggest that it is through asking questions of evidence that children gradually learn to consider and attempt to explain the viewpoints of people who lived in other times. It also seems likely that the experimental groups were better able to do this because they had been taught through discursive teaching strategies, which encouraged them to make a range of valid suppositions about evidence.

### Experimental groups

#### *Written test*

**I How was it made?**

HC  Exp 1. Qu 1 NVR 97
'They had metals . . . they could make things.'

JG  Exp 2. Qu 1 NVR 120
'They could smelt iron and bronze . . . they had a furnace for getting iron out of rock.'

#### *Discussion tapes*

**I How was it made?**

JH  Exp 2. NVR 100
'They made it carefully with the right kind of metals. Certainly they used a mould and little rivets.'

MF  Exp 2. NVR 129
'They had the right tools to shape the metal.'

IW  Exp 1. Qu I NVR 123
'They had charcoal to separate
metal from ore.'

ML  Exp 1. Qu 3 NVR 102
'I would like to know if the
horns were hollow, because if
they are it would be lighter.'

RL  Exp 1. Qu I NVR 107
'They must have had good minds
to remember things . . . They
knew how to get to learn.'

## II  What was it used for?

### (a) For protection in battle

HG  Exp 1. Qu 2 NVR 129
'They wore it to protect their
heads . . . they had fights.
They made it . . . they made
weapons. They had wars.'

MF  Exp 2. Qu 3 NVR 129
'I would like to know how
they got the idea of armour,
and why did they fight?'

### (b) As a ceremonial symbol or trophy

KC  Exp 2. Qu 2 NVR 111
'It might be made for a chief
. . . he would wear it at
ceremonies to look special.'

NH  Exp 1. Qu 2 NVR 105
'They might have used it at
chariot races . . . they might

NH  Exp 1. NVR 105
'They could print patterns on it.
They had a habit of putting circles
on their working.'

GP  Exp 1. NVR 133
'They had weapons – shields and
swords too. At the British Museum,
I copied a sword with a bronze
hilt.'

## II  What was it used for?

### (a) For protection in battle

NH  Exp 1. NVR 105
'They invented things. They knew
how to smelt metal.'
Exp. 1.
'It's got horns. It looks fierce –
like an ox that could kill. Like a
Stone Age hunter's deer antlers –
to hide in the bushes. The pattern
could show what side you were on
so you didn't kill your own men.'

'They fought for food. If there
was a bad winter and cattle died
. . . to steal another tribe's cattle,
or to cut another tribe's corn if
they didn't have enough.'

### (b) As a ceremonial symbol or trophy

NH  Exp 1. NVR 105
'Maybe the more metal you had it
showed how high up you were.
They'd start with a bracelet 'til
they were all covered in metal
then they'd be a chief.'

Exp 2.
'It may have been awarded for
extreme  bravery in battle. Or in

have had it as a medal. They might have liked beautiful things and had it as an ornament.'

SH  Exp 1. Qu 2 NVR 104
'It might have been for a goddess.'

a contest for new warriors. Maybe they had races and contests, and the armour was awarded for use in a battle.'

Exp 1.
'If they found other things in the River Thames, they may be offerings to a water goddess, to thank her for water to drink.'

### (c) A commodity to trade

ES  Exp 1. Qu 3 NVR 129
'How did the archaeologists come to find it, because it would tell me if it was made there, or if they traded them.'

RL  Exp 1. Qu 3 NVR 107
'And was there one people in the place who made them? if he did he would be rich.'

### (c) A commodity to trade

Exp 2.
'They could have traded it for helmets made in another land. Or maybe for metal to make more weapons. Maybe, as we learned in a lesson, Julius Caesar wrote they used rods of equal weight, or coins, to trade. They could have traded it for bronze or iron – probably for metal of some kind.'

## III What did it mean to the people who wore it?

PC  Exp 2. Qu 1 NVR 114
'They were not afraid of going into battle . . . they looked fierce . . . they put fierce patterns on them.'

## III What did it mean to the people who wore it?

Exp 2.
'The patterns make it look sort of mysterious – they look like flowers . . . it might mean something like "long live our tribe" or "our tribe is the horse tribe". Or special orders from their God. Or a magic helmet to help them in battle. Or the wearer's name. Or to describe the wearer – how good he was at hunting or fighting.'

ML  Exp 1. Qu 2 NVR 102
'I guess it had a kind of strap.'

KL  Exp 1. Qu 3 NVR 107
'Did they make different shapes and sizes, because it would have to fit . . . ?

Exp 2.
'The strips at the side probably had vines or strings attached to hold it on to the wearer . . . they must have put something on it to make

it shine . . . maybe it was measure for the wearer's head.'

DS  Exp 1. Qu 3 NVR 8
'I would like to know what it felt like to put it on. It must have been heavy to handle.'

Exp 1.
'It's so heavy they probably took it with them and put it on when they got there.'

When the study was planned, it had seemed that making deductions from evidence and historical imagination were different and discrete aspects of historical thinking, and for this reason, separate evidence and story-writing tests were devised. However, analysis of the evidence tests suggested that historical imagination develops through making valid suppositions about how things were made and used in the past and so considering what they may have meant to people at the time, and that this is the vehicle through which historical empathy may develop. Since historical imagination and historical empathy are defined in innumerable ways, their relationship as defined in this study is given in Figure 12.4.

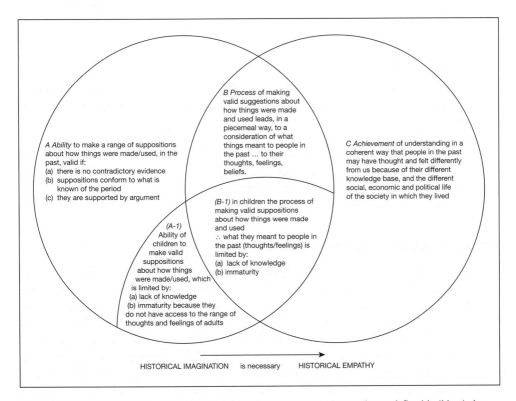

**FIGURE 12.4** Relationship between historical imagination and historical empathy as defined in this study.

## Assessing levels of argument

### The written evidence tests

In the written evidence tests, the children were given an answer paper that they were told to fill in, pretending they were archaeologists reporting on the evidence. Figure 12.5 shows how Andrew filled in his 'archaeologist's' report on the petroglyphics at the end of the Stone Age unit.

Answer papers were laid out to encourage the highest levels of response, based on the ten-point scale described on page 211.

They made a distinction between 'knowing', 'guessing', and 'not knowing', and encouraged children to make two statements for each of these categories, to follow each with a sequential argument and to write a 'conclusion'.

However, it was frequently necessary to look for the underlying logic of the thinking processes behind an answer in order to assess the level of thinking. Often this was obscured by poor spelling or handwriting. An answer may span several levels and would then be scored on the basis of the highest scoring statements within the answer and lower levels ignored. The logic of the answer does not always correspond to the divisions on the paper, so that the statements need to be carefully considered.

### The oral evidence tests

Figure 12.1 (pp. 208–10) shows how the oral evidence tests were also analysed on the ten-point scale. These synopses refer to the written evidence used in the Iron Age unit (Strabo 1.4.2).

> Most of the island is level and well-wooded, but there are many hilly districts. It produces corn, cattle, gold, silver and iron. They are all exported, together with leather, slaves and good hunting dogs. The Gauls use these dogs, and their own, for war as well.

## Making a distinction between 'knowing' and 'supposing'

In the written evidence tests, the children were asked three questions about each piece of evidence: question one, what do you know for certain? Question two, what reasonable 'guesses' can you make? Question three, what would you like to know? It is interesting that they were able to make these distinctions. Analysis of the unled discussion tapes – where they were not specifically asked to differentiate between knowing, guessing and not knowing – nevertheless show the discussions dominated by probability words (could be, maybe, unlikely, I wonder, what do you think?). The children occasionally make certainty statements. 'They [the axe-heads] were all chipped and smoothed' and sometimes these are challenged by other children: 'It's got two heads' (cave painting). 'That could be a tail.' 'Bit thick for a tail.'

The unled groups also sometimes mentioned things that they would like to know. 'It must have been for some reason?' 'How do you think they made the banks?'

**Experimental Group 1**

NAME _Andrew_     DATE 6.12.85

UNIT ONE     THE STONE AGES

EVIDENCE .writing

| What do you know FOR CERTAIN from this evidence?     Level 9 | | |
| --- | --- | --- |
| they communicated | **Therefore** they made signs for communicating | **Conclusion** they needed other people |
| they draw | **Therefore** They had thing to draw with | |

| What reasonable GUESSES can you make about it?     Level 8 | | |
| --- | --- | --- |
| they may of had speshells thing to do writing with | **Therefore** | **Conclusion** they might of had Spcshell hunting Signs |
| I think it had a meaning | **Therefore** It migh of taken them a long time to get the writing | |

| What would you LIKE TO KNOW about it?     Level 6 | | |
| --- | --- | --- |
| What it ment | **Because** then we could make little word | **Conclusion** |
| had they got to know what the signs ment | **Because** then we could do stone age writing | |

**FIGURE 12.5** Andrew's 'archaeologist's' report on petroglyphics at the end of the Stone Age unit.

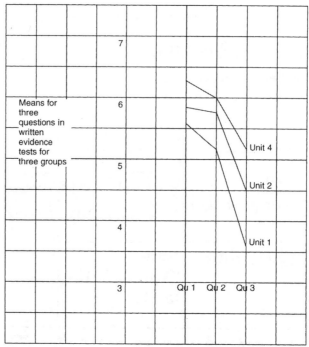

Question 1  What do you know FOR CERTAIN, from this evidence?
Question 2  What REASONABLE GUESSES can you make from this evidence?
Question 3  What WOULD YOU LIKE TO KNOW about this evidence?

**FIGURE 12.6** Graph showing means of scores for questions 1, 2 and 3 for units 1, 2 and 4. (Unit 3 was taught and tested but the results were not analysed due to shortage of time.)

It is interesting that in the written evidence tests the children were able to make 'certainty' statements, and reasonable guesses (questions 1 and 2) with almost equal ease. The graph (Figure 12.6) based on analysis of variance tests to compare groups, questions and types of evidence in each unit, shows a significant difference between the types of question, with question 3 (what would you like to know?), by far the most difficult. The Sheffe test of multiple comparison shows the difference between the first two questions and question 3 to be significant. These children then are able to make a distinction between knowing and valid suppositions, and they find both types of inference equally easy, but they find it far harder to say what they 'would like to know' about evidence.

Although these results were statistically significant, there were exceptions to the main effects. There were significant interactions between the questions and types of evidence. In unit 1, for example, there was little difference in difficulty between knowing and guessing about the cave painting, the plan of the stone circle, or the map. This is not surprising because not much is known about how these things were made or used or what they meant to Stone Age people, even by archaeologists, so there are fertile opportunities for reasonable guesses. On the other hand, it was easier to make certainty statements about axe-heads because these are central to a study of the Stone Age. The experimental groups had three lessons on tools and weapons and had seen them made at Grimes Graves. This is important because it shows how statistically significant main effects are blurred by other variables, by a particular example of a type of evidence, by interest and by motivation.

There do however, seem to be implications for teachers in the general finding that children are equally able to say what they know, and to make reasonable suggestions, but find it difficult to say what they 'would like to know'. It suggests that children of this age do not need to be restricted to repeating 'facts' and that they are able to become actively involved in historical problem-solving. They can learn to control their own thinking, and become increasingly aware of what constitutes a valid supposition. This is an important staging post on the way to true historical understanding. However, 'what would you like to know?' is a question with an unknown starting point, and is too open. It does not encourage children to control their own investigation. This is significant because children are frequently told to 'find out about . . .', particularly at the ends of chapters in history books, assuming this encourages motivation and independent learning. These tests suggest that such a question is too unstructured.

## Different types of evidence

The study set out to investigate whether children find it easier to make deductions about artefacts and pictures than about more abstract evidence, diagrams, maps and written sources. The relationship between groups, questions and evidence in each unit was statistically analysed using analyses of variance. The findings are shown in Figure 12.7.

Although in unit 1 there was a significant difference between the levels of response to the five types of evidence, and the children found the diagram and the map the most difficult, it is interesting that by unit 2, and again in unit 4, there was no significant difference in their ability to interpret 'concrete' and 'abstract' evidence. This is not to suggest that it is not very important for children to be introduced to artefacts and pictures (which are, at the very least, stimulating sources), but rather that if they are given more abstract evidence as well, as part of a continuum, and have learned to discuss evidence, they can interpret abstract sources equally well. This seems to be because, having learned how to discuss evidence and the kinds of responses required, they can relate abstract evidence to 'concrete' evidence – maybe through visits to sites or museums. The experimental groups had visited Grimes Graves, the British Museum and local sites, and related these to maps, geology, vegetation and relief. They could therefore draw on these experiences in interpreting, for example, the Stone Age axe-heads, the Waterloo Helmet, the plans of the stone circle, the Iron Age hut, and the maps.

Their level of response depends, not on the level of abstraction of the evidence, but on language, on concepts and on argument, because remains of the past are only evidence to the extent that they can tell us about the people who made and used them. Children need to experience physical evidence, and to learn to discuss it, if it is to have meaning for them. They are then able to transfer this process to new evidence, and to more abstract evidence.

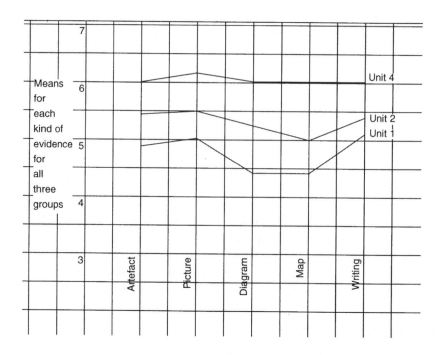

**FIGURE 12.7** Graph showing means of scores for questions 1, 2 and 3 for units 1, 2 and 4. (Unit 3 was taught and tested but the results were not analysed due to shortage of time.) The marking scale is outlined on page 211.

There are implications here for older students. It has often been assumed that artefacts and pictures are more appropriate for younger children who cannot read and write easily. However, if tangible sources are not easier to interpret, this strengthens the case for using a range of sources at any level of study.

Again, it is important to bear in mind that while the main effects shown in Figure 12.7 are statistically significant, there were variations in this pattern, influenced by particular examples of evidence, and by teaching strategies. In unit 4, the level main effect across the five kinds of evidence resulted from opposite trends across the experimental and control groups, although the span was only across one mark. It is likely that the control group found the *Beowulf* extract easier to interpret than the other evidence because they had more experience of 'comprehension exercises', but they had not learned how to interpret historical evidence.

## Using learned concepts

The concepts that children had been taught in each unit as 'spellings' and that they had learned to use in discussing key evidence during class lessons the following week were used spontaneously by at least some of the children both in the written tests and the taped discussions. It was also encouraging that in unit 4, they were using vocabulary that they had learned in connection with previous units, transferring it to a new period and new material. Not surprisingly, the children in the control group who had not learned specific concepts only used those that were labelled in the evidence, and these were rarely abstract concepts. Figures 12.8 and 12.9 show how children used concepts they had learned in previous units in both written and oral evidence tests.

Although no claim is made that the children totally understood the abstract concepts they used (e.g. vegetation, belief, power, agriculture, transport, society, religion), it seemed that these concepts were becoming part of their own vocabulary.

It may be that the experimental groups were able to make a far greater range of valid suppositions about the evidence because they had a conceptual framework of both concrete and abstract concepts to which they could relate new pieces of evidence, even if the concepts themselves were not mentioned in their answers. Freedman and Loftus (1971) concluded that concepts play an important part in organising semantic memory. For example, in interpreting the written evidence in the Iron Age unit (see pp. 216–19) many children made deductions concerned with trade, agriculture, metal production and social structure.

*1 cm represents the use of the concept in one evidence test on one or more occasions*

■ represents led discussion groups (Exp 1)
▨ represents unled discussion groups (Exp 2)

| *Led* (Exp 1) | Concrete | 11 | | *Unled* (Exp 2) | Concrete | 9 |
|---|---|---|---|---|---|---|
| | Abstract | 9 | | | Abstract | 8 |
| | Superordinate | 10 | | | Superordinate | 1 |

This bar chart shows how both the led and unled groups used their taught vocabulary in unit 2 discussions and, when appropriate, used concepts learned in unit 1. The led groups, however, used more superordinates than the unled groups.

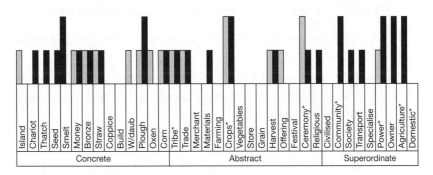

Note: *concepts learned in unit 1

**FIGURE 12.8** Concepts taught in unit 2 that were used in the discussion tapes.

This bar chart shows how children in both experimental groups retained concepts learned in units 1 and 2 and applied them in their answers to unit 4. The control group used no abstract key concepts.

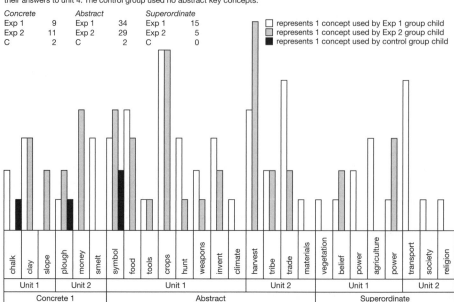

| Concrete | | Abstract | | Superordinate | |
|---|---|---|---|---|---|
| Exp 1 | 9 | Exp 1 | 34 | Exp 1 | 15 |
| Exp 2 | 11 | Exp 2 | 29 | Exp 2 | 5 |
| C | 2 | C | 2 | C | 0 |

□ represents 1 concept used by Exp 1 group child
▨ represents 1 concept used by Exp 2 group child
■ represents 1 concept used by control group child

**FIGURE 12.9** Concepts taught in units 1 and 2 that were used in written evidence tests in unit 4 by Exp 1, Exp 2 and control group children.

*IW* 'We know that Grece people traded with us … they must have had something to trade with.'

*FF* 'We know that gold, silver and iron are all exported across the sea.'

*NH* 'They had corn and cattle … they could farm and so they had learned to live in one place.'

*MF* Guessed that 'since they had gold, silver and iron, they had miners' and he wondered how they mined and transported it because he had seen neither mining tools nor Iron Age boats in pictures.

Similarly, in interpreting the illuminated Saxon manuscript showing harvest, children in the experimental groups focused on ideas connected with agriculture, community, and communication. They discussed crops, farming methods and the cycle of the farming year.

*RD* 'The people seem to be cutting logs and transporting them maybe to trade them – if they lived near a forest.'

They refer to the jobs people are doing and the relationship between them, and make various suggestions about the meaning of the writing.

It seems then that not only do children enjoy learning to use and spell 'hard words', but that learning key concepts gives them a reference point, or framework, to apply to new material, and that this helps to generate a range of new ideas about it.

## Led and unled group discussion

The content of the discussion was similar in both the led and unled groups. It was concerned with how the evidence may have been used and what it may have meant to those who created it, although the children had not been asked at any point to consider these aspects. However, the groups differed in the way they expressed their ideas. The led groups tended to make general statements and seemed to assume that the teacher knew where the discussion was leading, whereas the unled groups paid more attention to physical description, and sometimes explained their ideas through valid stories and images, about brave warriors for example, who may be commemorated by a stone circle, or who may have hidden their treasure there and defended it. However, in both the led and unled groups, there was genuine argument. They both made some illogical points. In the unled groups, they were either ignored or corrected, with respect, by another child. In the led groups, it was usually the teacher who queried them. In both groups, the children developed each other's points and the quality of the discussion improved over the four units. There was an increase in the numbers of points made and in the number of sequential arguments, and a decrease in the number of illogical points. The structure of the discussions differed slightly in the led and unled groups. The led groups tended to explore all the possibilities suggested by one point, then move on to the next point whereas the unled groups usually followed up a point with one further argument, then made a fresh point. Sometimes they backtracked, and ideas were less systematically explored.

It seems then that both led and unled discussions have a place in helping children to interpret evidence. If children have learned the thinking patterns required, discussion in small groups without the teacher may sometimes be more valuable than teacher-led discussion; children are more able to explain their ideas in their own way, to defend them and so to make them their own. This has implications for classroom organisation and for the value of group work not directly led by the teacher.

## Teaching strategies

### Visits

The children were able to transfer information learned on visiting a site to new evidence. For example, on the visit to Farthing Down, they had been asked how, if they had lived there in Neolithic times, they could have made a dry, warm, comfortable shelter, what they could have eaten, where they might have found water, how they might have made tools, weapons and pots. When given a map of another similar area of the North Downs they were able to apply these points to the new map and make a range of

**TABLE 12.2** Examples of written answers, showing how visit to Farthing Down helped children to interpret the map.

| Evidence discussed on visit to Farthing Down | Children's use of this evidence applied to the map (Exp Group 1) Written Evidence |
|---|---|
| *Examples. Experimental Group 2. Unit 1. Test 4. Showing use of visit in interpreting map* | |
| *Geology:* chalk/flint, clay, slope, wind, river | PC (level 8) Qu 1. They found that chalk sucks the water through it . . . we know it was dry. They lived in places like Farthing Down. DF (level 9) Qu 2. They lived near to chalk and clay areas . . . they didn't have to go far to get flints. They lived near slopes . . . they were in a place with not many trees. They knew exactly where to live. JG (level 8) Qu 2. I guess they could have shelter from the cliffs . . . they would be safe. They would have water . . . they could have land for farming on the chalk soil. FB (level 8) Qu 2. They probably went fishing in the river . . . they probably had quite a lot of fish. They probably had to wash in the river . . . they probably didn't wash much! JG (level 8) Qu 1. Neolithic people must have been in the area . . . they had camps there. Trees might be in great numbers on the clay soil . . . they had shelter. |
| *Vegetation* | MF (level 7) Qu 3. Why they chose that place. What animals lived there, because I'd like to know what they ate. RF (level 7) Qu 2. I can guess there must have been a lot of woods . . . I can guess there must have been lots of animals nearby. I know there |
| *Animals* | must have been a lot of food nearby. |

deductions and suggestions in their written answers. Table 12.2 shows the information children had discussed on their visit to Farthing Down on the left. This visit stimulated their deductions about the map of a similar but unknown area, which are given on the right.

The scores were surprisingly high for such abstract evidence; this seems to be because the visit enabled the children to relate real experiences and images to the map. As AW wrote in his conclusion 'This is the best evidence game'!

Similarly, in the Iron Age unit, they had again visited Farthing Down to trace the lynchets, the soil banks formed by turning the plough, which indicate Iron Age field patterns. Figure 12.10 shows how they were able to transfer discussion of these to the Iron Age map fields at Butser, on the South Downs.

At the end of unit 2 the children were given a previously unseen map of Iron Age fields on Butser Hill in Hampshire. In their written answers, experimental group 2 developed between them many of the arguments inherent in this evidence, which showed lynchets and trackways.

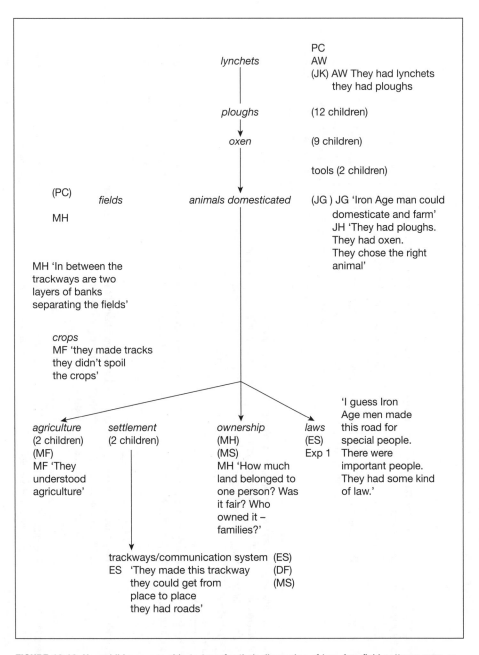

**FIGURE 12.10** How children were able to transfer their discussion of Iron Age field patterns seen on a visit to Farthing Down to a previously unseen map of field systems on Butser Hill, Hampshire.

TABLE 12.3 How children, in written answers, related new evidence about Butser to their visit to Farthing Down and also to their class discussion about Iron Age farming, and finally to their own ideas.

| Butser Map | Farthing Down Visit | Class Discussion | Own Ideas |
|---|---|---|---|
| PC There are bumps. We know where the fields were | They could use machinery like a plough. They farmed. They grew crops. | There was probably a settlement there. They probably grew vegetables (re: evidence of beans, vetch, crop rotation) | If they thought a horse was a god or something why did they not use it? (in farming) |
| JG They had ploughs | They understood how to grow crops. They could farm and domesticate | There might be tools or there might be bones of oxen still there. (re: evidence of bones found, and tools, at Glastonbury) (re: oxen bones similar to modern Dexter) | A cart could carry crops from the field. How long did it take to make (invent?) a cart? If there are bones there, archaeologists could make up an oxen like they make dinosaurs in Natural History Museum |
| RF I know for certain this map give us clues. I know some people can find these ditches (i.e. I know they exist and what they look like) | I guess they had patterns in soil and chalk (i.e. I know soil or chalk is thin – viz the Uffington Horse) | I guess they had lambs (re: sheep probably Soay, as at Butser) or as JK said 'sheep would give wool and meat and keep the grass down' | |
| MS They had fields. They must have had a plough | I guess the tracks were for taking the plough across | They might grow things like peas and beans (re: Butser evidence) | I guess the tracks were made of wood. There must have been timber to make them from. I would like to know what transport they had, and we would know what skills they had |
| SK They had roads | They could take the oxen across to another field because if the plough went over the corn it would crush it up and it would not grow again | I think had a field of *herbs* (re: discussion of flavouring and preserving) | They could eat them and (use them to) make other foods |
| MH In-between the two trackways are the two layers of banks separating the fields | They must transport the plough through gaps in the banks | The blank bits might be for *settlements* (re: post-hole evidence) | Maybe the owners might live there. Maybe ownership separated by trackways. I would like to know how much land belonged to one person; if they had the same amount and if they lived in families next to each other |

Table 12.3 analyses how children in the written answers related the new evidence about Butser to their visit to Farthing Down, and also to their class discussion on Iron Age farming, and finally to their own ideas. This shows how they were able to transfer the experience of the visit and following class discussion to new evidence, and, in so doing, also to form their own valid suggestions and questions.

The visits probably also helped them to discuss the plans of a stone circle, an Iron Age hut, and a Saxon church, although they had not visited similar sites, because they had considered geology, vegetation and relief, and the effects of these on a settlement in each period.

The stimulus of the 'further afield' visit to Grimes Graves and the British Museum probably helped the experimental groups to make a greater range of suppositions than the control group about artefacts, about the Stone Age axe-heads, for example, and the Waterloo Helmet.

## Language: discussion, concepts and language as an objective tool

### Discussion

Class lessons were based on discussion of selected evidence, using learned concepts. Each unit consisted of four such lessons taught over consecutive weeks. One of the four lessons was based on the local visit to an area of settlement, and one focused on ideas and beliefs.

This study endorsed the importance of learning through open-ended discussion, in which children learn the thinking processes of history. They learn that many suggestions are possible, and remain uncertain, and that arguments must be supported and can be contested. This is how criteria for validity become understood. It seems likely that this is the most important factor in the difference between the control group and experimental groups' responses. First, the experimental groups achieved both a higher level of inferential reasoning, and a wider range of valid suppositions. Second, the control and experimental groups used the factual information they had in different ways. They were not required to rehearse it in their answers but, nevertheless, it underpinned their answers. The control group, however, tended to repeat information given, which was only loosely related to the evidence, and when they went beyond it, they often revealed misconceptions. The experimental groups were more likely to test given knowledge against the evidence. Their suggestions, for example, about the Anglo Saxon sceptre were dependent on their knowledge of Anglo Saxon kings and kingdoms, laws and succession.

It seems, then, that discussion is important in the development of historical understanding. However the discussion must be based on selected key evidence. Children need key factual information, but if they learn it through discussion, they do not simply repeat it, but they both retain the information and are able to transfer the pattern of discursive thinking to new evidence.

## Concepts

The importance of teaching and using selected concepts of different levels of abstraction to interpret key evidence has already been discussed (pp. 216–19). It was seen that children were able to use abstract, learned concepts as an organising framework against which to test new evidence, even when they did not mention the concept itself. This helped them in discussing the Sutton Hoo sceptre to talk about the king, ceremonies, symbols and laws; *Beowulf* deductions involved power, vengeance, courage and beliefs. Learned concepts helped children to make a greater range of valid suggestions about evidence, to develop arguments, and so to make suggestions about different attitudes, behaviour and beliefs.

## Language as an objective tool

The experimental groups had also discussed the nature of language as a tool for communication. They were able to talk about the relationship between the written and spoken word, the symbolism of language and to suppose how language originated and changed. A child could say of the Stone Age petroglyphics, for instance, 'They made signs for communicating; they had things to draw with; they needed people.' Or 'They wrote strange writing . . . they had different words from today. This writing is found in Italy . . . it could have been found in other places.' One child wrote, 'They had to teach each other how to speak . . . they had to cooperate in making writing.' Another guessed that 'in different countries they had different signs . . . if someone went to a different country, he would not understand. It took a long time to carve the signs . . . they would not move from place to place.'

In considering the Strabo excerpt in unit 2, JG wondered 'how long after the Romans the Iron Age wrote'. AW observed that 'they had different language over different times. They did not have the same language everywhere . . . I would like to know how they made their languages up.'

## Acceleration

The study suggested that if children are taught consistently, applying the same teaching strategies to new material, they learn patterns of thinking that can be transferred, and the quality of their thinking improves. In unit 4, the experimental groups achieved higher levels of deductive argument than in previous units, and used more abstract concepts. It seems then that it is important for children to learn patterns of thinking, and for teachers to be clear what these should be. In unit 4, although the means for all three groups were higher than in the first two units, the means for the experimental groups were much higher than the control group mean (Figure 12.11).

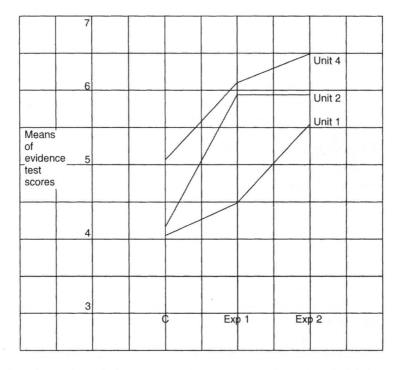

**FIGURE 12.11** Graph showing means of evidence test scores for control and experimental groups for units 1, 2 and 4.

## The integrated curriculum

The study did not aim to prove the benefits of learning history through an integrated curriculum. However, the links between responses to the history tests and other areas of the curriculum can be traced. From the science components, the children seem to have learned both to question and respect the technology of other societies.

They discuss how things were made and used. For example, the discussion of the Waterloo Helmet reflects their knowledge of iron smelting learned in the Iron Age unit. Their experience of historical fiction (e.g. *The Changeling*, Sutcliff 1974; and *The Bronze Sword*, Treece 1965) may well have helped children to recognise the difference between fact and imagination. There are many examples of children transferring their knowledge of geology, vegetation and relief to maps of other areas; geography probably also influenced their references to trade, transport, and migration of peoples. Art taught the experimental groups careful observation through drawing (slides of cave paintings, Iron Age artefacts in the British Museum, or Anglo Saxon pottery). It also seems to have taught them both an interest in the techniques and materials used in the past, and an understanding and respect for different interpretations. SH guesses that 'Stone Age people may have kept their oxides in pots and used their hands to paint'. The experimental groups suggest why the Uffington Horse may be unrealistic. DS NVR 88 (Exp 1. Qu 1(7)) owns a horse and brings her own keen interest to bear, in spite of difficulties with spelling!

> I kown that they had Horse Because it is a piter of one. They must of copid the Bones of the Horse And the shape of the Horse And it must of bein bukin because of its back legs and the sape of it . . .
>
> Two of the legs do not join up to the body. Therefore I think that is a special 3D effect. It has whiskers on a kind of chin. Therefore either they have not observed well, or their horse has whiskers.
>
> MH NVR 135 (Exp 2. Qu 1(9))

The dimension of religious education involved the discussion of the symbolism of light and dark in cave painting and in other cultures, the needs and fears of Iron Age people, the nature of Roman gods, the teachings of early Celtic and Roman missionaries. It may be that this helped children to consider reasons for beliefs and rituals in their own and other societies. The mathematics component may have encouraged deductions involving estimates. ('It might take 1,000 people to fill the church. The population must have been big.') They consider shape. One child says of the circle, 'They had another shape in maths', and the Uffington Horse has a 'special 3D effect'. The Iron Age fields are 'square or rectangular'.

A degree of integration, with a clear history focus seems the most economical way, in a crowded curriculum, to allow children to become steeped in a period. It also demonstrates that history involves the history of thought in all disciplines and in all aspects of society, and can, in turn, give a purpose to experiment in science and to calculations in mathematics.

## Ways in which teachers can evaluate and develop a statutory curriculum that meets the needs of their pupils

This research indicates some of the problems involved in assessing patterns in the development of children's thinking in history. However, the study was undertaken as an integral part of class teaching, and refined the thinking of the teacher and the quality of her teaching in the process, so that it suggests that action research by practising teachers is both possible and desirable, and should therefore be supported and encouraged.

It is not necessary for such detailed analysis to be carried out all the time, or by all teachers; the purpose of the study described was to indicate broad patterns of development, and the relationship between different aspects of historical thinking that could form a basis for planning and for ongoing assessment by teachers. It is essential that the broad brushstrokes with which a statutory curriculum aims to paint a map of the past is also balanced by detailed and carefully focused discussion of key evidence. Young children cannot grasp a holistic view of complex social structures; they do not understand the workings of adult minds, and cannot address difficult political and religious issues. The need to list and memorise 'causes and effects' killed school history for many people and there is still a danger that teachers will over interpret the content specified in the revised curriculum.

Experience suggests that children are interested in detail, and in problem-solving in which they can be validly and genuinely engaged: what did sailors on the Armada ships eat? What did the sailors on the *Mary Rose* do? Who lived in my home before I did?

Therefore, the curriculum must be taught in an economical way if it is not to be overloaded. Planning must be carefully focused to centre on real problem-solving in each curriculum area, and in a range of contexts. Planning, activities and evaluation must form a related sequence so that assessment is an integral part of all the work children do and of the constant interaction between teacher and child. Work planned in history must reflect the thinking processes of history, and allow for a range of differentiated outcomes. It should also involve learning history through the rich variety of activities on which good primary practice is based:

- information technology (simulations, word-processing and data-handling);
- art (drawing, printing, painting, embroidery, model-making);
- science and technology (cooking, spinning, weaving, grinding seeds, building and testing structures, using tools, moving loads, using a range of materials);
- language for different audiences (transactional and expressive writing, reading, discussion, role play, making video and audio tapes).

## In conclusion

There are many opportunities to interpret the curriculum for history in creative ways, planning activities that reflect an increased understanding of the nature of history, an articulate rationale for its importance, and the sharing of teachers' own enthusiasms. Nevertheless, the position of history in the curriculum is probably more precarious than before. The statutory requirement is minimal, with a recognition that some outline studies are inevitable; on the other hand, there is increasing emphasis on tests in 'basic skills' and on published league tables of the results. Yet,

> The present is where we get lost
> If we forget our own past and have
> No vision of the future.

> (Ayi Kwei Amah in Fryer 1989)

Whether or not this is allowed to happen will depend on the enthusiasm, efforts and expertise of all those who care about primary history, working together with conviction.

## Postscript – a Starkey contrast!

Of course you need not only to understand the process of historical enquiry but also to be able to articulate it with confidence to those who know nothing of history education, and certainly nothing of young children's thinking in history. The British Education Conference at the Institute of Historical Research in February 2005 brought together teachers, historians, film makers, television producers and policy makers to discuss how history should be taught in the future and its presence in British education safeguarded. Dr David Starkey spoke first, on 'What History should we be teaching in the twentieth century?'. I was invited to speak, on 'History in primary schools: identity, progression, dialogue'. All the papers can be found at www.history.ac.uk/education/conference.

Yes, there were other speakers – sixteen to be precise – and I did not follow on directly from Dr Starkey. I juxtapose here contrasting statements from each of our talks, in the form of the debate I should like to have had with him, if he had not escaped after giving his paper.

*DS* We can justify history at the centre of the curriculum by memory. Societies have a collective memory. A society that loses its collective memory has nothing.

*HC* But there is a problem with whose identity we are talking about. As Jerome Bruner (1996) has said, it is not easy, however multicultural your intentions, to help a ten-year-old create a story that includes him in a world beyond his family and neighbourhood, having just been transplanted from . . . wherever, so there are questions in looking at history in terms of identity. I should like to suggest that the way around this is to take a constructivist approach to history, to ensure that children are involved in the process of enquiry, from the very beginning . . . I am not saying that children create their own histories in their entirety. They should clearly work within what is known, a planned framework. It is the process that is important – there is no one story.

*DS* It leads to a universal scepticism which, I think, is profoundly dangerous . . . Simon Schama, Niall Ferguson and I all gave the same answer at the Summer School organised by the Prince of Wales, who plays a very important role in this area. What matters is **content**; what matters is **narrative**. And what goes on in schools has been deliberately modelled on university teaching. We have become research led, in a way that I think is entirely unsuitable for a subject which, we are arguing here, is worthy of a place in the curriculum . . . The first job is to be **confident** in **content**.

*HC* I would follow Collingwood's definition of the process of historical enquiry; making inferences and deductions about sources.

*DS* I am profoundly sceptical about the use of documents at early stages in teaching.

*HC* This process does not necessarily require documents. When you are three years old written sources might mean your birthday cards or hospital baby tag, artefacts or pictures. Children at Key Stage 2 can be introduced to the idea that sources are often incomplete and of differing status. And when children construct their own accounts of the past by selecting and combining sources, they gain an understanding, from the beginning, of why different accounts may be equally valid. Of key significance here is the role of dialogue. If you are talking about interpreting sources and recognising that very often, especially with ancient sources, there is no single correct answer, this involves listening to others, sharing ideas and possibly changing your mind as a result. I would argue that this is at the centre of learning history.

*DS* A skills-based approach consumes endless time. It is profoundly wasteful of time . . . The way we teach history is fundamentally wrong, or rather the dominant message of the way we teach history is catastrophic . . . leading to an utterly vulgar notion of relativism . . . In other words I get a bit worried about the emphasis on the critical . . . I think we have overdone the critical element of history.

*HC* Let me give you some examples of two four-year-olds reasoning about whether a story about dragons was true.

> 'I've seen pictures of dragons in books . . . dragons might have existed, since dinosaurs did, and they've died out now.'

> 'It might be the Loch Ness monster. That lives in Scotland and Robert's going on holiday and he's going to look for it . . .'

*DS* It is silly . . .

## References

Ashby, R. and Lee, P.J. (1987) 'Children's concepts of empathy and understanding in history', in C. Portal (ed.) *The History Curriculum for Teachers*. Lewes: Falmer Press.

Bruner, J. (1996) *The Culture of Education*. Cambridge, MA: Harvard University Press.

Collingwood, R.G. (1939) *An Autobiography*. London: Oxford University Press.

Freedman, J.L. and Loftus, E.F. (1971) 'Retrieval of words from long-term memory', *Journal of Verbal Learning and Verbal Behaviour*, 10, 107–15.

Fryer, P. (1989) *Black People in the British Empire: an introduction*. London: Pluto Press.

Piaget, J. (1932) *Moral Judgement and the Child*. London: Kegan Paul.

Sutcliff, R. (1986) *The Changeling*. London: Penguin.

Treece, H. (1965) *The Bronze Sword*. London: Hamish Hamilton.

# Appendix

**TABLE A.1** Professional needs analysis based on *History for All* (Ofsted 2011), *Primary History Survey* (2011), *Cambridge Review* (Alexander, 2010).

Completing this table will enable you to identify your existing areas of strength and areas you can develop as you read through the book

| Teacher's subject knowledge | Page ref. History 5–11 | Reference to reports on Primary History | Note on reading History 5–11 | Experience in practice | Plan to develop |
|---|---|---|---|---|---|
| **Content of topic being taught** | 13, 76, 125, 236 | **Ofsted: 5, 20** | | | |
| What period came before/after the topic I am teaching? | | | | | |
| What are the significant events in the topic? | 61, 63, 66, 71 | | | | |
| Who are significant people in the topic? | 63 | **Ofsted: 10** | | | |
| Significant dates in the topic? | | | | | |
| What are significant changes within the period? | | | | | |
| What did I know about daily life in the period? | | | | | |

**TABLE A.1** *continued.*

| Teacher's subject knowledge | Page ref. History 5–11 | Reference to reports on Primary History |
|---|---|---|
| **Broad chronological knowledge; 'mental map of the past'** Sequence of periods; (e.g. Romans, Saxons/Vikings, Medieval …) Similarities and differences between periods Causes and consequences | 42, 59, 175 47 | Ofsted: 5, 6, 7, 11, 20, 31, 32 *Cambridge Review:* **229, 272** |
| **Understanding of processes of historical enquiry** | 6, 28, 41, 61, 71 | *Cambridge Review:* **257** *PH Survey:* **16** |
| Using sources to find out about the past | see index, historical enquiry | Ofsted: 10 *Cambridge Review:* **229** |
| Using secondary sources to find out about the past: information books, narrative, internet | 15, 34, 36, 157 | Ofsted: 9, 11 |
| Primary sources: Interpreting sources: artefacts, visual sources, written sources, statistics, sites, plans, maps, oral sources Discuss validity/reliability | see index, historical enquiry 24, 37, 159, 231 | Ofsted: 19 |
| Understand why there can be different views about events Consider why events, people, changes are significant | 21, 37, 137, 159 50, 61, 63, 66, 71 | Ofsted: 10 |
| Combining sources to create accounts/interpretations | see index, interpretations and accounts | Ofsted: 10, 12, 19 |
| Presenting interpretations | see index, interpretations and accounts; reconstructions | Ofsted: 19, 30 |

**TABLE A.1** *continued.*

| Teacher's subject knowledge | Page ref. History 5–11 | Reference to reports on Primary History | Note on reading History 5–11 | Experience in practice | Plan to develop |
|---|---|---|---|---|---|
| Chronological understanding (including time span of period and intervals between periods studied) | see index, chronology | | | | |
| Discuss change and continuity | 2, 92, 96, 98, 106 | | | | |
| Identify anachronism | 216 | | | | |
| **Language** | | | | | |
| Differentiate between certainty, probability, what is not/cannot be known | 11, 28, 202, 222, 226 21, 23, 220 20, 221, 222 | | | | |
| Use historical terms correctly (e.g. Victorian, knight, monk, century, evidence) | | **Ofsted: 10** **19, 53** | | | |
| ICT | | | | | |
| Historical imagination | | **Cambridge Review: 257** **Ofsted: 17** | | | |
| Opportunities to work collaboratively | | **Ofsted: 9, 17, 19, 42** | | | |
| To question | | | | | |
| To discuss | | *Cambridge Review*: **238, 257** | | | |
| Consider hypotheses | | | | | |
| To analyse | | | | | |
| Methods of monitoring | | | | | |
| Methods of recording | | | | | |
| **Collaboration with other schools** | | **Ofsted: 31** | | | |
| Primary schools | | | | | |
| Primary/secondary transition | | **Ofsted: 6, 7** **PH Survey: 21–2** | | | |

**TABLE A.1** *continued.*

| Teacher's subject knowledge | Page ref. History 5–11 | Reference to reports on Primary History | Note on reading History 5–11 | Experience in practice | Plan to develop |
|---|---|---|---|---|---|
| Subject specific training for teachers across schools | 140–5 | *PH Survey:* 22–5, 26 | | | |
| **Classroom organisation to promote enquiry, discussion, construction of accounts/interpretations, presentation of interpretations** | | Ofsted: 18, 19 *Cambridge Review:* 257 | | | |
| Whole class | 22–3, 155–7, 179 | | | | |
| Groups | 128, 151, 157, 175, 227 | Ofsted: 19 | | | |
| Individuals | 59, 176 | | | | |
| Pairs | 59, 144, 162 | | | | |
| **Local/family history/visits/ museums related to taught period** | | Ofsted: 30, 33–4, 57 *Cambridge Review:* 256, 262 *PH Survey:* 12, 14, 16 | | | |
| School/home/community links | 61–6, 100, 180, 191, 235 | | | | |
| **Planning and assessment** | | Ofsted: 12, 18, 19, 20, 27–8, 31 *PH Survey:* 18–23, 26 | | | |
| Methods of assessment | 82–5, 164, 178, 187 | Ofsted: 17, 19 | | | |
| Methods of monitoring and recording | 80, 84–5 | Ofsted: 0, 2, 43 | | | |
| Planning for progression in pupils' thinking: | 5, 23, 79, 85, 141 | Ofsted: 19, 20 | | | |

**TABLE A.1** *continued.*

| Teacher's subject knowledge | Page ref. History 5–11 | Reference to reports on Primary History | Note on reading History 5–11 | Experience in practice | Plan to develop |
|---|---|---|---|---|---|
| Medium-term plans | 76, 78, 80–1, 86 | | | | |
| Cross-curricular links | see index, cross-curricular approaches | **Ofsted: 19, 31, 33** **PH Survey: 10, 26** | | | |
| Lesson plans | 7, 72, 76, 78, 86 | **Ofsted: 18–19** | | | |
| Balance between teacher led and pupil led activities | 49, 88, 93 | **Ofsted: 19** | | | |
| Imaginative variety of activities (including hands-on activities) | throughout! | ***Cambridge Review: 218*** | | | |

# Index